Data Exfiltration Threats and Prevention Techniques

Data Exfiltration Threats and Prevention Techniques

Machine Learning and Memory-Based Data Security

Zahir Tari
RMIT University
Melbourne, Australia

Nasrin Sohrabi
RMIT University
Melbourne, Australia

Yasaman Samadi
RMIT University
Melbourne, Australia

Jakapan Suaboot
Prince of Songkla University
Phuket, Thailand

IEEE PRESS

WILEY

Library of Congress Cataloging-in-Publication Data applied for:
ISBN: 9781119898870 (HB); ePDF: 9781119898887; epub: 9781119898894

Cover design by Wiley
Cover image: © jijomathaidesigners/Shutterstock

Set in 9.5/12.5pt STIXTwoText by Straive, Chennai, India

To our dear parents.

Contents

About the Authors

Zahir Tari is a full professor of distributed systems at RMIT University (Australia) and research director of the Centre for Cyber Security Research and Innovation (CCSRI). His expertise is in the areas of *system's performance* (e.g. P2P, Cloud, IoT) as well as *system's security* (e.g. SCADA, SmartGrid, Cloud, IoT). He is the co-author of eight books (John Wiley, Springer), and he has edited over 25 conference proceedings. Zahir is or has been an associate editor of *ACM Computing Surveys, IEEE Transactions on Computers (TC), IEEE Transactions on Parallel and Distributed Systems (TPDS)*, and *IEEE Magazine on Cloud Computing*.

Nasrin Sohrabi received a PhD degree in Computer Science from RMIT University in early 2022. She is currently a Postdoctoral Research Fellow in Cloud, Systems and Security discipline at the School of Computing Technologies, RMIT University (Australia). She is also a core member of the RMIT Centre for Cyber Security Research and Innovation (CCSRI). She is an expert in distributed ledger (e.g. blockchain) and cybersecurity (e.g. network and system security) technologies, as well as in scalability and performance of large-scale distributed systems.

Yasaman Samadi is a PhD student in computer science at RMIT University, Australia, and a researcher in quantum cybersecurity. Yasaman has a Master's in Computer Architecture and worked as a quantum engineer at QBee. Her research interests include security, low-level control electronic systems, FPGAs, and micro-architecture for intelligent devices.

Jakapan Suaboot received BEng and MEng (research) degrees in Computer Engineering from Prince of Songkla University (Thailand) and a PhD degree in Computer Science from RMIT University (Australia) in 2007, 2010, and 2021, respectively. He is a lecturer at the College of Computing, Prince of Songkla University. His research interests include malware detection, data breach prevention, machine learning technologies, and digital financial security.

Acknowledgments

The enormous work done in this book will not be able to get done without the continual support of our families, friends, and colleagues.

Zahir Tari, Nasrin Sohrabi, Yasaman Samadi, and Jakapan Suaboot

Acronyms

ACC	accuracy
AMAL	AutoMal and MalLabel
ANN	artificial neural network
API	application programming interface
APT	advanced persistent threat
ARP	address resolution protocol
BEC	business email compromise
C2	command and control
CBA	classification based on associations
CFG	control-flow graph
CHS	Community Health Systems
CI	critical infrastructure
CIA	confidentiality, integrity, availability
CMAR	multiple association rules
COTS	commercial-off-the-shelf
CRA	Canada Revenue Agency
CRF	conditional random field
CRT	classification and regression tree
DFA	deterministic finite automaton
DLP	data leakage prevention
DNS	domain name service
DoS	Denial of Service
FBoW	Fast lookup Bag-of Words
FPG	frequent pattern growth
FN	false negative
FP	false positive
GSP	generalized sequential pattern
HID	host-based intrusion detection
HMM	hidden Markov model

HMI	human machine interface
HTM	hierarchical temporal memory
ICS	industrial control system
ICT	information and communication technologies
IDS	intrusion detection system
IED	intelligent electronic device
IoT	Internet of Things
IR	incident response
IS	information system
IT	information technology
LAN	local area network
MFA	multi-factor authentication
MIST	Malware Instruction Set
MITM	Man-in-the-Middle
NB	naïve Bayes
NID	network-based intrusion detection
OCSVM	one class support vector machine
OT	operational technology
PLC	programmable logic controller
PR	precision
RAM	read access memory
RAT	remote administration Trojan
RC	recall
RF	random forest
RIPPER	repeated incremental pruning to produce error reduction
RTU	remote terminal unit
SCADA	supervisory control and data acquisition
SDR	sparse distributed representation
SLQ	supervised learning in quest
SQL	structured query language
SVM	support vector machine
TLS	transport layer security
TP	true positive
TMBoW	Temporary Memory Bag-of-Words
TN	true negative
UTF	Unicode Transformation Format
VM	virtual machine
WAN	wide area network

Abstract

Data exfiltration is a type of cyberattacks that causes breaches of sensitive information. It is undoubtedly a critical issue for the modern world of data-centric services. In particular, the sectors of critical infrastructure (CI), information technology (IT), and mobile computing are the targets of advanced persistent threat (APT). Data breaches cause huge losses every year to a wide range of industries, including large enterprises such as Google, Facebook, Microsoft, to name a few. Furthermore, such breaches can have major impacts on national security if government departments or the military are targeted. Since the adversary constantly attacks the target using various system vulnerabilities (e.g. unknown or zero-day exploits), a prevention-based measure alone is not sufficient to thwart the adversary. To address such a problem, in this book, a holistic approach for data exfiltration detection based on three approaches for the detection of data breaches will be discussed in detail.

We begin the description of the technical content by providing basic background so to enable readers understand some of the fundamental and technical concepts/models covered in the remaining chapters of the book. The background covers, for example, basic knowledge of hidden Markov model (HMM), memory forensics, bag-of-words (BoW) model, and sparse distributed representations (SDRs). Cybersecurity threats are also covered, as these can cause a wide range of damage, including the physical destruction of an entire information systems facility. Recognizing different types of data security threats and the way that they steal sensitive information from individuals and organizations will give readers a clear understanding on how to protect their data. Hence, data security threats are explained, and various attacks are discussed, such as malware, denial of service (DoS), SQL injection, Emotet (malspam), social engineering and phishing, and man-in-the-middle (MITM) attacks. These attacks often access the high-value targets, such as nation states and major corporations, to steal the crucial data.

To better grasp the importance of addressing the various topics of this book, a few use cases (examples) of data leakage attacks over the last three years across all continents are discussed in a separate chapter. This helps readers to under-stand the real-world cases of cyberattacks and the damage they caused. According to various reports, several attacks (e.g. ransomware, server access, business email compromise (BEC), data theft, credential harvesting, remote administration Tro-jan (RAT), misconfiguration, and malicious insider) are among the most known attacks that occurred over the period of 2020–2021. This chapter provides all the information, including statistical information, about these use cases.

We later examine the major technologies that have a strong potential to be used as the basis for data leakage prevention technologies. The literature review revealed numerous advanced intrusion detection methods that use similar core technologies for the data exfiltration detection solution. Industrial control systems (ICSs), especially the ones with supervisory control and data acquisition (SCADA), are the most challenging ones for researchers and practitioners as they are constantly subject to cyberattacks. In the systematic literature review we carried out, over a hundred peer-reviewed articles were examined. This study illustrated the development of supervised-based learning approaches from the industrial perspective that target various data auditing sources and attacking methods. Based on this extensive review, both qualitative and quantitative benchmarks for several machine learning methods were conducted in 10 dif-ferent categories. Furthermore, future directions for the development of new algorithms/methods and facilitating the selection of algorithms/methods for industrial-based intrusion detection system (IDS) were identified.

Following the extensive review, the technical aspects of a holistic data exfil-tration detection approach were considered. First, the data exfiltration problem caused by malicious software is examined in detail, as malware is a critical tool used by attackers to steal sensitive information. For the real-time detection of sus-picious data-stealing behaviors, an innovation method, called Sub-Curve HMM, is described, and this is based on the HMM to extract the sub-contained mali-cious behavior from a long application programming interface (API) call sequence. This method is intended to detect malicious activities that occur only over a short period. By projecting a series of matching scores into a curve, this approach dis-tinguishes malignant actions from other system's activities using discontinuities in the slope of the curve. When testing the long API call sequence, malicious and benign activities obtain different matching scores for an adjoining set of API calls. Experimental results show that the Sub-Curve HMM method outperforms existing solutions in detecting six families of malware: the detection accuracy of Sub-Curve HMM is over 94% compared to 83% for the baseline HMM approach and 73% for information gain.

After that, we move away from behavioral-based to the sensitive-data-oriented methods. In particular, the common belief of this research field is challenged here by discussing new ways of monitoring the physical memory for sensitive information instead of checking for malicious activities or scanning the network traffic. Essentially, the main memory is a single point of data flow in the computer system; hence, the adversary cannot evade the detection system by using other channels. This approach helps to shortlist processes that involve sensitive data; using anomaly detection systems, advanced hackers who use a legitimate program to commit data exfiltration can be detected. To efficiently monitor sensitive text-based files in the memory space of the running processes, the Fast lookup Bag-of Words (FBoW) method will be discussed in detail. This method transforms a text document into a BoW sequence and then builds a Deterministic Finite Automaton (DFA) to match content in the read access memory (RAM) with the database of sensitive text documents. Experimental results show that FBoW is the most scalable method compared to other state-of-the-art, pattern-matching methods when the size of sensitive data is increasing. Specifically, it uses 31–400 times less memory than the Aho–Corasick method, with a trade-off of less than a 2% drop in the detection accuracy for the non-memory-based dataset. When tested with memory-based datasets, FBoW distinctively outperformed the state-of-the-art methods in terms of memory efficiency, runtime, and robustness.

Finally, this book will look at one of the most challenging data exfiltration problems, namely *temporal data exfiltration*. A sophisticated adversary could delay the data-stealing activity by exfiltrating tiny pieces of information over a long period instead of transferring a lot of information at once. Although one can detect small fractions of sensitive data in the RAM, if a piece of information is too small, the detection could return a false-negative result. This research is the very first attempt to mitigate temporal data exfiltration by proposing a novel Temporary Memory Bag-of-Words (TMBoW) method, which combines SDR and BoW representation to efficiently detect the temporal patterns of the time-delayed data exfiltration. Experimental results show that TMBoW has 100% accuracy when the minimum detection threshold is only 0.5, and the analytical result shows that the probability of TMBoW reporting a false alarm is approximately zero.

1

Introduction

The high penetration of data-centric services has markedly increased the risk of exposing sensitive customer and corporate data. In particular, the sectors of critical infrastructures (CIs), information technology (IT), and mobile computing are those which are constantly targeted by sophisticated adversaries, insiders, or bribed workers who launch an attack using advanced malware and hacking tools [1]. The main purpose of these attackers is to gain long-term access to a system and steal critical sensitive data from the enterprise. This causes data breach or data leakage, also known as *data exfiltration*, which poses huge losses every year to a wide range of industries including many technology giants such as Google, Facebook, and Tesla. Google alone stores an enormous volume of sensitive data derived from sources worldwide [2]. Despite the Covid-19 pandemic, in 2020, of the reported 32,002 incidents, 3950 involved data breaches [3], of which 86% were financially motivated. Recent outbreaks of ransomware are good examples of new data exfiltration-based attacks for the purpose of financial gain [4]. Not only are attack methods becoming increasingly sophisticated, but most of the advanced hacking is conducted by state-sponsored hackers [5]. Moreover, the consequences of data leakage could pose a critical threat to security and the privacy of users, particularly those who work for the government or the military. For instance, the recent leakage of the subcontractor database of the Australian Defence Force had severe implications for national security as the design of military combat aircraft was compromised [6].

Intruders take the opportunity to exploit the unknown vulnerabilities of security systems in order to penetrate an organization. Stuxnet worm [7] was one of the most well-known attack tools created by the intelligence agencies of the United States and Israel and was intended to thwart the Iranian nuclear development program. Indeed, this worm virus could be classified as a military-grade weapon considering its origin and sophistication. Stuxnet was used to exploit several undiscovered bugs in the Windows operating system to wirelessly spread itself and install a rootkit on the Siemens' programmable logic controllers (PLCs),

Data Exfiltration Threats and Prevention Techniques: Machine Learning and Memory-Based Data Security, First Edition. Zahir Tari, Nasrin Sohrabi, Yasaman Samadi, and Jakapan Suaboot.

which were manipulated and used to destroy the delicate equipment at the targeted nuclear power plant. Another example of the widespread vulnerability of security systems is the OpenSSL Heartbleed [8]. There was no clear evidence indicating whether the bug was discovered and used by hackers before 2014, and for how long. Despite having a mathematically robust design, the implementation bug was accidentally embedded in the widely used OpenSSL cryptography library for decades. Since OpenSSL is the core of Transport Layer Security (TLS) encryption, vital services like secure web pages, email, or the secure shell protocol had been affected. Unfortunately, the security patching process took several months or more to fix the widespread vulnerability in several million devices worldwide. This resulted in several data breach incidents, such as the data breaches involving the Community Health Systems (CHS), which was the giant private hospital chain in the United States, and the Canada Revenue Agency (CRA) incident that impacted millions of Canadian taxpayers.

Since attack prevention measures might not be adequate, the detection-based approach plays a crucial role in minimizing damages resulting from data breaches. Generally, a malicious program (known as malware) is the primary tool employed by adversaries to help them gain access to a system or even automatically exfiltrate sensitive information. In spite of numerous malware detection approaches proposed in the literature, few works focus on data exfiltration. On the other hand, the studies that propose solutions for data breach detection focus only on a single data leakage channel: network monitoring, unsafe data exportation, or user authorization, to name a few. Such atomistic solutions give attackers opportunities to exfiltrate sensitive data via alternative channels. This suggests the need for a holistic data exfiltration detection approach. Hence, this research investigates several methods for detecting data exfiltration, which is crucial for various corporate sectors as the modern world is evolving toward the adoption of data-centric services.

Generally, off-the-shelf antivirus scanners primarily use known signatures to detect malicious programs. The signature-based solution has a very low false alarm rate, as it uses a hash of the program or signature strings contained in the malware binary to match with the virus signature. However, advanced hackers could develop a new unseen malware for the well-protected target or even use the benign program to steal the data. Furthermore, some sophisticated malware does not need to be installed on the disk storage at all (e.g. Code Red worm [9]). Instead, this malware could run in the memory to perform the malicious activity for the entire time. This is where the real-time behavior detection method plays an important role. However, detecting a nefarious purpose from a series of the program's actions is challenging, as there are too many possibilities that the program's actions infer the malicious transaction, especially in a real-time context. Hence, behavior-based data exfiltration is one issue that needs a careful and systematic investigation.

Apart from using malware to steal sensitive data, some attackers might simply exploit the benign program to exfiltrate the sensitive information. In some cases, the monitoring system cannot detect the unforeseen malware. Hence, the malicious behavior-monitoring approach alone might not be sufficient. Therefore, by taking different perspectives, we may be able to obtain a list of processes used to access sensitive data, which could cause data leakage. To do so, one will need to search for sensitive data in the memory space of those processes. This will allow sensitive files to be read, and other inputs such as keystrokes containing sensitive keywords, to be detected. Ultimately, all data in the computer system needs to be loaded into the main memory before it can be processed; hence, the adversary cannot avoid having the sensitive data in the main memory. Moreover, the data can remain in the memory even if the process has already been terminated [10]. Hence, if those processes can be listed, it will be easier to narrow down and identify the root cause of the data breach regardless of whether the program is classified as malicious or benign. However, to the best of the authors' knowledge, this idea has not been closely examined by previous studies, and therefore this book will elucidate new ways of addressing such issues.

A sophisticated adversary could obfuscate the data exfiltration even more by using a temporal attack [11] to evade the detection system. Here, the data-stealing activity is delayed so as to trick the monitoring system into "thinking" that it is just a false alarm (false positive). In other words, the hacker could minimize the chance of being discovered by the monitoring system by stealing a minuscule amount of sensitive data at a time. Over a period of time, the attacker could reassemble those small amounts to form the original sensitive file. Even though these time-delay attacks have been reported for over a decade, few researchers have attempted to address the issue (e.g. [11, 12]). If this method is used to penetrate the critical systems of government departments or the military, the consequences will be devastating. Hence, this book looks at the data exfiltration detection issue by **holistically** approaching the problem from several perspectives, namely by: (i) examining the program's behavior, (ii) monitoring sensitive data program is accessing, and (iii) monitoring the collective activities of the process related to fractions of sensitive information being collected over a period of time.

1.1 Data Exfiltration Methods

The prevention of data exfiltration is a broad and complex issue. To examine this issue more closely, current methods can be categorized into four areas: (i) state-of-the-art survey, (ii) behavior-based data exfiltration solution, (iii) memory-based data exfiltration solution, and (iv) temporal-based data exfiltration prevention. The shortcomings of each of these methods are discussed here.

1.1.1 State-of-the-Art Surveys

To begin with, this book surveyed technologies that have a high potential to be used as a fundamental building block for data leakage prevention (DLP) methods, and data exfiltration prevention solutions shared similar core technologies that are used for intrusion detection systems (IDSs). While an IDS is a standard measure to protect computer systems from outsider and insider attacks, DLP is a more specialized and advanced security solution that can provide a better protection against security breaches. DLP aims to detect abnormal access to sensitive data, and this is based on the use of either machine learning (ML) or temporal reasoning algorithms.

Industrial control systems (ICSs), especially supervisory control and data acquisition (SCADA) systems, are a constant target by cyberattacks as their inability to function can have serious impact on people's daily lives. This obviously creates a nightmare to the security community to find the right solutions that could protect ICSs' essential services, so these can provide the required functionalities. IDSs, when tailored to deal with specific requirements (e.g. real-time detection and reliability), can provide an appropriate protection to ICSs.

Despite several attempts to address SCADA security, only a few of the studies reported in the literature have focused on the development of appropriate ML solutions for SCADA systems. Many of the researchers examined, from different perspectives, the design of specific IDS for CIs. For example, the survey conducted in [13] focused on the design of IDS architecture for SCADA systems. In the other hand, the work in [14] looked at classifying IDS solutions based on detection methods and audit materials. In [15], a review is conducted to gather information about the testbeds used for ICSs. Therefore, it is crucial to conduct a survey based on the supervised ML methods, focusing on CI which has the potential to contribute to the research on efficient methods and technologies for the prevention of data leakage.

1.1.2 Malicious Behavior Detection Methods

Malware has become one of the most effective tools for searching and stealing users' sensitive information. Over several decades, numerous malware detection methods have been proposed in the literature. However, only a few current malware detection solutions focus directly on the detection of data exfiltration; instead, they are used to detect different types of virus/malicious programs. Intuitively, if a Trojan horse software accesses sensitive data, it is highly likely to cause data leakage. Hence, observing the behavior of all running processes (to identify potential malware) is the key to detecting data breaches.

Nevertheless, in most cases [16], data is stolen by malware but remains undetected for two reasons [17]: the signature of the malware is new to antivirus programs, and the anomaly-based systems cannot detect variations in the malware behavior and therefore cannot differentiate between legitimate and exfiltration activities. Based on a sequence of application programming interface (API) calls invoked by a process, hidden Markov model (HMM) has been used extensively to discriminate between malicious and benign behavior (e.g. [18–20]). However, the dynamic behavior analysis of a malware can generate a very long sequence of API calls. For example, in the experiments carried out by our team, Keylogger malware (MD5 hash value d4259130a53dae8ddce89ebc8e80b560) generated more than 300,000 series of API calls in less than two minutes. Also, HMM seems to perform poorly with such long sequences of API calls. This allows the exfiltration-based malware to pose as a benign software for most of the time and perform malicious activities only for a very short period of time to avoid detection. Hence, the effect of the sequence length on the detection accuracy which has not been fully studied in the context of malware detection will be examined in more detail in this book.

1.1.3 RAM-Based Data Exfiltration Detection Methods

The detection of suspicious activities is one approach used to prevent data exfiltration. However, the behavior-monitoring approach has two significant limitations: (i) it covers only certain types of malicious activity (e.g. searches for user identity/credentials, installation of a keystroke-capturing service, and attempts to contact or export the user's documents to the malicious server). However, the adversary could pass on the data through several legitimate services by, for instance, attaching the sensitive file with email or putting in the email content, inserting the sensitive data into the untrusted database server, storing the sensitive data in files which will be exported later. (ii) The behavior-monitoring system cannot totally guarantee the detection of all suspicious incidents. Therefore, one needs a detection method that monitors the system from different angles. Specifically, the idea of monitoring the random-access memory (RAM) for the sensitive data has great potential as a solution that protects the system from attacks coming from nearly all channels. Intuitively, any computer program needs to load the stored sensitive data into the memory before any processing activity can be conducted. In other words, RAM is a sole gateway for the processing of computer data, including the sensitive data that needs protection.

The monitoring of sensitive data in the memory is however a challenging task, since the size of the sensitive data to be monitored (i.e. patterns) could be large, in some cases even larger than the size of the main memory itself. Existing text-searching methods are designed for using a small-size patterns to search against a larger-size database, e.g. Smith–Waterman [21], Aho–Corasick [22], and regular expressions [23]. Unfortunately, existing string-matching methods are not designed for the monitoring of a large set of sensitive documents. In the context of this book, the searching patterns could be bigger than the size of the memory. Therefore, a new search approach will be provided here to allow a large database of searching patterns to be summarized/compressed into a smaller representation. This will enable more sensitive files to be monitored in real time, particularly in the memory.

There are several challenges to be addressed to build such a system. Firstly, sensitive data could include various information and therefore not only limited to personal information. It can also include organizational information such as hospital patient medical records, government CI sites detail, corporate intellectual property, and organization internal information. Sensitive data can be also classified into various formats, for example, a corpus of text documents (e.g. ASCII, Unicode UTF-8/16/32) and database files (e.g. comma separated values, spreadsheet, and JavaScript Object Notation). Dealing with different format of sensitive data, indeed, requires different monitoring methods. As the type of data search is directly related to the design of a monitoring algorithm, the discussion here will first focus on sensitive data that is a corpus of text documents, giving that the text is pre-decoded (i.e. using standard Unicode) from the raw memory data/snapshot.

1.1.4 Temporal Data Exfiltration Methods

Much research work focused on monitoring sensitive data using various methods, such as creating and tracking data signatures of sensitive documents [24, 25], tagging sensitive files with additional meta-data [26, 27], or classifying/detecting sensitive documents using advanced ML methods [12, 28, 29]). However, sophisticated espionage might use highly advanced methods to hide malicious software from being detected while still be able to spy on a victim.

Temporal-based data exfiltration is one of the hardest attack detection problems and remains one of the most challenging threats [11], because a spy software keeps collecting small fragments of sensitive information over an interval of time (hence, a temporal attack). Consequently, a malicious process could avoid being detected by the security system. Only a few solutions have dealt with temporal data exfiltration attacks by, for example, monitoring the network traffic over a period of time [12]. Interestingly, the hierarchical temporal memory (HTM) technology, which mimics the behavior of neocortex cells in the human brain [30], has been able to recognize a pattern in temporal input data. This technology has not yet been investigated fully to determine whether it can be applied to memory-based data leakage patterns to detect temporal-based data exfiltration. At this stage, related work attempting to detect temporal data exfiltration attacks cannot be found, especially by monitoring the RAM's sensitive data, which is also the main focus of this book.

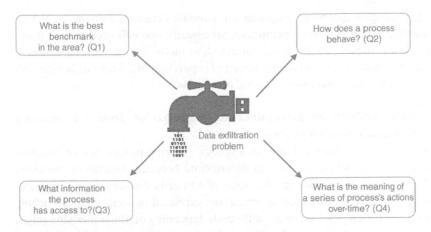

Figure 1.1 Overview of data exfiltration problems.

1.2 Important Questions

This book comprehensively addresses the data exfiltration issues by answering the following four important questions, as depicted in Figure 1.1.

- What is a survey and benchmark of existing methods?
- How does a process behave or how to detect the malicious behavior of the process?
- What information the process has access to or how to efficiently detect if any process has access to the sensitive data?
- What is the meaning of series of process's actions over time or how to efficiently detect the temporal data exfiltration?

A detailed description of each data exfiltration problem is given in the following section.

(Q1) What are the limitations of existing supervised learning methods for data leakage prevention (DLP) and/or intrusion detection system (IDS) for industrial control systems (ICSs)?
To address the first problem, an extensive literature survey is conducted to find and investigate the state-of-the-art technologies that have been used in data leakage and/or IDSs. Over the past decade, various ML methods have been used to train artificial intelligence to detect abnormal behaviors, including data exfiltration. The supervised-based machine learning (supervised ML) methods are more common in the anomaly detection system than the unsupervised methods (known as clustering). This is because the patterns of the attack vector are known. To contribute to the current knowledge regarding supervised ML for DLP/intrusion detection, a survey is conducted to examine existing supervised

ML technologies that were proposed for anomaly detection systems, including data exfiltration and other cyberattacks. Specifically, one will need to: (i) categorize existing Supervised-ML based on detection methods and auditing material; (ii) identify system-specific requirements of supervised ML; and (iii) benchmark supervised ML methods from a holistic perspective.

(Q2) How to effectively detect data-stealing behaviors from the sequence of API instructions of a process?

Detecting the malicious activities of a specific running process is a challenging task, particularly when we need to differentiate between patterns of malicious and legitimate processes using a sequence of API calls. Unlike text or image processing where all features are observed and extracted by examining the whole picture, a running process can act differently depending on the underlying stages or task it is doing. Therefore, the program behavior, which changes expeditiously, could easily hide fractions of malicious instructions over a brief period of execution time. Hence, it is very challenging for the malware detection technology to detect the malicious behavior that is carried out within seconds or milliseconds. Therefore, the methodology tailored for detecting data exfiltration behavior will require a new method and algorithm to address this problem. This will particularly look at the feature extraction problem, in particular, for the long sequence of API calls that indicate a stream of ongoing activities currently being executing by the program.

(Q3) How to efficiently inspect the sensitive information on the random-access memory space to which a process has access?

This problem is related to the monitoring of data in the memory space of a process in order to detect the presence of sensitive information. In a computer system, data needs to be loaded into the RAM before it can be processed or transferred; hence, a malicious software will not be able to hide from the detection system if it is accessing sensitive information. Thing et al. [10] suggest that attackers have even tried to evade the memory forensic tool itself to prevent their malicious software from being detected. Even though data in the RAM is changing all the time, the unused data will stay in the RAM until the address space is recycled by the operating system. For instance, they capture up to 75–100% of conversation on instant messages by analyzing the mobile phone memory. On the other hand, Wang et al. [31] identified up to 98.6% of the kernel rootkit by using memory images. The monitoring of sensitive data on the RAM will be a more robust way of mitigating various data exfiltration incidents. However, monitoring memory-based data is challenging in terms of scalability issue, especially when there is a large number of sensitive documents. The robustness of the method is also an important issue, particularly when the monitoring system directly accesses data from the program's memory.

(Q4) How to efficiently mitigate with a sophisticated temporal-based data exfiltration?

The last problem relates to a particularly sophisticated attack, namely temporal-based data exfiltration. This threat might occur when the target information is highly protected, such as military or business databases. Despite the tight surveillance, the hacking bot steals sensitive documents from the compromised machine by splitting them into chunks. The bot then exports pieces of the sensitive data one by one through single or multiple data leakage channels. Even though the small fraction of sensitive data can still be detected, the matching probability could be lower than the detection threshold and considered as a false negative (i.e. not detected). This enables attackers to evade the detection system by collecting several pieces of sensitive data over a period. The hackers then reconstruct the pieces of data to obtain the complete original sensitive file. Furthermore, the delay of data exfiltration action could also return a false positive (i.e. false alarm) when the small part of sensitive data is detected repeatedly. For instance, if a fraction from the sensitive text file is found twice, it could be the same instance that has been detected previously or the new data that has just been loaded into the memory. Unfortunately, the current DLP technology is not adequate in preventing temporal data exfiltration.

1.3 Book Scope

The main purpose of this book is to address the problems stated in Section 1.2: exhaustive survey (Q1) and specialized data exfiltration detection methods (Q2–Q4). For (Q1), state-of-the-art supervised ML methods have been surveyed here and describe the intrusion detection methods/systems proposed in the literature for over the past decade. Existing supervised-ML-based methods are categorized and evaluated on specific requirements, namely the requirements of CI systems (i.e. SCADA), as such systems are those that are used in our daily life (i.e. critical) and therefore need to be fully, strongly, and properly protected. Ultimately, such an assessment and evaluation of (critical) systems will help the reader understand the key research challenges and ideas about the use of supervised ML methods in IDSs, in particular, for critical systems. On the other hand, Q2–Q4 relate to data exfiltration detection method from three different perspectives, namely behavior-based (Q2), memory-based (Q3), and temporal-based (Q4). Since they are all technical methods that share similarities with existing data leakage/intrusion/malware detection methods, the scope of the Q2–Q4 questions is summarized by comparing them with the mentioned methods based on the following categorization criteria: (i) the detection source, (ii) detection method, and (iii) input characteristics. Figure 1.2 depicts such a categorization.

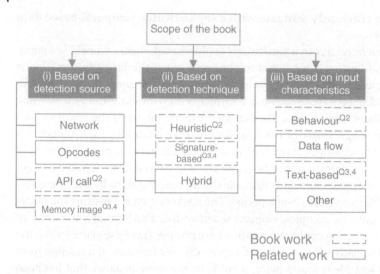

Figure 1.2 Scope of the work for Q2–Q4 compared to related work based on three different listed aspects.

To address RQ2, the goal is to detect the program's suspicious behavior, in particular, the data scraping and stealing actions. The sequence of API calls is chosen as the detection source because it indicates the ongoing activities of a program. This is known as a heuristic approach and is very flexible compared to the static method. In the behavior-based model, the number of command sequences issued by a program to steal sensitive data could be very large, making it impossible to find all possible signatures of the malicious command sequences. Also, the signature-based approach suffers from zero-day attack, or variant of polymorphic malware where their signatures are unknown. Indeed, the delay in generating the new signature consumes a lot of time and budget. Therefore, the heuristic-based approach is being developed, facilitated by artificial intelligence and data mining technology.

RQ3 and RQ4, on the other hand, refer to signature-based methods. The explanation is as follows: to detect a sophisticated malware or a corrupted employee exporting sensitive data using ordinary software, the sensitive data will be monitored regardless of whether or not the program is classified as malicious. The main advantage of the signature-based method is that it has a very high true positive rate compared to the heuristic-based method. Here, the static signature or fingerprint is used instead of the generic pattern used by the heuristic approach. However, because sensitive data is text-based (i.e. unformatted text), the signature-based method is not scalable. For instance, when the size of the signature database is large, the memory footprint and runtime could be affected.

Moreover, the signature-based method becomes less effective when the input data contains too much noise. In this case, RQ3 and RQ4, which relate to the monitoring of data leakage by examining the physical memory, will definitely need to deal with noise from the RAM's data extracted (Chapter 7). These scalability and robustness issues are primary targets of the research addressing RQ3 and RQ4.

1.4 Book Summary

By addressing the four problems, this book describes new methods that address various limitations of current state-of-the-art methods that prevent them from detecting data exfiltration incidents from the four different aspects mentioned earlier.

1.4.1 Data Security Threats

Data security refers to preserving data against unwanted access, corruption, or theft across all stages of its life cycle. This also refers to covering every aspect of security, including the logical security of applications, administrative and access controls, and the physical security of hardware and storage devices. Specific policies and procedures are used to guarantee data security. However, data can be still vulnerable to various attacks and threats. Data security threats refer to activities that have the potential to compromise the confidentiality, integrity, and availability of the data and have therefore considerable damage and harm to organizations. *Confidentiality* refers to ensuring that the data is kept secret or private, and accessing it must be controlled to prevent any malicious or accidental unauthorized sharing of data. *Integrity* refers to ensuring that the data is reliable and immutable. *Availability* means that the data should be available for the users in the entire life cycle of the data. Chapter 3 aims to cover data security threats in detail, and more specifically it will cover the most known cyberattacks, e.g. Malware, denial of service (DoS), SQL Injection, Emotet (malspam), Man in the Middle (MITM), Password Attacks, and Social Engineering & Phishing. This will provide readers with a good understanding of existing cybersecurity threats.

1.4.2 Use Cases

Studying data security can be seen as "boring" (and thus not convincing) when the focus is only on the theoretical aspects and concepts cybersecurity. This study will hopefully convince readers about the importance of properly understanding as well as dealing with cyberattacks through the description of some real-world use cases. Thus, to make this book more interesting to readers, Chapter 4 will study several use cases of data leakage attacks that occurred over the last three years across all the continents. More specifically, it first introduces the cyberattack types and categorized them based on the objectives and attackers intend to accomplish. Some of these cyberattacks (e.g. ransomware, server access, business email compromise (BEC), data theft, credential harvesting, remote administration Trojan (RAT), misconfiguration, and malicious insider) are all grouped based on attackers ultimate goals. Ransomware is considered as the most common attack in the recent three years. After ransomware, the server access attacks are ranked the most frequent common ones. They occur when an attacker gains unauthorized access to a server. The third most frequently used attack is BEC. After discussing the cyberattack types in detail, the chapter explains the initial infection vectors, i.e. the method through which a network is breached and compromised. It is important to note that the cyberattack types and initial infection vectors are two different concepts and not be confused. Phishing, stealing credentials, and exploiting vulnerabilities are considered initial infections vectors. Reports show that in 2021, phishing alone achieved the highest record of 222,127. The effect of this attack vector can be reduced by monitoring suspicious connections.

1.4.3 Survey

After covering all the necessary background in the early chapters of the book, a survey of various supervised ML methods is thoroughly conducted to provide information how such methods are used in intrusion detection and DLP systems. This review focuses on specific applications, namely CIs (i.e. ICSs such as electrical/power/water systems), as these need to be protected from major disruptions. It addresses Q1, and over a 100 of peer-reviewed articles were reviewed, which gave an insight into current research trends regarding supervised ML methods to implement anomaly detection systems (i.e. DLP and IDS). This study illustrates the development of such systems from industry perspectives and provides a comprehensive study of supervised ML methods for SCADA-based IDS systems using specific criteria and properties. A framework is described to categorize various supervised ML methods and made qualitative and quantitative comparisons of various state-of-the-art research methods to identify the directions of research that target different data auditing sources and attacking methods. Additional issues and challenges are discussed for industrial-based IDS systems using supervised learning methods and illustrated the trends in developing such systems to identify the future directions for the development of new algorithms and to guide the selection of algorithms for industrial IDS systems. The survey not only provides a framework enabling administrators to choose the right ML method for a prevention system, but it also provides a comparison of various supervised ML algorithms.

1.4.4 Sub-Curve HMM

The work related to Q2 has led to the design of a method that accurately detects data exfiltration behaviors that occur at any time a process is executing. This method is called Sub-Curve HMM, and it is an innovative feature extraction method based on HMM, which makes use of API call sequences by extracting the subcontained behavior from a long API call sequence. Sub-Curve HMM is probably one of the early attempts to extract the subcontained pattern from a long API call sequence to detect data exfiltration malware. This enables small pieces of malicious activities contained in the long API call sequence to be detected. The limitations of current detection solutions are also considered here, especially in terms of a long API call sequence. Compared to existing methods, Sub-Curve HMM outperforms baseline methods across several datasets with various average API sequence lengths. The experimental results confirm the ability of Sub-Curve HMM to match interesting behaviors from subsequences of all observed activities. Unlike the previous works that focused on using all information gathered from executable binaries, Sub-Curve HMM requires only parts of detection activities. Hence, this method can be applied in a real-time context where it is not possible to gather all information from the executable binary. In addition, to prevent data exfiltration incident, Sub-Curve HMM can be used to monitor only those programs that are accessing sensitive information.

1.4.5 Fast Lookup Bag-of-Words (FBoW)

To address Q3, an efficient way to monitor sensitive data in real time on a RAM is described. This is probably the first attempt to challenge existing data leakage detection methods by monitoring sensitive data in the RAM. The method described here, called Fast lookup Bag-of-Words (FBoW), is an approximate multi-pattern matching method for text documents. FBoW addresses several aspects in matching the RAM's textual sensitive data, such as scalability and noise. When there is a large number of sensitive documents in a database, the problem is that existing pattern-matching methods, e.g. Aho–Corasick [22] and Smith–Waterman [21], cannot be used, and regular expression methods, e.g. [23], do not meet the scalability requirements of RAM data files. The second issue is that the text extracted from memory contains noise. For instance, the noise is produced by decoding the non-textual elements in the memory to extra characters or re-ordering the content according to memory paging [32]. This issue poses a serious practical impediment to use exact matching algorithms, e.g. Knuth–Morris–Pratt [33], Boyer–Moore [34], Aho–Corasick [22], or Commentz–Walter [35]. Although approximate matching is more robust in this context, approximate matching methods are either runtime-inefficient (e.g. Smith–Waterman [21]) or unable to accurately identify free-form text (e.g. using regular expression [23]). By addressing Q3, this book will provide the followings: (i) an innovative pattern-matching algorithm for multiple corpora or a large corpus, that is, memory- and runtime-efficient; (ii) a customizable approximate search algorithm that allows a user to fine-tune a trade-off between scalability (i.e. memory footprint and processing time) and the detection accuracy; and (iii) a series of experimental evaluations that benchmark single and multiple pattern-matching algorithms (e.g. inference of regular expressions [RegEx] [23], Smith Waterman [21], and Aho–Corasick [22]) for both exact and approximate solutions in the context of matching sensitive data in three different formats: keywords only, whole text files, and sensitive data in the physical RAM.

FBoW is efficient in the way it monitors RAM sensitive data in real time. It addresses issues in matching the RAM's textual sensitive data as follows. The first aspect is the scalability problem when the database of sensitive data contains many documents, which prevents existing pattern-matching methods (i.e. Aho–Corasick [22], Smith–Waterman [21], and using regular expression [23]) from being scale enough to match the RAM content with the files in the database. The second issue is that the text content extracted from memory contains noise, for instance, the noise from decoding the non-textual elements in the memory to extra characters or re-ordering the content as per memory paging [32]. This issue raises a serious practical impediment to use the exact matching algorithms, e.g. Knuth–Morris–Pratt [33], Boyer–Moore [34], Aho–Corasick [22], or Commentz–Walter [35]. Although approximate matching is more robust in this context, the approximate matching methods are either runtime-inefficient (e.g. Smith–Waterman [21]) or unable to accurately identify free-form text (e.g. using regular expression [23]). RQ3's details can be summarized as follows: (i) an innovative pattern-matching algorithm for multiple long text corpus that is memory and runtime-efficient; (ii) a customizable approximate search algorithm that allows a user to finetune a trade-off between scalability (i.e. memory footprint and processing time) and the detection accuracy; and (iii) a series of experimental evaluations that benchmark single and multiple pattern-matching algorithms (e.g. inference of RegEx [23], Smith–Waterman [21], and Aho–Corasick [22]) for both exact and approximate solutions in the context of matching sensitive data in three different formats: only keywords, whole text files, and sensitive data in the physical RAM.

1.4.6 Temporary Memory Bag-of-Words (TMBoW)

Q4's will deal with one of the long discovered sophisticated data exfiltration threats [11]: temporal data exfiltration; yet not many research works have proposed solution to this problem. This book will describe TMBoW – Temporary

Memory Bag-of Words – to capture time-delay data exfiltration activities. The design of TMBoW is based on bag-of-words (BoW) and sparse distributed representation (SDR) to represent textual sensitive documents. TMBoW allows a large number of sensitive documents to be added to the detection model. This is because the SDR and BoW shrink unique words that appear in the sensitive database to only one-bit-per-word frequency. The sensitive data-matching process is performed via multiple bitwise operations. Its design enables parallel programming to be done on a modern system with a multicore processor. As a result, TMBoW can more quickly match sensitive data that appear in the memory with of a multicore CPU system. Hence, both memory and runtime efficiency can be achieved simultaneously. Put simply, the feature of temporary memory and the multiple time-step detection framework enable temporal or time-delay data exfiltration to be detected, even though the operation has been extended over a long period of time. Furthermore, the new data structure that contains the sensitive database with BoW and SDR representation allows noisy data from the RAM to be monitored efficiently with a very low probability of returning a false positive (i.e. false alarm). To summarize, by addressing Q4, this book will describe the followings: (i) a method to detect the leakage of the sensitive data in the memory using time-delay channel, (ii) the scalability issue of the multi-pattern-matching algorithm for text-based sensitive data will be discussed, and (iii) the issue of noises associated with extracting strings from the memory snapshot will be addressed.

1.5 Book Structure

Figure 1.3 depicts the structure of this book, which consists of nine chapters. The arrow depicts the flow of the research steps. The chapters with main contributions are highlighted in the dotted trapezoid. Chapter motivates the issues as well as the methods described in the book. Chapter 2 provides background knowledge on various cybersecurity threats associated with the data leakage issues. Details of the data security threats are provided in Chapters 3 and 4 reports on recent real-world data leakage and top cybersecurity attacks from 2020 to 2021 in all five continents. A comprehensive literature survey of existing supervised machine learning technologies is presented in Chapter 5. Afterward, three data exfiltration detection approaches are presented. Chapter 6 discusses the approach based on software behavior. Chapter 7 discusses a novel approach based on monitoring the physical memory. Finally, a solution to the advanced temporal data-stealing threat is described in Chapter 8. Chapter 9 concludes the book.

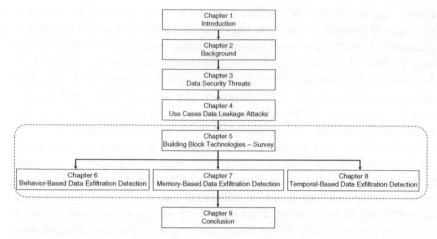

Figure 1.3 Book structure.

References

1 Faheem Ullah, Matthew Edwards, Rajiv Ramdhany, Ruzanna Chitchyan, M. Ali Babar, and Awais Rashid. Data exfiltration: a review of external attack vectors and countermeasures. *Elsevier Journal of Network and Computer Applications*, 101:18–54, 2018.

2 Scott Wilson, Susan Maphis, Helga George, Rebecca Turley, Steven Carver, and Hannah Coffman. Top 5 Most Technically Advanced Hacking Attacks of All Time. https://www.cybersecurityeducationguides.org/2017/11/top-5-most-technically-advanced-hacking-attacks-of-all-time/, 2017.

3 Verizon. 2020 Data Breach Investigations Report. https://enterprise.verizon .com/resources/reports/2020-data-breach-investigations-report.pdf, 2020.

4 Kevin Savage, Peter Coogan, and Hon Lau. The evolution of ransomware. Technical report, Symantec Corp., Mountain View, CA, USA. https://www .symantec.com/content/en/us/enterprise/media/security_response/whitepapers/ the-evolution-of-ransomware.pdf, 2015.

5 National Cyber Security Centre. Russian state-sponsored cyber actors targeting network infrastructure devices. https://www.ncsc.gov.uk/pdfs/blog-post/ malicious-russian-cyber-activity-what-does-it-mean-small-organisations.pdf, 2018.

6 Dan Conifer. Defence contractor's computer system hacked, files stolen, cyber security report reveals. https://www.abc.net.au/news/2017-10-10/defence-contractors-files-stolen-in-hacking:-security-report/9032290, October 2017.

7 Nicolas Falliere, Liam O. Murchu, and Eric Chien. W32. stuxnet dossier. *White paper, Symantec Corp., Security Response*, 5(6):29, 2011.

8 Zakir Durumeric, Frank Li, James Kasten, Johanna Amann, Jethro Beekman, Mathias Payer, Nicolas Weaver, David Adrian, Vern Paxson, Michael Bailey,

et al. The matter of heartbleed. In *Proceedings of the 2014 Conference on Internet Measurement Conference*, pages 475–488, 2014.

9 Hal Berghel. The code red worm. *Communications of the ACM (CACM)*, 44(12):15–19, 2001.

10 Vrizlynn L. L. Thing, Kian-Yong Ng, and Ee-Chien Chang. Live memory forensics of mobile phones. *Digital Investigation*, 7:S74–S82, 2010.

11 Annarita Giani, Vincent H. Berk, and George V. Cybenko. Data exfiltration and covert channels. In *Sensors, and Command, Control, Communications, and Intelligence (C3I) Technologies for Homeland Security and Homeland Defense V*, volume 6201, page 620103. International Society for Optics and Photonics, 2006.

12 Brian A. Powell. Malicious Overtones: hunting data theft in the frequency domain with one-class learning. *ACM Transactions on Privacy and Security (TOPS)*, 22(4):1–34, 2019.

13 Bonnie Zhu and Shankar S. Sastry. SCADA-specific intrusion detection/ prevention systems: a survey and taxonomy. In *Proceedings of the 1st Workshop on Secure Control Systems (SCS)*, volume 11. Berkeley University of California, 2010.

14 Robert Mitchell and Ing-Ray Chen. A survey of intrusion detection techniques for cyber-physical systems. *ACM Computing Surveys*, 46(4):55, 2014.

15 Hannes Holm, Martin Karresand, Arne Vidström, and Erik Westring. A survey of industrial control system testbeds. In *Proceedings of the 20th Nordic Conference on Secure IT Systems (NordSec 2015)*, pages 11–26. Springer International Publishing, October 2015.

16 Check Point Research. H2 2017 Global Threat Intelligence Trends Report. Technical report, Check Point Technologies Ltd. https://research.checkpoint .com/h2-2017-global-threat-intelligence-trends-report, 2018.

17 Symantec Corporation. Symantec internet security threat report 2017. Technical report, Symantec Corp. https://www.symantec.com/content/dam/ symantec/docs/reports/istr-22-2017-en.pdf, 2017.

18 Chinmayee Annachhatre, Thomas H. Austin, and Mark Stamp. Hidden Markov models for malware classification. *Springer Journal of Computer Virology and Hacking Techniques*, 11(2):59–73, 2015.

19 Gerardo Canfora, Francesco Mercaldo, and Corrado Aaron Visaggio. An HMM and structural entropy based detector for android malware: an empirical study. *Elsevier Journal on Computers & Security*, 61:1–18, 2016.

20 Anusha Damodaran, Fabio Di Troia, Corrado Aaron Visaggio, Thomas H. Austin, and Mark Stamp. A comparison of static, dynamic, and hybrid analysis for malware detection. *Springer Journal of Computer Virology and Hacking Techniques*, 13(1):1–12, 2017.

21 William R. Pearson. Searching protein sequence libraries: comparison of the sensitivity and selectivity of the Smith–Waterman and FASTA algorithms. *Elsevier Journal of Genomics*, 11(3):635–650, 1991.

22 Alfred V. Aho and Margaret J. Corasick. Efficient string matching: an aid to bibliographic search. *Communications of the ACM (CACM)*, 18(6):333–340, 1975.

23 Alberto Bartoli, Andrea De Lorenzo, Eric Medvet, and Fabiano Tarlao. Inference of regular expressions for text extraction from examples. *IEEE Transactions on Knowledge and Data Engineering (TKDE)*, 28(5):1217–1230, 2016.

24 Yuri Shapira, Bracha Shapira, and Asaf Shabtai. Content-based data leakage detection using extended fingerprinting. *arXiv preprint arXiv:1302.2028*, 2013.

25 Hao Zhuang, Rameez Rahman, Pan Hui, and Karl Aberer. Optimizing information leakage in multicloud storage services. *IEEE Transactions on Cloud Computing*, 8(4):975–988, 2018.

26 Hao Li, Zewu Peng, Xinyao Feng, and Hongxia Ma. Leakage prevention method for unstructured data based on classification. In *Proceedings of the Springer International Conference on Applications and Techniques in Information Security*, pages 337–343, 2015.

27 Chunwang Zhang, Ee-Chien Chang, and Roland H. C. Yap. Tagged-MapReduce: A general framework for secure computing with mixed-sensitivity data on hybrid clouds. In *Proceedings of the 14th IEEE/ACM International Symposium on Cluster, Cloud and Grid Computing*, pages 31–40, 2014.

28 Sultan Alneyadi, Elankayer Sithirasenan, and Vallipuram Muthukkumarasamy. Detecting data semantic: a data leakage prevention approach. In *Proceedings of the IEEE Trustcom/BigDataSE/ISPA International Conference*, volume 1, pages 910–917, 2015.

29 Shuaiji Li, Tao Huang, Zhiwei Qin, Fanfang Zhang, and Yinhong Chang. Domain Generation Algorithms detection through deep neural network and ensemble. In *Proceedings of the World Wide Web Conference (WWW)*, pages 189–196, 2019.

30 J. Hawkings and S. Blakeslee. On intelligence: how a new understanding of the brain will lead to the creation of truly intelligent machines. *An Owl Book*, Henry Holt and Company, New York, 2004.

31 Xiao Wang, Jianbiao Zhang, Ai Zhang, and Jinchang Ren. TKRD: Trusted kernel rootkit detection for cybersecurity of VMs based on machine learning and memory forensic analysis. *Mathematical Biosciences and Engineering*, 16(4):2650–2667, 2019.

32 Abraham Silberschatz, Peter B. Galvin, and Greg Gagne. *Operating System Concepts*. John Wiley & Sons, 2006.

33 Donald E. Knuth, James H. Morris, Jr., and Vaughan R. Pratt. Fast pattern matching in strings. *SIAM Journal on Computing*, 6(2):323–350, 1977.

34 Robert S. Boyer and J. Strother Moore. A fast string searching algorithm. *Communications of the ACM (CACM)*, 20(10):762–772, 1977.

35 Beate Commentz-Walter. A string matching algorithm fast on the average. In *Springer International Colloquium on Automata, Languages, and Programming*, pages 118–132, 1979.

2

Background

2.1 Hidden Markov Model

2.1.1 Definition

The HMM is essential to understand the methods described in Chapter 6. It is basically a statistical Markov model [1]. The modeling assumes that the system is a Markov process [2] with unobservable states. HMM explains the possibility of sequential events by assuming that the state of the system generating the event is hidden or unable to be observed. Given each underlying state, the system emits several observable events when the system is at a particular state. The emission can be described in terms of the probability of being emitted during a particular state. In contrast, each individual hidden state can also be described in terms of probability of transition from the previous hidden state. Notations listed in Table 2.1 are presented for clarification and will be used to formally describe the HMM later in this section.

HMM have three components: (i) state transition probability matrix A, (ii) state-related observation probability matrix B, and (iii) initial state probability matrix π. Overall, three probability matrices define the relationship between the sequence of the observable events and the hidden states, especially, the relationship between the hidden state Q and observations O. A explains the probability of hidden state q_i transforming to q_j at anytime t and $t + 1$, whereas $b_i(o_k)$ shows the likelihood of o_k being observed at time t if the hidden state is q_i, as illustrated in Figure 2.1.

Formally, let $Q = \{q_1, q_2, \ldots, q_N\}$ is a set of N hidden states, $V = \{v_1, v_2, \ldots, v_M\}$ is a set of M emissions, and $O = \{o_1, o_2, \ldots, o_T\}$ is a sequence of T observations, where $O \in V$. We can define HMM λ as:

$$\lambda = (A, B, \pi). \tag{2.1}$$

Data Exfiltration Threats and Prevention Techniques: Machine Learning and Memory-Based Data Security, First Edition. Zahir Tari, Nasrin Sohrabi, Yasaman Samadi, and Jakapan Suaboot.
© 2023 John Wiley & Sons, Inc. Published 2023 by John Wiley & Sons, Inc.

Table 2.1 HMM notation.

Notation	Description
N	The number of hidden states
M	The number of observable value or emission
T	The number of observation or sequence length
O	An observations vector size of T
Q	A set of N hidden states
V	A set of M possible observable value
A	State transition $N \times N$ matrix
B	State-related observation probability $N \times M$ matrix
π	Initial state probability $N \times 1$ vector

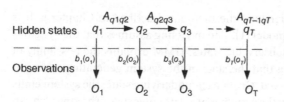

Figure 2.1 Relationship of HMM hidden state Q and observable event O in the Markov process.

The first probability matrix A describes the likelihood of the current hidden state being transferred to the next hidden state. The state transition matrix A is defined as:

$$A = (a_{ij}), \tag{2.2}$$

$$a_{ij} = P(q_{t+1} = j | q_t = i), \tag{2.3}$$

$$\sum_{j=1}^{N} a_{ij} = 1, \tag{2.4}$$

where $1 \leq (i,j) \leq N$, and A is a $N \times N$ matrix which represents transition probability between state i^{th} and j^{th}.

Second, the probability of each hidden state emitting the particular observable is described by the state-related observation probability matrix B. It is formally defined as:

$$B = (b_i(o_k)), \tag{2.5}$$

$$b_i(v_k) = P(v_k | q_i), \tag{2.6}$$

$$\sum_{k=1}^{M} b_i(o_k) = 1, \tag{2.7}$$

where $1 \le k \le M$, and B is a $N \times M$ matrix which shows that the probability of emission o_k being observed is generated by the hidden state q_i.

The last HMM component is the probability of the system being initialized with the particular hidden state. It is described as initial state probability matrix π, and formal description is as follows:

$$\pi = (\pi_1, \ldots, \pi_N), \tag{2.8}$$

$$\sum_{i=1}^{N} \pi_i = 1, \tag{2.9}$$

where π_i is the probability that states i^{th} is an initial hidden state of the system.

2.1.2 HMM Applications

HMM modeling faces the following three problems [2]:

- *Learning problem* is about HMM training by maximizing HMM λ parameters to best fit the training set. There are two well-known methods: Baum–Welch which uses the expectation maximization (EM) algorithm to find the maximum likelihood, and the Viterbi method which applied the dynamic programming algorithm to find the best hidden states [2].
- *Decoding problem* examines how to calculate the highest probable sequence of hidden state q that generates emission set of observable O. This can be used to simulate the possible system output from the trained HMM model.
- *Evaluation problem* aims to calculate probability that model λ has generated sequence O. This can be solved using forward (α-pass) or backward (β-pass) methods which are interchangeable [3].

The decoding problem is not considered here as the aim is to detect the unknown behavior using the known patterns of malware. This book analyses the limitations of the HMM evaluation method, and later describes a feature extraction method based on the HMM evaluation approach (i.e. forward algorithm [2]), details of which are given in Chapter 6. Hence, a standard approach (Baum–Welch algorithm [3]) is used for training the HMM model. Details of the Baum–Welch and forward algorithms are presented in the following section.

2.1.3 HMM Training Method

Baum–Welch algorithm is a method used to build HMM models from the observable behavior (i.e. HMM training algorithm), and the software application programming interface (API) call sequence is used to train the model.

This learning problem aims to find HMM parameters that maximize $P(O|\lambda)$ [3]. Specifically, we calculate the best A, B, π parameters that fit the training observable.

Since finding the best-fit parameters or global maximized values is an NP-hard problem, Baum–Welch uses iterative *EM* method [3] to find the local maximum instead. The algorithm estimates the maximum value of λ as follows:

- *Step 1*: Set up the initial values $\lambda = (A, B, \pi)$,
- *Step 2*: Compute $\alpha_t(i)$, $\beta_t(i)$, $\gamma_t(i)$, and $\gamma_t(i,j)$,
- *Step 3*: Re-estimate the model $\hat{\lambda}$,
- *Step 4*: Update parameters $\lambda \leftarrow \hat{\lambda}$, and
- *Step 5*: Repeat steps 2–4 until the threshold *tol* is satisfied or the maximum iteration is reached.

In **Step 1**, random value could be assigned to A and B as per conditions in Eqs. (2.4), (2.7), and (2.9). If the initial states are known, the π could be set to reflect the real-world probability. Otherwise, it could be set to equal likelihood for all the possible states.

In **Step 2**, details of each function mentioned are described in [4], summarized as follows. Let $\alpha_t(i)$ is the probability of the partial observation sequence up to time t, formally defined as:

$$\alpha_t(i) = \begin{cases} \alpha_1(i) = \pi_i b_i(o_1) & t = 1 \\ \alpha_{t+1}(j) = \left\{ \sum_{i=1}^{N} \alpha_t(i) a_{ij} \right\} b_j(o_{t+1}) & t > 1, \end{cases} \qquad (2.10)$$

where q_i is the hidden state. Second, $\beta_t(i)$ function denotes the probability similar to $\alpha_t(i)$, but the calculation starts from time T backward, defined as follows:

$$\beta_t(i) = \begin{cases} \beta_T(i) = 1 \\ \beta_t(i) = \sum_{j=1}^{N} a_{ij} b_j(o_{t+1}) \beta_{t+1}(j), \\ \beta_1(i) = \pi_i b_i(o_1) \end{cases} \qquad (2.11)$$

where $t = (T-1), \ldots, 1$. Third, $\gamma(i)$ calculates the most likely hidden state of the system at time t as follows:

$$\begin{aligned} \gamma(i) &= P(v_t = i | O, \lambda) \\ &= \frac{\alpha_t(i) \beta_t(i)}{P(O|\lambda)}. \end{aligned} \qquad (2.12)$$

Figure 2.2 The illustration of $\gamma_t(i,j)$ functions (so-called Di-gammas).

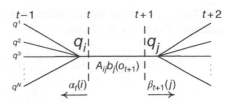

Figure 2.2 depicts the Di-gammas function, i.e. $\gamma_t(i,j)$, which is the probability being in state q_i at time t and state q_j at time $t+1$. The function is defined as follows:

$$\gamma(i,j) = P(v_t = i, v_{t+1} = j | O, \lambda)$$
$$= \frac{\alpha_t(i)a_{ij}b_j(O_{t+1})\beta_{t+1}(j)}{P(O|\lambda).} \tag{2.13}$$

In **Steps 3 and 4**, $\hat{\lambda} = (\hat{A}, \hat{B})$ are estimated in iterations. For each $i = 1, \dots, N$ and $j = 1, \dots, N$, the $\hat{a}_{ij}$ is computed by:

$$\hat{a}_{ij} = \frac{\sum_{t=1}^{T-1} \gamma_t(i,j)}{\sum_{t=1}^{T-1} \gamma_t(i)}. \tag{2.14}$$

Similarly, for each $j = 1, \dots, N$ and $k = 1, \dots, M$, $\hat{b}_j(k)$ is also computed by:

$$\hat{b}_j(k) = \frac{\sum_{t=1,o_t=k}^{T-1} \gamma_t(j)}{\sum_{t=1}^{T-1} \gamma_t(j)}. \tag{2.15}$$

In **Step 5**, the new estimation of $(\hat{A}, \hat{B})$ continues until the terminating criteria is met. The threshold *tol* (i.e. tolerance) is considered to stop the training process, and if this condition is satisfied the learning will stop. Here, the description of $P(O|\lambda)$ function is provided in Section 2.1.4. The stopping criterion is described as:

$$\log P(O|\lambda) - \log P(O|\hat{\lambda}) < tol.$$

Baum–Welch algorithm has a time complexity of $\mathcal{O}(NK^2)$. Obviously, this process is not runtime-efficient. Nevertheless, this training process is supposed to be a prerequisite of the monitoring phase. Hence, the accuracy of the detection model is more important than the runtime of the algorithm.

2.1.4 HMM Testing Method

Forward algorithm (so-called α-pass) is used to evaluate the testing samples with the trained HMM model, in context of this book, API call sequence of the unknown program. The goal of the forward algorithm is to test how likely the observation O being generated from HMM model λ, which is denoted by $P(O|\lambda)$. Formally, let

Q is the sequence of hidden states $Q = \{q_1, q_2, q_3, \dots, q_T\}$. The naïve method to calculate $\mathcal{P}(O|\lambda)$ is as follows:

$$\mathcal{P}(O|\lambda) = \sum_{t=1}^{T} \pi_{q_1} b_{q_1}(o_1) a_{q_1 q_2} b_{q_1}(o_2) \dots$$
$$a_{q_{T-1} q_T} b_{q_{t-1}}(o_T). \tag{2.16}$$

Unfortunately, the calculation method in Eq. (2.16) is inefficient due to time complexity of $\mathcal{O}(2TN^T)$. Hence, the forward algorithm offers a more efficient computation method that requires only $\mathcal{O}(N^2 T)$, detailed as follows:

$$\mathcal{P}(O|\lambda) = \sum_{i=1}^{N} \alpha_T(i), \tag{2.17}$$

where $\alpha_{t+1}(j)$ is defined in Eq. (2.10). However, as the number of observation T is growing large, the value of $\mathcal{P}(O|\lambda)$ will fall exponentially close to zero. In general, the *log-likelihood*, i.e. $\log \mathcal{P}(O|\lambda)$, will be used instead of the actual $\mathcal{P}(O|\lambda)$. This allows a longer observation sequence to be tested for the matching likelihood.

2.2 Memory Forensics

Memory forensics sits under the umbrella of *digital forensics*, which includes recovering and investigating material found in digital devices, frequently related to cybercrime [5]. However, memory forensics uses only volatile memory (i.e. random-access memory [RAM]) as a source of evidence. Memory *acquisition* and information *analysis* are crucial processes of memory forensics. This book focuses primarily on the *analysis* of the data already extracted from the memory, specifically detection of the sensitive data (see Chapters 7 and 8). Various memory acquisition strategies are described in this section to show the reader how the methods described in this book are applicable to real-world scenarios, even though companies have different computer systems.

2.2.1 Memory Acquisition Strategies

The physical memory data can be acquired by means of various methodologies. The decision can be made with regard to system-specific requirements. To implement a suitable memory acquisition strategy, one needs to consider several factors. Figure 2.3 depicts a decision tree showing how to apply the right memory acquisition strategy to the particular computer system. First, if the system is running on the virtual machine (VM), the memory snapshot can be captured simply by using hypervisor software utilities, such as snapshot, clone, host disk,

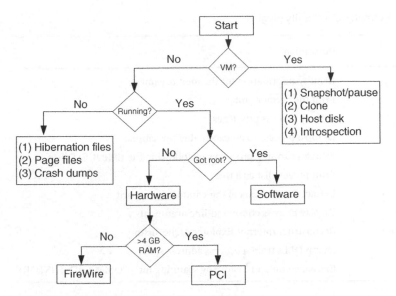

Figure 2.3 The decision flowchart of choosing memory acquisition strategies. Source: Adapted from "The art of memory forensics: detecting malware and threats in Windows, Linux, and Mac memory," by M. H. Ligh, A. Case, J. Levy, and A. Walter, 2014. John Wiley & Sons, page 71.

or introspection [6]. On the other hand, if the computer system is running on the physical machine or bare-metal server, the memory acquisition strategy varies depending on other factors. If the system is not running, very few options are available. Mainly the operating system's temporary files, such as hibernation files, page files or crash dumps, are saved on the hard drive. If the system is running and the administrator's privilege is available, then many memory acquisition software could be used, such as Linux Memory Extractor (LiME) [7], Linux Memory Grabber [8], WindowsSCOPE software suite [9], Belkasoft Live RAM Caputer [10], and Goldfish [11].

If the system is running, but the administrator privilege is unavailable, the security team requires special hardware to obtain the data from the physical RAM, such as the FireWire interface [12]. This interface allows access to the physical memory as the FireWire device has the privilege of direct memory access (DMA). However, the FireWire trick only allows up to 4 GB of memory to be accessed. If the system has RAM larger than 4 GB, a special peripheral component interconnect (PCI) device is required. Although it allows the examination of an unlimited memory size, the special PCI device has a high price: the one sold by the WindowsSCOPE company costs around 8000 USD [6].

The memory-based methods have been evaluated by using memory data acquired from the VM; hence, only hypervisor tools are used. The focus of this

Table 2.2 Examples of Volatility plugins.

Plugin	Description
imageinfo	Identify information for the memory image
memmap	Print the memory map
privs	Display process privileges
procdump	Dump a process to an executable file sample
pslist	Print all running processes by following the EPROCESS lists
pstree	Print process list as a tree
clipboard	Extract the contents of the windows clipboard
cmdline	Display process command-line arguments
iehistory	Reconstruct Internet Explorer cache/history
dlldump	Dump DLLs from a process address space
cmdscan	Extract command history by scanning for _COMMAND_HISTORY

book is on the development of a memory analysis approach rather than a memory acquisition method. Furthermore, free open-source VM software is also available (e.g. Oracle VirtualBox [13]).

2.2.2 Memory Analysis Tool

The open-source Volatility software [14] is the main memory analysis tool used in this research. Based on the extracted memory image (so-called memory snapshot), Volatility reconstructs the meta-data into a binary memory image. In other words, it interprets the binary image and presents it as a human-understandable data structure, for instance, basic data types (e.g. char, int, and double), abstract data types (e.g. arrays, bitmaps records, linked-list, hash-table, and trees) [6]. This basic data structure helps Volatility plugins to rebuild usable evidences from aspects of operating systems or software programs, such as messages, images, encryption keys, and so on.

Table 2.2 shows examples of many useful Volatility plugins [15] for memory analysis. For instance, imageinfo is a very useful plugin for identifying the exact version of the operating system. Having an accurate version of the OS is very important because it indicates the specific data structure used by the particular version of the OS. Also, Volatility rebuilds the usable information from the binary image by using the preconfigured data structure types. Other plugins help to visualize the status of the system while it is running. For example, pslist and pstree help to identify the processes that are running, making it easier to pinpoint the process that we want to investigate further. Obviously, other plugins (listed in Table 2.2) are also very useful for the manual or automatic analysis and detection of sensitive data exfiltration. In fact, Volatility has several more plugins that are not mentioned here. In particular, those plugins are designed for other memory forensics tasks; a full list of the plugins and usage details is available at [15].

In this book, *Volatility* has been chosen as a RAM analysis program because it has a complete collection of tools needed to analyze the program's behavior (i.e. used in Chapter 6). Also, it helps to extract string content from the specific memory region of a running process for the methods described in Chapters 7 and 8. Moreover, *Volatility* is open source and free to use. Also, it is the most popular memory analysis tool among digital forensics research [5], allowing practitioners to design their plugins to perform specific tasks as required by the particular project.

2.3 Bag-of-Words Model

The focus in Chapters 7 and 8 is on detecting sensitive data in textual (i.e. plain text) documents. For several decades, the BoW method [16] has been extensively used to represent the text document in various research fields, such as documents classification, natural language processing, and information retrieval. The important advantage of BoW is that it reduces the size of the original text document, especially a long document, by replacing paragraphs with a set of unique word–frequency pairs. In other words, it stores a term that is used multiple times throughout the document as one object. This object consists of the term and the number of times the term appears in the document. This not only shrinks the size of the data storage capacity required for multiple documents but also allows any two documents to be compared based on their BoW model.

Say, once has two paragraphs and wants to generate BoWs:

Paragraph 1: Yesterday I saw a deer. Today I have a test.

Paragraph 2: He wants to pass a test, so he does not go out.

To transform these paragraphs into BoWs, the string of each paragraph needs to be broken down into individual terms. Also, the punctuation (e.g. ".", ",", "",";","-", etc.) and letter case are discarded. Specifically, all capital letters are converted to lower case, and the punctuation is replaced with the space character. The processed paragraphs are as follows:

Paragraph 1: "yesterday", "i", "saw", "a", "deer", "today", "i", "have", "a", "test"

Paragraph 2: "he", "wants", "to", "pass", "a", "test", "so", "he", "does", "not", "go", "out"

After that, pairs of term-frequency are stored in the BoW. In this example, we show the BoW in JSON format, so it is easy to read. One JSON object represents one paragraph. The resulting BoWs from paragraphs 1 and 2 are as follows:

BoW 1: {"yesterday":1, "i":2, "saw":1, "a":2, "deer":1, "today":1, "have":1, "test":1};

BoW 2: {"he":2, "wants":1, "to":1, "pass":1, "a":1, "test":1, "so":1, "does":1, "not":1, "go":1, "out":1};

BoW 1 and BoW 2 have only term frequency {"test":1} in common. Hence, the size BoW dictionary, which contains all unique term frequency, is 18 pairs. This BoW dictionary will be updated when more paragraphs are added to the text database. When comparing unknown text to the known text in the database, term frequency that is not in the BoW dictionary is discarded as it cannot be matched.

In this book, the BoW dictionary can be stored in a more efficient data structure, such as a hash map. The hash map allows the BoW lookup operation to be very efficient with constant runtime complexity, i.e. $\mathcal{O}(1)$. This allows us to design an efficient filter for extracting terms associated with the sensitive document, more details of which are given in Chapters 7 and 8.

2.4 Sparse Distributed Representation

SDR is one of the data representation methods. Initially, the SDR method emerged from the idea of imitating the natural visual cortex cells [17]. SDR is fundamentally an array of binary, representing attributes of the objects. The array contains mostly zero values (i.e. OFF) with a few ON bits (hence, sparse) [18]. In Chapter 8, the SDR is used as a fundamental representation of a text document, because it can represent temporal-observable patterns, including temporal data exfiltration. Furthermore, SDR offers several useful operations that are needed for the temporary memory method (discussed in Chapter 8).

To give basic idea of how SDR represents a text document, let take example from Section 2.3. The BoW dictionary, which is built from a combination of BoW 1 and BoW 2, consists of 18 term-frequency pairs, as the following:

BoW dictionary: {"yesterday":1, "i":2, "saw":1, "a":2, "deer":1, "today":1, "have":1, "test":1, "he":2, "wants":1, "to":1, "pass":1, "a":1, "so":1, "does":1, "not":1, "go":1, "out":1};

Let x and y denote SDR vectors of BoW 1 and 2. The size of SDR vector is equal to the size of the BoW dictionary, which is 18 bits. Each bit represents the presence or absence of the particular term-frequency pair at its position in the BoW dictionary. Hence, x and y vectors are as follows:

x: [1 1 1 1 1 1 1 1 0 0 0 0 0 0 0 0 0 0]

y: [0 0 0 0 0 0 0 1 1 1 1 1 1 1 1 1 1 1]

One can easily compare similarity between x and y by finding the number of overlapping bits. In this context, the similarity is equivalent to the dot product of x and y [18]:

$$overlap(x, y) \equiv x \cdot y.$$

The temporal pattern is detected by combining several observations over a period of time. Hence, the union of SDRs vector observed in different time points could be used to recognize the temporal pattern that occurs over time. The union operation of two or more SDRs can be done using the bitwise logical OR operation [18], for example:

x_1: [1 0 0 0 0 0 0 1 0 0 0 0 0 0 0 $\cdots$ 0 0 0]

x_2: [0 0 0 0 0 0 0 1 1 1 0 0 0 0 1 $\cdots$ 0 0 1]

$$\vdots$$

x_n: [0 1 0 0 0 0 0 1 0 1 0 0 0 0 1 $\cdots$ 0 1 1]

$$X = x_1 \vee x_2 \vee x_3 \ldots x_n$$

X: [1 1 0 0 0 0 0 1 1 0 0 0 0 0 0 $\cdots$ 0 1 0]

As can be seen, the SDR operations are very intuitive when it comes to representing the temporal patterns. On top of that, the bit-level operations allow an application to be runtime- and memory-efficient, especially, when the application is running on the modern multicore processor. In particular, when the parallel programming is used, several bitwise operations could be improved even further.

2.5 Summary

This chapter presented both general and technical information which should enable a reader to better understand the methods that will be described in the remaining chapters of the book. Fundamental operations of the HMM were described, which is necessary for understanding the method elaborated in Chapter 6. Afterward, basic information about memory forensics was provided, especially regarding the acquisition and analysis of data from RAM, which are essential for the methods described in Chapters 7 and 8. The concepts of BoW model and SDRs are illustrated with examples.

References

1 Kristie Seymore, Andrew McCallum, Roni Rosenfeld, et al. Learning hidden Markov model structure for information extraction. In *AAAI Workshop on Machine Learning for Information Extraction*, pages 37–42, 1999.

2 M. Bishop Christopher. *Pattern Recognition and Machine Learning*. Springer, 2016.

3 Gernot A. Fink. *Markov Models for Pattern Recognition: From Theory to Applications*. Springer, 2nd edition, 2014.

4 Mark Stamp. A Revealing Introduction to Hidden Markov Models. http://www.cs.sjsu.edu/faculty/stamp/RUA/HMM.pdf, 2018.

5 Tobias Latzo, Ralph Palutke, and Felix Freiling. A universal taxonomy and survey of forensic memory acquisition techniques. *Elsevier Journal of Digital Investigation*, 28:56–69, 2019.

6 Michael Hale Ligh, Andrew Case, Jamie Levy, and Aaron Walters. *The Art of Memory Forensics: Detecting Malware and Threats in Windows, Linux, and Mac Memory*. John Wiley & Sons, 2014.

7 Joe Sylve. Lime-Linux memory extractor. https://github.com/504ensicslabs/lime, 2012.

8 Hal Pomeranz. Script for automating Linux memory capture. https://github.com/halpomeranz/lmg/, 2020.

9 WindowsSCOPE Group. WindowsSCOPE Windows memory forensics tools. http://www.windowsscope.com/, 2020.

10 Belkasoft. Belkasoft RAM Capturer: Volatile Memory Acquisition Tool. https://belkasoft.com/ram-capturer, 2020.

11 Digital Forensics Investigation Research Laboratory. Goldfish. http://digitalfire.ucd.ie/?page_id=430/, 2020.

12 Carsten Maartmann-Moe. Inception is a physical memory manipulation and hacking tool exploiting PCI-based DMA. https://github.com/carmaa/inception, 2020.

13 Oracle Corporation. Oracle VirtualBox. https://www.virtualbox.org/manual/ch08.html, 2017.

14 Aaron Walters. Volatility Wiki. https://github.com/volatilityfoundation/volatility/wiki, 2020.

15 Aaron Walters. Volatility plugins developed and maintained by the community. https://github.com/volatilityfoundation/community, 2021.

16 Zellig S. Harris. Distributional structure. *Word*, 10(2–3):146–162, 1954.

17 Michael Weliky, József Fiser, Ruskin H. Hunt, and David N. Wagner. Coding of natural scenes in primary visual cortex. *Neuron*, 37(4):703–718, 2003.

18 Subutai Ahmad and Jeff Hawkins. Properties of sparse distributed representations and their application to hierarchical temporal memory. *arXiv preprint arXiv:1503.07469*, 2015.

3

Data Security Threats

Computer systems are vulnerable to a variety of potential threats, which can cause considerable financial damage and harm to resources [1]. Security threats can cause a wide range of damage, including the physical destruction of an entire information system (IS) facility due to a fire or flood, and database integrity security breaches [2]. These threats can occur from unauthorized actions taken by "reliable" employees, hacker attacks, unintentional data entry errors, etc. [2]. A security threat is anything that has the potential to compromise the confidentiality, integrity, or availability of information or cause other types of information system resources to be compromised. Since the effects of security threats are varied, some have an impact on the accuracy or dependability of data that has been saved, while others have an impact on the operation and effectiveness of the overall information system [1]. Security threats can be identified and categorized using a variety of methods and standards.

A group of attackers may move slowly and deliberately in some attacks to achieve their objective, which is typically to steal the target's data secretly. Advanced persistent threats (APTs) is the name given to this category of attacks (APT). Although APT attackers may employ well-known methods to gain access to their target entity's network, the tools they use are unfamiliar [3]. As the word implies, sophisticated tools are utilized, which is necessary for an attacker to remain persistent in the network for a long time. They remain undetected while gradually spreading their influence over the organization's network, gathering information along the way and exporting it to their command and control center in a structured way [3].

There are different main data security threats such as Malware, Denial of Service (DoS), SQL injection, Emotet (malspam), social engineering and phishing, Man-in-the-Middle (MITM), and password attacks. Each of these data security threats has its specific features for stealing the data and compromising any given system. For instance, a malware means unauthorized actions on the victim's system.

Data Exfiltration Threats and Prevention Techniques: Machine Learning and Memory-Based Data Security, First Edition. Zahir Tari, Nasrin Sohrabi, Yasaman Samadi, and Jakapan Suaboot.

DoS disables, shut down or disrupt a network, website, or service. SQL injection gives unauthorized access to a web application database. Emotet (malspam) is kind of Trojan that is primarily spread through spam emails. Social engineering and phishing attack steal user data, including login credentials and credit card numbers. MITM listen to the messages between two parties. Password attacks tries to steal user's password. Each of these data security threats are of various types, and they are explained in Sections 3.1–3.4.

This chapter provides details of security threats so to enable readers to have a better understanding of the various concepts related cybersecurity threats.

3.1 Data Security

The term *information security* means protecting sensitive information and systems from unauthorized access, use, disclosure, disruption, modification, or destruction in order to provide confidentiality, integrity, and availability [1]. *Data security* refers to preserving digital data against unwanted access, corruption, and theft across all stages of its life cycle [4]. It is a concept that covers every aspect of information security, including the logical security of applications, administrative and access controls, and the physical security of hardware and storage devices. Specific policies and procedures are used to guarantee data security. Robust data security strategies help to protect an organization's information system (IS) against cybersecurity activities such as insider threats like downloading or accessing unnatural amounts of data, accessing sensitive data not associated with their job, and human errors like poor hygiene habits or misdelivering emails. Another strategy could be utilizing/deploying the current technologies, methods, and tools which can help to increase the control over the data. These tools can increase the organization's visibility into where its critical data are located and how they are being used. Preferably, these tools should be qualified to apply protections like encryption, data masking, and redaction of private information; and reporting should be automated to speed up audits and ensure compliance with legal standards [5].

The CIA triad of Confidentiality, Integrity, and Availability is a common model that serves as the foundation for security system development [4]. Figures 3.1 and 3.2 depict the CIA triad model and their relations. They are used to identify vulnerabilities and to develop cybersecurity strategies for problem solving. This separation is necessary since it directs security teams to determine the many approaches they might take to each issue [6]. Whenever all three standards are implemented, any system will be much more robust and better equipped to face any data security threats.

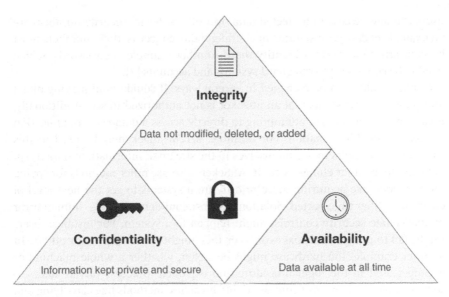

Figure 3.1 CIA Triad.

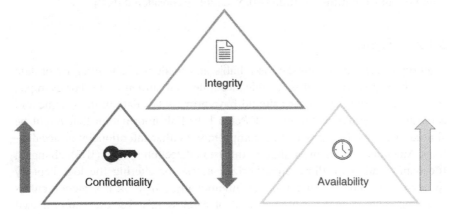

Figure 3.2 CIA Triad relations.

3.1.1 Confidentiality

Confidentiality in data security triads ensures that the data are kept secret or private [6]. Accessing the data must be controlled to prevent any purposeful or accidental unauthorized data sharing. A crucial component is that only authorized users can access information, and any other unauthorized use should be banned. A reliable system must guarantee that only the qualified/authorized users can have access to protected data over others. Social security numbers are an example of data with significant confidentiality concerns; these numbers must be kept private to prevent identity theft. Another example is passwords, which need to be kept secret to safeguard systems and accounts [7].

Confidentiality can be breached in several ways. It could entail making direct attacks to access systems that an attacker is not authorized to see. Additionally, it can involve an attacker attempting to directly access a database or application to steal or alter information. For example, MITM attack may be used in this case, where attackers locate themselves in the stream of information to intercept data and then either change/steal it. Attackers also use other methods for spying on networks, like acquiring more priority from systems to get the next level of clearance. Other unexpected violations against confidentiality, e.g. human error or inadequate security controls, might happen to a system. For instance, users might fail to protect their passwords, or they might share them with others. In another example, the hardware might be stolen, whether a whole machine or a gadget used in the login procedure and exploited to access private data. To secure a system in terms of confidentiality breaches, methods like classifying and labeling-restricted data, enabling access control policies, encrypting data, and using multifactor authentication (MFA) could be considered [6, 7].

3.1.2 Integrity

Integrity ensures that your data is reliable and unaltered. The integrity of data can only be preserved if it is reliable, accurate, and authentic [6]. For example, in an organization, employees should have primary key data of their name and a particular "employee number." Foreign keys link information that might be shared or empty. Integrity can be compromised either intentionally or accidentally. Attempts such as bypassing an intrusion detection system (IDS), changing file configuration to allow unauthorized access, or altering the logs kept by the system to hide the attack occur intentionally. However, if someone enters a wrong code or makes another kind of careless mistake, the compromised integrity is accidental. Also, if the security policies of a company are weak, integrity can be abused without any one individual in the company taking responsibility [7].

There are different methods/algorithms that can be applied to provide integrity, such as hashing and encryption algorithms, digital certificates, and digital signatures. Companies can use trustworthy certificate authorities (CAs) to obtain a digital certificate for their websites so that their users can be assured they are accessing a trusted website. Nonrepudiation, which refers to when something cannot be disputed or repudiated, is a method for confirming integrity. For example, providing digital signatures is popular among organizations when sending emails. Digital signatures prevent denial from senders and receivers [6, 7].

3.1.3 Availability

This is the most significant component in this triad since data should be available for users; otherwise, confidentiality and integrity of the data are useless. This requires that all systems, networks, and applications operate properly and at the appropriate moments [6]. Users who work with specific data should easily have access to it at any time. For instance, if electricity is cutoff in an organization and there is no disaster recovery system, the availability of the data will be compromised. Other examples such as intentional sabotage like ransomware or DoS attacks might jeopardize availability[1] [7].

Organizations can guarantee the availability of the data by using extra networks, servers, and applications as backup systems. These can be set up to become available if the main system is down or broken. Also, availability is increased by improving software packages and security systems. By considering availability issues like backup systems and extra network, and servers that are mentioned above, the possibility of malfunction of a program or any breach in data will be reduced. Backups and disaster recovery strategies could also assist systems in quickly regaining availability following data threats [6, 7].

3.2   Security vs. Protection vs. Privacy

Data security, data protection, and data privacy are three different terms that are mostly confused with each other. As mentioned, data security preserves private information against unauthorized access or usage, where it might be compromised, lost, or corrupted. For example, encryption methods are used for securing data against hackers. Data protection refers to protecting the data from unintentional loss or destruction. Therefore, any backup of the data is considered a data protection example. Concerns about how much data is processed, like data sensitivity, regulatory requirements, consent, and notifications related to data privacy. The use of a separate, secure database for personally identifiable information is an illustration of data privacy [8]. Figure 3.3. provides a summary of the different aspects related data protection.

---

1 Ransomware and DoS attacks will be explained further in this chapter.

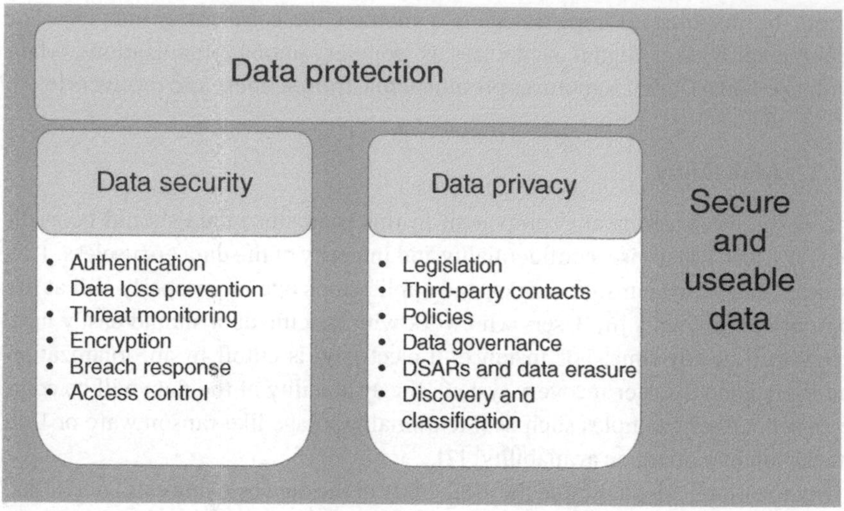

Figure 3.3 Data security, privacy, protection.

3.3 Advanced Persistent Threats Attacks

The idea of an attack using a variety of sophisticated methods intended to steal the company's crucial data is what keeps corporate cybersecurity professionals up at night, if there is one thing that does [3]. APTs can enter a system and stay there for a long time with potentially damaging consequences by employing continuous, discrete, and sophisticated hacking methods. APTs are directed at high-value targets, such as nation-states and major corporations, due to the effort required to carry out such an attack. The ultimate goal of these attacks is to steal information over an extended period, as opposed to "dipping in" and leaving quickly, as many black hat hackers do during lower-level cyberattacks. Businesses everywhere should be aware of the APT attack method. Small- and medium-sized firms should not disregard this kind of attack, though. To reach large organizations, APT attackers are increasingly leveraging smaller businesses that are a part of their target organization's supply chain. They employ these businesses as stepping stones because they are often less well defended. Figure 3.4 shows how a typical APT attacks moves in five stages [9].

- *Access*: Hackers can spread malware using phishing emails, fake applications, social engineering, and infected files.
- *Settle*: Once the infection is active, hackers can quickly access your systems. Hackers may use their coding skills to hide their activities because the purpose is to avoid detection.

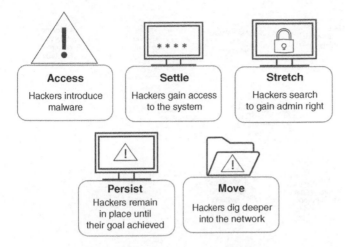

Figure 3.4   How advanced persistent threats work.

- *Stretch*: Hackers look for ways to access administrator rights.
- *Move*: Hackers access deeper areas of your network and connect to other sites.
- *Persist*: Hackers remain in place until they've accomplished a certain objective. Even then, they might make it possible for them to come back if necessary.

The main objective of APT attacks is to access systems, and attackers employ the following five steps. Figure 3.5 depicts an APT attack life cycle [3, 9].

- *Gain access (stage #1)*: Cybercriminals typically use networks, infected files, spam emails, or applications vulnerabilities to insert malware into a target network.
- *Establish a foothold (stage #2)*: Malware that is installed by cybercriminals allows the creation of a network of backdoors and tunnels that are used to move around in systems undetected. To help hackers hide their tracks, malware frequently use known methods like code rewriting.
- *Deepen access (stage #3)*: Once inside, hackers employ strategies like password cracking to achieve administrator rights, which they can use to take over more of the system and gain even more access.
- *Move laterally (stage #4)*: Hackers can move freely deeper inside a system if they have administrator rights. They could even try to enter other secure areas of the network, such as other servers.
- *Look, learn, and remain (stage #5)*: From within a system, hackers can fully comprehend how it functions and its points of vulnerability, giving them the freedom to gather any data they desire. Hackers can try to continue this procedure indefinitely or stop once they've achieved their objective. They frequently leave a back door open, so they can enter the system again later.

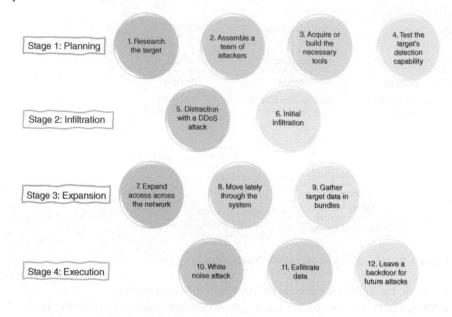

Figure 3.5 Advanced persistent threats life cycle.

3.4 Cybersecurity Threats

Cybersecurity threats are a reflection of any breach and weakness in the security of the sensitive data or information of a system. Deliberate and malicious activities to break the systems of organizations or individuals are considered a breach of cybersecurity. These activities occur for different goals such as information theft, financial gain, spying, or sabotage [10]. Reports show that cyberthreats are quickly expanding, and there are various types of data threats; hence, organizations and individuals are unable to protect themselves against all of these threats. Malicious software is one of the major threats that can lead to successful/desired damages on the targeted systems. Security threats include a malicious network attack accessing a port on the firewall, a process accessing data security policy improperly, a tornado wiping up a facility, or a user accidentally exposing sensitive data or destroying the integrity of a file [11, 12]. Figure 3.6 depicts the various types of data security threats and their definitions.

Protecting systems, networks, and programs from digital attacks is the practice of cybersecurity. Today, there are more devices than humans, and hackers are getting more creative, making it hard to implement efficient cybersecurity measures. In the connected world, cutting-edge cyber defense programs are beneficial to everyone. A cybersecurity attack can lead to any type of attack, from identity theft to extortion attempts to the loss of crucial information like health-related data or personal data revealing racial or ethnic origin, political opinions, religious,

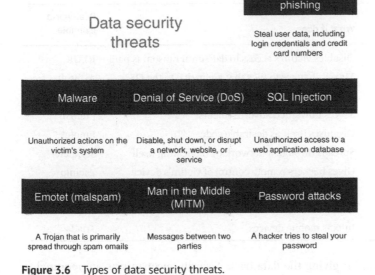

Figure 3.6 Types of data security threats.

or philosophical beliefs. Protecting critical information, such as power plants, hospitals, and financial service providers, is essential for everyone. Therefore, for an efficient society, it is crucial to secure these organizations [12].

3.4.1 Malware

The term "malicious software," or simply "malware," refers to a variety of suspicious or intrusive software [13]. Cybercriminals use malware to steal information, access restricted accounts, access a computer, or damage the target computer, its data, or its programs [14]. The multiplication of malware attacks resulted in an exponential increase in the number, types, and complexity of malware produced [13]. Additionally, generic antivirus software on its own is unable to recognize malware mutations and their variants which leaves the user and system open to attack at all times [15]. A malware describes by Vasudevan and Yerraballi in as "a generic term that encompasses viruses, trojans, spywares and other intrusive code" [16]. Malware canonical examples include Trojan horses, worms, viruses, spyware, and ransomware. Table 3.1 provides an overview on the most common types of malware and their real-world examples.

3.4.1.1 Ransomware

A malware, which is known as *Ransomware*, is used by cybercriminals to stop users from accessing their data until they pay a ransom. If a computer system or network has been infected with ransomware, ransomware prohibits access to the system or encrypts its data [17]. Attackers request ransom money from their

Table 3.1 Types of malware.

Type	What it does	Real-world example
Ransomware	Disables victim's access to data until ransom is paid	RYUK
Fileless malware	Makes changes to files that are native to the OS	Astaroth
Spyware	Collects user activity data without their knowledge	DarkHotel
Adware	Serves unwanted advertisements	Fireball
Trojans	Disguises itself as desirable code	Emotet
Worms	Spreads through a network by replicating itself	Stuxnet
Rootkits	Gives hackers remote control of victim's device	Zacinlo
Keyloggers	Monitors user's keystrokes	Olympic Vision
Bots	Launches a broad flood of attacks	Echobot
Mobile malware	Infects mobile devices	Triada

victims in return for giving the data back. Security mechanisms are required to protect the system from this kind of attack. Victims face three different options after they are infected with the ransomware attack. They can either pay the ransom, attempt to get rid of the malware, or restart the device [18].

The Remote Desktop Protocol, phishing emails, and software vulnerabilities are frequent attack methods employed by extortion Trojans. A ransomware attack can therefore target both individuals and companies [17, 19]. Figure 3.7 shows the ransomware life cycle steps.

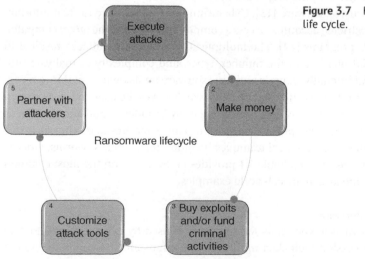

Figure 3.7 Ransomware life cycle.

Attackers usually ask for a huge amount of ransom money, especially if the blocked data represents a significant financial loss for the company or the individual being attacked. For example, in *WordPress ransomware* and *The Wolverine case*, the cyberattack victim is, or was, more important than the type of ransomware used [17]. "WordPress ransomware" targets WordPress website files. As it is typical in ransomware, the victim is required to pay a ransom. In "Wolverine case," the malware encrypted a large number of the company's files, making it impossible for employees to open them. Thus, a significant amount of patient's data was compromised and information such as names, addresses, medical data, and other personal data might have been obtained by cybercriminals [17, 19].

The most commonly applied ransomware are

- *Locker ransomware*: This type of malware blocks fundamental computer functions and does not usually target critical files. For instance, the desktop may be unavailable to the victim while the keyboard and mouse are still partially working. This only allows the victim to proceed with interacting with the window displaying the ransom demand so that the victim can make a payment.
- *Crypto ransomware*: This type of malware encrypts users' sensitive data such as documents, pictures. Users can see their files, but there is no access to them. Attackers mostly add a countdown to their ransom request and threaten users by deleting their data if they do not pay the ransom. Crypto ransomware can have a disastrous effect since many users are ignorant of the necessity for backups in the cloud or on external physical storage devices. As a result, many victims pay the ransom to access their files.

3.4.1.2 Fileless Malware

Fileless malware is a kind of malicious activity that uses native, legitimate tools built into a system to execute a cyberattack [20]. Current fileless malware uses a reliable and legitimate process, while traditional file-based malware uses real malicious executables. Fileless malware attacks do not download malicious files or write any content to the disk. To directly inject malicious code into the main memory, the attacker only uses the vulnerable application as a point of attack. Using native Windows administration tools such as Microsoft Office or WMI to execute scripts and inject malicious code into volatile memory are examples of fileless malware attacks. In these examples, the attacker can also make use of widely and trustworthy applications. Fileless malware life cycle includes three different phases and Figure 3.8 shows the infection flow of fileless malware [21].

- *Attack vector*: This includes methods the attacker uses to target their victims.
- *Execution mechanism*: The malicious code's initial execution mechanism may attempt to build a registry entry for its persistence or WMI object with VBScript/JScript to invoke an instance of PowerShell.

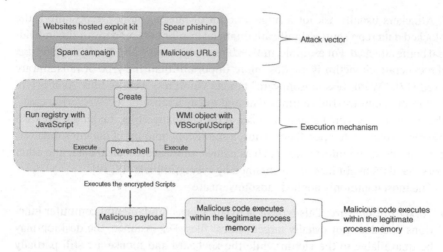

Figure 3.8 Infection flow of fileless malware.

- *Compromised host running malicious program in memory*: PowerShell can execute malicious code directly into the memory of a legitimate process without transferring any files to the file system, making its target vulnerable to fileless malware.

3.4.1.3 Spyware

Malware known as spyware comes from indirect penetration, such as monitoring software that has been covertly installed on computers, rather than direct attacks by viruses or hackers. "Spyware" is the term for these monitoring tools, which keep track of a user's online activities and share it with outside parties. Spyware can help to direct targeted advertising to computers and is frequently used by marketers to gather customer data for segmentation and targeting purposes. Since installations can be approved as a part of the licensed "clickwrap" agreement that users agree to when installing free utility and file-sharing applications from the Internet, spyware is frequently employed legally. In certain circumstances, spyware is installed as a component of genuine computer software companies sell to their clients to give application users updates and communication features. It would seem that the chance to monitor remotely and connect with computers is appealing enough to draw the interest of outside parties with malicious intentions [22]. Spyware is software that takes control of a user's computer without the user's permission. Spyware includes Adware, Keyloggers, and Trojan Horses. These programs consume resources and bandwidth on the user's computer, and, at worst, seriously compromise its security [22].

3.4.1.4 Adware

Applications classified as adware carry out a variety of tasks, including the following:

• They keep track of user's online activity and provide relevant adverts to their desktops depending on that behavior.
• Installing "browser assistance objects" adware can alter how a user's web browser operates.
• They can alter Web browsers' basic settings to display various home pages, bookmark lists, and search engine redirects.

Many remote monitoring adware programs are described by their developers as having legitimate commercial purposes and are designed by particular business models intended to present users with tailored pop-up adverts since they are engaged in Internet browsing and search activity [22].

3.4.1.5 Keyloggers

Before the era of personal computers, various types of user monitoring software were available. There are applications to record login ID and password data from terminals. Some keyboard loggers are marketed as legal tools for monitoring coworkers or family members, but despite their claim of authenticity, this type of spyware is nevertheless quite common and dangerous. The usage of "activity monitors" is used for a variety of reasons, from the highly illegal (such as identity theft or blatant spying) to the highly legitimate (such as parents or employers monitoring their charges for acceptable Internet use). Hackers also employ keyloggers to access the networks and capture passwords and are mostly part of Trojan Horses attacks. Mechanical keyloggers attached to computer keyboards are another type of keystroke logger [22].

3.4.1.6 Trojan Horse

The term "Trojan" comes from the Greek history of the Trojan Horse, and it is called Remote Administration Trojan (RAT) for its spyware features [23, 24]. Trojans are malicious code or pieces of code that sneak into a computer and pretend to be a legitimate program before taking control of it without the user or IT administrator ever realizing it. A Trojan is technically a type of malware instead of a virus. There is a difference between Trojan malware and Trojan viruses since a Trojan cannot be executed by itself and must be executed by the user, whereas viruses can execute and replicate themselves [23]. In this type of spyware, there is an unknown and unexpected delivery in a package that a user may usually accept. These packages typically contain free software downloads, such as peer-to-peer file sharing programs or computer games. Trojans entail the installation of programs that can be accessed by other computers and give the attacker control of the host computer [24]. Their dangers range from straightforward dialer programs made to activate user modems and incur high toll fees to more nefarious modifications of network administration tools like Back Orifice or SubSeven that take advantage of flaws in the Microsoft operating system to allow unauthorized users to capture screen displays and keyboard input or take over a remote computer [22].

Although authorized network administrators frequently utilize remote administration to monitor and manage the networks they are in charge of, Trojans do not use specific applications to attack systems. A Trojan needs a user to download the client side of the application for it to function. Trojan cannot attack a device unless the executable file (.exe) is used and the program is installed. Trojans function by posing as trusted files and tricking users into clicking, opening, or installing them. As soon as this happens, the Trojan starts to download malware onto the device and runs every time the infected device is switched on [13]. For example, an email Trojan uses social engineering strategies to look like a normal email attachment and trick them into downloading the attached file. However, the typical RAT is an example of viral malware that enters through a drive-by download or an email attachment. RATs attack by taking advantage of flaws in the Microsoft browser or operating system to install themselves on the target computer and then launch the installation of utilities that monitor and control the target computer for malicious purposes as mild as website redirects and as dangerous as zombie-like production and transmission of bulk email spam [22]. Depending on the Trojan type and the process used to create it, the infection could disappear, go dormant, or continue to function even after the hacker's intended action is completed [23, 24]. Different types of Trojan malware are shown in Table 3.2. Popular examples of Trojan malware attack are ZeuS and Shedun which are explained below.

- ZeuS first appeared in a data theft attack against the US Department of Transportation in 2007. ZeuS, which is recognized today as a banking Trojan, is frequently used to steal financial information using two browser-based methods:
  - *Keylogging*: When users enter information into their browser, the Trojan records their keystrokes.
  - *Form grabbing*: ZeuS can intercept their username and password when users log into a website.

  ZeuS eventually infected millions of machines through its widespread use of phishing emails and automatic drive-by downloads from malicious websites. As a result, it was used to build one of the most infamous botnets ever, Gameover ZeuS. Figures 3.9 depicts this malware with some details [23].
- Shedun is an Android adware Trojan that repackages trusted Android apps with fake adware and then hosts them on third-party download websites. When users download an app from these sites, they also get adware. Once this app installed on the user's system, the user's device is spammed with ads that produce money for the attacker. Because it's difficult to get the spyware off your Android device, most victims decided to buy new ones [23].

Table 3.2 Trojan malware.

Type	What it does
Backdoor Trojans	A way to access your computer without your knowledge
Banking Trojans	Infiltrate your devices and steal your financial login credentials
DDoS Trojans	Aim to conscript your device into a botnet (a network of linked devices controlled remotely by a hacker known as bot herder)
Dropper or Downloader Trojans	Infects your device and sets the stage for the loader, which in turn installs a rootkit that gives a hacker access to your device
Exploit Trojans	Software tricks designed to leverage a known software or hardware vulnerability to infect your device
Fake antivirus Trojans	Fake AV Trojans pretended to detect viruses and other malware on your device, then urge you to pay for security software which is either useless or actively malicious
Gaming Trojans	Target online gamers and steal their login information
Infostealer Trojans	Comb through your device for sensitive personal data, then send it back to the hacker who attacked you
Instant message Trojans (IM Trojan)	Hijack your login credentials and help themselves to your contact list
Mail finder Trojans	Target email applications like Microsoft office and plump them for email addresses
Ransomware Trojans	Blocks your access to your data or device, then threatens to either publish, permanently withhold, or destroy the data unless you pay a ransom
SMS Trojans	Infect mobile devices, usually Android, and either send expensive SMS messages coming to and from your phone

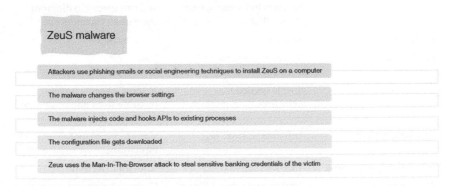

Figure 3.9 ZeuS malware.

3.4.1.7 Viruses

A virus is a piece of malicious software that is attached to a file or document and uses macros to run its code and spread from one host to another. The virus will remain dormant after it has been downloaded until the file is used and opened. Viruses are made to interfere with a system's functionality. Consequently, infections might result in serious operational issues and data loss [13].

3.4.1.8 Worms

Worms are a type of malicious software that quickly spread to all devices connected to a network. Worms can spread without a host application, unlike viruses. A worm enters a system through a network connection or a downloaded file, where it then multiplies and spreads at an exponential rate. Worms, like viruses, can severely damage a device's functionality and data loss [13]. Table 3.3 shows the difference between a virus and a worm.

3.4.2 Emotet (Malspam)

Emotet is a very advanced modular Trojan malware that primarily targets financial systems and Internet users to steal personal and financial information by sending phishing emails to the recipients and propagating itself [21]. Emotet additionally drops and downloads extra banking Trojans like Trickbot, Ursnif, and IceDiD.

Table 3.3 Difference between virus and worm.

Basis for comparison	Virus	Worm
Meaning	The virus attaches itself to executable files and transfers from one system to the other	A worm is a malicious program that replicates itself and can spread to different computers via network
Human action	Needed	Not required
Speed of spreading	Slower as compared to worm	Fast
Requirement of host	Host is needed for spreading	It doesn't need a host to replicate from one computer to another
Removing malware	Antivirus, formatting	Virus removal tool, formatting
Protect the system using	Antivirus software	Antivirus, firewall
Consequences	Corrupt and erase a file or program	Consumes system resources and slows down it and can halt the system completely

It also encrypts a large chunk of the victim's sensitive data using Ryuk ransomware payloads for the benefit of cybercriminals [21]. Emotet started as a banking Trojan first in 2014. In regards to malicious Emotet campaign attackers, the United States Computer Emergency Readiness Team (US-CERT) has previously issued an alert. The Emotet malware, according to US-CERT, is the most destructive and costly malware that affects federal, state, local, tribal, and private businesses, nonprofit organizations, and individuals [25]. Emotet mainly spreads through emails when a user downloads phishing files and clicks on malicious URL links, bogus PDFs, and Microsoft Word documents with macro functionality. Since 2014, with the distribution and dropping off of more banking Trojans like Trickbot, Ursnif, Ryuk payload, and IceDiD, Emotet has developed into a multinational threat distributor that serves as Malware-as-a-Service (MaaS) [21].

In most organizations, people communicate with each other through email. Emotet malware can compromise the system and communications between businesses and individuals that are sent through email. Emotet will infect the system with malicious payloads and seize control of the user machine after gaining initial access via email attachments or links. It will then spread over the network like a worm without human involvement [21, 25]. Figure 3.10 depicts the Emotet attack chain, and the steps are explained below.

- *Step #1*: An Emotet is sent to the user as a Microsoft Word attachment in an email.
- *Step #2*: By accepting the license agreement when opening a Microsoft Word document, the user allows Emotet macros.
- *Step #3*: Macros execute the document's obfuscated code in the background of the system using Command Prompt (cmd.exe).
- *Step #4*: PowerShell will also be started via Command Prompt to connect to malicious Emotet sites.
- *Step #5*: Malware Emotet sites provide Emotet payloads to the victim's machine.
- *Step #6*: To steal users' financial and personal information, Emotet also distributes additional Trojan modules onto the victim Computer system, including Trickbot, IceDiD, and Ursnif.
- *Step #7*: Emotet uses a C2C connection to send the attacker the stolen data.

Basically, phishing emails with links to infected PDFs, files, or Word attachments are how the Emotet malware is distributed. Furthermore, the most recent version of Emotet can hijack active email threads and insert a malicious link or

Figure 3.10   The Emotet attack chain.

file without affecting the text of the email threads. A self-executing copy of the Emotet malware is installed on the computers when the infected link is clicked, opening doors for more advanced attacks such as targeted Ryuk and Maze ransomware attacks. Moreover, Emotet can avoid antivirus tools and signature-based detection pattern features. Emotet can also keep its existence and pass over the network using its persistence features after removal, like random services, auto-start registry key values, and loaded Dynamic Link Libraries (DLLs) [21, 25].

3.4.3 Denial of Service Attack (DoS)

This is an attack that shuts down a machine or network and prevents its intended users from using it. DoS attacks achieve that by providing the victim with an excessive amount of traffic or information that causes a crash. In both cases, the DoS attack denies the service or resource that legitimate users (such as employees, members, or account holders) expected [26]. Victims of DoS attacks are often emails, online banking, websites, or any other service relying on a targeted network or computer [27]. DoS attacks can cost the victim a lot of time and money to deal with, even though they generally do not result in the theft or loss of important information or other assets [26]. There are various types of DoS attacks:

- *Flooding services*: Flood attacks happen when the system receives excessive traffic that the server cannot buffer, which causes it to slowly and eventually cease. Flood attacks send an overwhelming number of packets that exceed server capacity. Popular flood attacks include
  - *Buffer overflow attacks* is the most common DoS attack. It aims to send more traffic to a network address than the system can handle.
  - *ICMP flood* also known as the smurf attack or ping of death. Uses misconfigured network devices to ping every computer on the targeted network rather than just one particular machine by sending fake packets. The network is then triggered to amplify the traffic.
  - *SYN flood* sends a connection request but never completes the handshake with the server. It continues until all open ports are fully utilized by requests and none are left accessible for authorized users to connect to.
- *Crashing services*: Crashing attacks exploit vulnerabilities that lead to the target system or service crashing. In these attacks, input is received that exploits vulnerabilities in the target and causes the system to crash or become very unstable, making it impossible to access or utilize the system.

3.4.4 Distributed Denial of Service (DDoS) Attack

Distributed Denial of Service (DDoS) is a kind of DoS attack where the traffic used to overwhelm the target comes from a variety of dispersed sources [28].

The Internet is severely threatened by DDoS attacks. This attack uses the specific capacity restrictions that apply to all network resources, including the processing systems of a company's website [29]. For example, network resources such as web servers can process a limited number of requests simultaneously. If the number of requests exceeds more than their limits, the servers are unable to process. Additionally, the channel that connects the server to the Internet is also limited in bandwidth and capacity. Hence, a DDoS attack may send several requests to the attacked web server to process more requests than the website can handle and prevents a website from properly operating [29].

A DDoS attack can be carried out in different ways. The attacker sends a stream of packets to a victim. To prevent the victim's legitimate clients from accessing some crucial resource, the attacker delivers a stream of packets to the victim. Another approach is that the attacker sends malformed packets to the application or a protocol that confuses them and forces the victim's machine to freeze or reboot. Most typical targets for DDoS attacks include: Internet shopping sites, online casinos, and any business or organization that depends on providing online services [28, 29].

A DDoS performs in several phases. Firstly, the attacker uses slave machines which perform automatically through scanning of remote systems to find a security hole that will enable subversion. Then, vulnerable machines use the identified vulnerability and may be infect it with the attack code. The infect phase is automated, and the infected systems can be used for the recruitment of new agents. Attack packets are sent by these agent machines. Attackers typically spoof the source address field in attack packets to conceal the identification of subverted machines during the attack. Spoofing is not always required for a successful DDoS attack. In all other attack types, except reflector attacks,[2] rely only on spoofing to prevent agent machine discovery and attack detection [28]. Figure 3.11 shows a comparison between DoS and DDoS attacks.

3.4.5 Man in the Middle Attack (MITM)

This occurs when a delinquent puts himself/herself in a conservation between a client and a server to eavesdrop or pretend to be one of the participants to appear as though a typical information exchange is taking place [30, 31]. MITM attack steals personal data like login information, account details, and credit numbers. Users of financial applications, SaaS companies, e-commerce websites, and other websites that require signing in are often the targets [31]. Captured data by attacks

---

2 In a reflection attack, the attacker sends a request for information, typically using the User Datagram Protocol (UDP) or, in some cases, the Transmission Control Protocol, while spoofing the target's IP address (TCP). The server then replies to the request by delivering a response to the IP address of the destination.

Parameter	DoS	DDoS
Full Form	Denial of Service	Distributed Denial of Service
Source of attack	DoS attack uses one computer and one Internet connection to flood a targeted system or resource	DDoS attack uses multiple computers and Internet connections to flood the targeted resource
Protection	System can be stopped/protected easily	Difficult to protect against DDoS attack
Threat level	Low threat level	Medium to high threat level
Malware involvement	No malware involved	A botnet is mostly made up of thousands of infected computers
Cost and management	Easier to operate and manage	Not easy to manage and operate

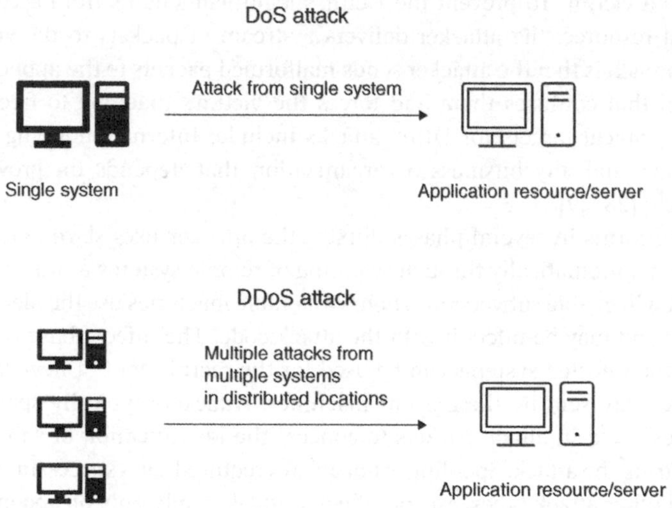

DoS attack

DDoS attack

Figure 3.11 A comparison between DoS and DDoS attacks.

could be used for different purposes, such as identifying theft, unapproved fund transfers, or an illicit password change. The infiltration phase of an APT attack can also employ it to obtain access to a secured perimeter [30]. Figure 3.12 shows a man in the Middle attack. There are two main aspects to successful MITM execution, and Figure 3.13 gives a clear representation of it:

- *Interception*: Before it reaches its target location, the first step intercepts user traffic passing via the attacker's network. In a passive attack, attackers put free and malicious WiFi hotspots available to the public, and they usually don't have password protection, and their names usually match their current location. When a victim connects to one of these hotspots, the attacker has complete access to any online data transfer. Attackers who want to engage in more direct interception may carry out one of the following actions:

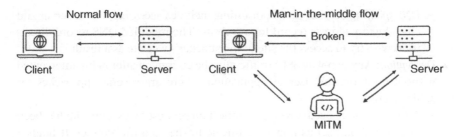

Figure 3.12 Man-in-the-Middle flow.

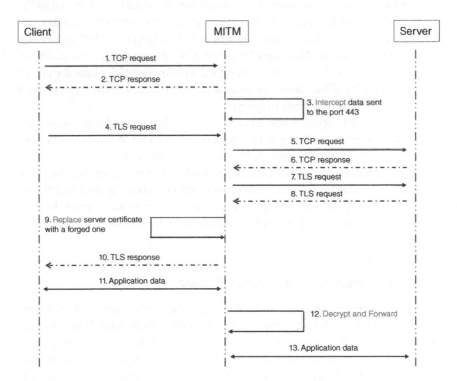

Figure 3.13 Successful MITM execution steps.

- *IP spoofing* involves changing packet headers in an IP address to mask an attacker as an application. Because of this, users who try to access a URL linked to the program are routed to the attacker's website.
- *ARP spoofing* is the act of utilizing fake ARP messages to connect the IP address of a legitimate user on a local area network with the attacker's MAC address. As a result, information that the user intended to send to the host IP address is instead transferred to the attacker.

- *DNS spoofing* or DNS cache poisoning, includes accessing a DNS server and changing an address record for a website. The modified DNS record directs users who try to access the site to the attacker's website as a result.
- *Decryption*: Any two-way SSL[3] traffic must be encrypted after being intercepted without notifying the user or application. There are several approaches for achieving this:
  - *HTTPS spoofing* occurs when a connection request to a secure site has been established and sends a fake certificate to the victim's browser. It holds a digital thumbprint linked to the threatened application, which the browser checks using a list of trustworthy websites. Any information submitted by the victim before it delivers to the program is then accessible to the attacker.
  - *SSL BEAST* or browser exploit against SSL/TLS targets a TLS[4] version 1.0 vulnerability in SSL. Malicious JavaScript has infected the victim's machine, intercepting cookies sent by an encrypted web application. Then, the cipher block chaining (CBC) of the application is compromised, allowing its cookies and authentication tokens to decrypt.
  - *SSL hijacking* happens when an attacker gives the user and application fake authentication keys during a TCP handshake. As a result, what seems to be a secure connection is controlled by the man in the middle.
  - *SSL stripping* intercepts the TLS authentication sent by the application to the user, converting an HTTPS connection to HTTP. While the user is still connected to the program through a secure session, the attacker sends them an unencrypted version of the application's website. Meanwhile, the user's entire session is visible to the attacker.

3.4.6 Social Engineering Attacks and Phishing

The term "social engineering" is used to describe a wide range of malicious behaviors carried out through interactions with other people [32]. It uses various manipulations to trick users into making security breaches or revealing private data. Social engineering attacks might occur in one or more steps. An attacker first looks into the target to obtain background information, such as possible points of entry and weak security protocols needed to carry out the attack [33, 34]. The attacker then attempts to obtain the victim's trust to offer motivation for later actions that break security protocols, including revealing private information or

---

3 Secure Sockets Layer or SSL, is a protocol for web browsers and servers that allows for the authentication, encryption, and decryption of data sent over the internet.
4 A cryptographic method called Transport Layer Security (TLS) is intended to guarantee communications security over a computer network. Although the protocol is widely used in voice over IP, email, and instant messaging, its use to secure HTTPS is still the most publicly visible.

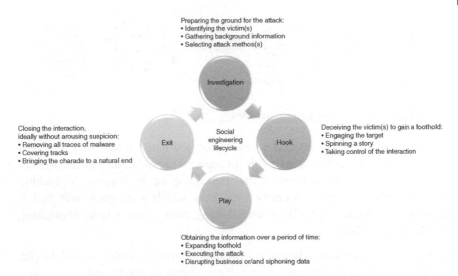

Figure 3.14 Social engineering life cycle.

allowing access to critical resources. Figure 3.14 shows the social engineering attack life cycle.

The fact that social engineering relies on human error rather than vulnerabilities in software and operating systems makes it more dangerous. Legitimate user errors are much less likely to be predicted, making them harder to recognize and prevent than malware-based attacks. One of the main risks of social engineering is that the attacks do not have to work against everyone. An attack that may impact the entire business might start with one victim who is tracked successfully. Social engineering attacks have become more complex over time. The following are the most common forms of social engineering attacks [32–34].

3.4.6.1 Phishing

One of the most popular social engineering attacks is phishing which steals users' data such as login credentials and credit card numbers [35]. It happens when an attacker deceives a victim into opening an email, instant message, or text message by disguising themselves as a reliable source. Then the victim is tricked into clicking a malicious link, which may start installing malware, freezing the system as a part of a ransomware attack, or sharing sensitive data and information. An attack can have disastrous consequences like theft of funds or identity and unauthorized transactions. Figure 3.15 shows how a phishing attack occurs.

Furthermore, phishing is frequently used as part of a larger attack, like an APT attack, to compromise business or governmental networks. Employees are compromised to bypass security perimeters, distribute malware inside a closed

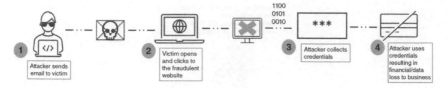

Figure 3.15 How a phishing attack happens.

environment, or gain privileged access to secured data. A company that falls victim to such an attack suffers significant financial losses like diminished market share, reputation, and customer trust. Depending on its domain, a phishing attempt could turn into a security issue from which a company will find it challenging to recover [32, 35]. In the following, most common types of phishing attacks are described.

- *Spear phishing* attacks individuals instead of targeting a wide range of people. The attackers can then personalize their communications and seem more authentic. The initial stage in a targeted attack to get through a company's defenses is frequently spear phishing. Spear phishing attacks account for 95% of all attacks on enterprise networks. Three steps of how spear phishing works are
  1. A cybercriminal identifies a piece of data they want and identifies an individual who has it.
  2. The cybercriminal researches the individual and poses as one of their trusted sources.
  3. The cybercriminal convinces their victim to share the data and uses it to commit a malicious act.
- *Microsoft 365 phishing* attacks use a fake email from Microsoft, and attackers get access to a Microsoft 365 email account. There is a log-in request in the email that asks for a new password to set. Also a URL is provided, tempting the user to click in order to fix the problem.
- *Voice phishing* or *Vishing* is a type of social engineering. It is a phony phone call intended to get access to private data, such login credentials. For example, the attacker may contact the victim and pretend to be a support agent or corporate representative, and new employees are especially vulnerable to these types of scams.

3.4.6.2 Baiting

Baiting attacks use a phony promise to spark a victim's curiosity or sense of greed. They trick consumers into falling into a trap that takes their data or infects their computers with malware. The most reviled form of baiting uses physical media to disperse malware such as when attackers put the bait (typically malware-infected flash drives) in significant places where potential victims will certainly see them. The bait has a legitimate appearance, including a label that presents it as the business's payroll list. The bait is picked up by victims and then put into their home or office computers, where it causes the system to download malware automatically. There are also online forms of baiting consisting of enticing ads that lead to malicious sites or encourage users to download a malware-infected application [35].

3.4.6.3 Scareware

Scareware attacks, also known as deception software, rogue scanner software, and fraud, overwhelm victims with fake threats and misleading alarms. Users are tricked into believing their computer is infected with malware, which leads them to install software that either serves only to profit the perpetrator or is malware in and of itself. The legitimate-appearing popup ads that show in your browser as you browse the internet and contain text such as "Your computer may be infected with harmful spyware applications" are a frequent type of scareware. Either it offers to install the malicious tool for you or it sends you to a malicious website where your machine is infected. Additionally, spam emails that provide false alerts or urge recipients to purchase useless or dangerous services are a common type of scareware to spread [35].

3.4.6.4 Pretexting

In this kind of attack, an attacker gathers information by telling a string of cleverly constructed lies. The scam is frequently started by a perpetrator who poses as someone who needs the victim's private information to complete a crucial task. The attacker establishes trust with their victim by impersonating police, co-workers, bank and tax officials, or other persons who have the right to know authority. The pretext asks inquiries that are necessary to verify the victim's identity to obtain crucial personal information about the victim. This scam is used to get all kinds of sensitive data and records, including social security numbers, individual addresses, and phone numbers; phone records; dates of staff vacation; bank records; and even security data about a physical plant [35].

3.4.7 SQL Injection Attack

An online security flaw known as SQL injection (SQLi) enables an attacker to inter- fere with the database queries that an application makes [36]. In most cases, it enables an attacker to view data that they would not usually be able to access. This includes the data and any information that the application can access. In most examples, an attacker can update or remove this data, permanently alter- ing the application's behavior or content. An attacker may sometimes use a DoS

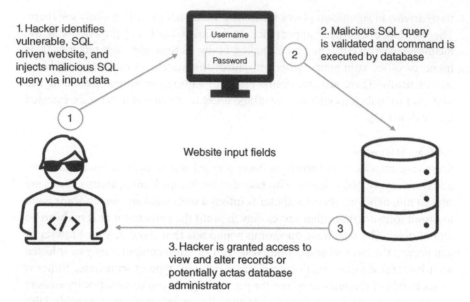

1. Hacker identifies vulnerable, SQL driven website, and injects malicious SQL query via input data

2. Malicious SQL query is validated and command is executed by database

Website input fields

3. Hacker is granted access to view and alter records or potentially actas database administrator

Figure 3.16 SQL injection attack.

attack or escalate an SQL injection attack to compromise the underlying server or other back-end infrastructure.

Passwords, credit card numbers, and other sensitive data can be improperly accessed as a result of a successful SQL injection attack. SQL injection attacks have been the cause of numerous high-profile data breaches in recent years, which have resulted in reputation damage and regulatory fines. In some circumstances, an attacker can gain access to a persistent backdoor, which results in a long-term breach that can go undetected for a long time [36]. Figure 3.16 shows a SQL injection attack.

SQL injection vulnerabilities, attacks, and methods come in a wide variety and are used in various contexts. Typical examples of SQL injection include

- Retrieving hidden data, where you can modify an SQL query to return additional results.
- Subverting application logic, where you can change a query to interfere with the application's logic.
- UNION attacks, where you can retrieve data from different database tables.
- Examining the database, where you can extract information about the version and structure of the database.
- Blind SQL injection, where the results of a query you control are not returned in the application's responses.

3.4.8 Password Attacks

These use automatic password attack tools to speed up password guessing and cracking while also taking advantage of a system authorization vulnerability [37]. The attacker assumes the identity and privileges of the valid user to access and expose their credentials. Given that the username–password combination is one of the more known means of account authentication, attackers have developed a variety of methods for getting passwords that are easy to guess. Additionally, given that the vulnerabilities are known, applications that rely solely on passwords for authentication are open to password attacks. To compromise a web application, malicious users need unauthorized access to a single privileged account or a small number of user accounts. Compromised passwords can lead to the exposing of sensitive data, distributed DoS, financial fraud, and other complex attacks depending on the data that the application hosts [37]. To get and authenticate with a legitimate user's password, hackers use methods such as

- *Phishing attacks*: They, by far the most common type of password attack, use a social engineering method in which the hacker sends the victim a fake link while impersonating a reliable website. The victim clicks on this link, believing they are connecting to a valid web server, giving the attacker access to their account information. Phishing attacks, in addition to stealing identities, also help APTs grow by enabling threat actors to access internal users' accounts and infiltrate increasingly complex system components undetected. To deceive the user into clicking the infected link in phishing attacks, the enemy frequently employs a variety of methods, including
  - *DNS cache poisoning*: Attackers use vulnerabilities in the DNS server of the program to reroute user queries to a malicious website with a domain name that looks similar.
  - *URL hijacking/typosquatting*: The attacker produces a URL that strongly matches the target website while having minor differences. Users' spelling errors are then used by the attacker to direct them to the infected page.
  - *Tabnabbing*: Unattended browser tabs are hijacked by the attacker and replaced with malicious websites that imitate trustworthy web pages.
  - *UI redressing/iFrame overlay*: By using transparent layers, the attacker covers a real, clickable button with a link to the malicious page.
  - *Clone phishing*: In this attack, the sender sends a copy of a legitimate email containing malicious website URLs in place of the links in the original email.
- *Brute-force password attacks*: To guess a user's login information, this kind of password attack uses trial-and-error methods. To accurately guess the user's password, the malicious party runs as many variants through automated programs as they can. Brute force attacks are still used in attempts to breach accounts because they are automated and simple, despite being an outdated

method that takes a lot of time and patience. There are various kinds of brute force attacks, including

- *Simple brute force attacks*: To determine the most likely password, a hacker employs reasoning and information about a user. This method is used for relatively easy passwords, such as those that include a pet's name with the year and month of birth.
- *Credential stuffing*: Using login combinations that were maliciously stolen from vulnerable websites and previously made public. In these attacks, hackers typically gain from the fact that organizations mostly reuse their username–password combinations across many services.
- *Hybrid brute force attacks*: To find complex passwords, an attacker uses automated software that does credential stuffing along with simple weak password guessing. Entities typically utilize modest changes of passwords on many websites in production systems. To increase the accuracy of their credential stuffing tools, attackers often rely on user data patterns across different services.
- *Reverse brute force attacks*: In this type of attack, a hacker starts with a well-known password and looks for usernames with similar characters. It is simple to find common passwords among a certain set of users since threat actors frequently have access to several databases of compromised credentials.

- *Dictionary password attacks*: A predetermined list of terms that a given target network is most likely to use as passwords is used in this attack method. A website user's online behavior patterns and passwords stolen from past data breaches are used to create the predetermined list. The lists are made by changing the case of frequent word pairings, adding numerical suffixes and prefixes, and using frequent phrases. An automated tool receives these lists and attempts to authenticate against a list of recognized usernames.
- *Password spraying attack*: A hacker starts by trying the same password on several other accounts to authenticate, then switches to a different password. Password spraying is most effective since most website users use easy passwords, and because it uses many accounts, it is not against lockout policies. The majority of password spraying attacks are planned by attackers on websites where the administrator has established a default password for new users and unregistered accounts.
- *Keylogging*: A hacker installs monitoring software on the user's computer during a Keylogging attack to secretly record the keys the user presses. Any data that users enter into input fields are recorded by a keylogger and sent to the malicious third party. While keyloggers frequently serve functions in business environments (UX improvement, employee monitoring, etc.), attackers utilize them to extract data, such as login passwords for maliciously unauthorized access.

3.5 Conclusion

The usage of specific security threat classification is one of the fundamental criteria for a successful information system security management process. In a secure information system, it is possible to identify the information system from which we are protecting it and efficiently use the limited resources like time, money, and employees. Recognizing different types of data security threats and the way that they steal sensitive information from individuals and organizations give everyone a clear overview of how to protect their data.

References

1 Sandro Gerić and Željko Hutinski. Information system security threats classifications. *Journal of Information and organizational sciences*, 31(1):51–61, 2007.

2 Dorothy E. Denning. An intrusion-detection model. *IEEE Transactions on Software Engineering*, (2):222–232, 1987.

3 Adel Alshamrani, Sowmya Myneni, Ankur Chowdhary, and Dijiang Huang. A survey on advanced persistent threats: techniques, solutions, challenges, and research opportunities. *IEEE Communication Surveys and Tutorials*, 21(2):1851–1877, 2019.

4 Mouna Jouini, Latifa Ben Arfa Rabai, and Anis Ben Aissa. Classification of security threats in information systems. *Elsevier Journal of Procedia Computer Science*, 32:489–496, 2014.

5 What is data security? https://www.ibm.com/topics/data-security.

6 Wesley Chai. What is the CIA triad? https://www.techtarget.com/whatis/definition/Confidentiality-integrity-and-availability-CIA, 2022.

7 Peng Gao, Fei Shao, Xiaoyuan Liu, Xusheng Xiao, Haoyuan Liu, Zheng Qin, Fengyuan Xu, Prateek Mittal, Sanjeev R. Kulkarni, and Dawn Song. A system for efficiently hunting for cyber threats in computer systems using threat intelligence. In *Proceedings of the 37th IEEE International Conference on Data Engineering (ICDE)*, pages 2705–2708, 2021.

8 Lei Xu, Chunxiao Jiang, Jian Wang, Jian Yuan, and Yong Ren. Information security in big data: privacy and data mining. *IEEE Access*, 2:1149–1176, 2014.

9 Advanced-persistent-threat-apt. https://www.okta.com/identity-101/advanced-persistent-threat-apt/.

10 What-is-data-security-threats-controls-and-solutions. https://satoricyber.com/data-security/what-is-data-security-threats-controls-and-solutions/.

11 Orion Cassetto. Data security threats. https://www.exabeam.com/information-security/cyber-security-threat/, 2022.

12 Luca Caviglione, Michał Choraś, Igino Corona, Artur Janicki, Wojciech Mazurczyk, Marek Pawlicki, and Katarzyna Wasielewska. Tight arms race: overview of current malware threats and trends in their detection. *IEEE Access*, 9:5371–5396, 2020.

13 Nwokedi Idika and Aditya P. Mathur. A survey of malware detection techniques. *Purdue University*, 48(2):32–46, 2007.

14 Mohammed N. Alenezi, Haneen Alabdulrazzaq, Abdullah A. Alshaher, and Mubarak M. Alkharang. Evolution of malware threats and techniques: a review. *International Journal of Communication Networks and Information Security*, 12(3):326–337, 2020.

15 Macdonald Chikapa and Anitta Patience Namanya. Towards a fast off-line static malware analysis framework. In *Proceedings of the 6th IEEE International Conference on Future Internet of Things and Cloud Workshops (FiCloudW)*, pages 182–187, 2018.

16 Amit Vasudevan and Ramesh Yerraballi. SpiKE: engineering malware analysis tools using unobtrusive binary-instrumentation. In *Proceedings of the 29th Australasian Computer Science Conference*, pages 311–320, 2006.

17 Kasperskey. Ransomware attacks and types - how encryption Trojans differ. https://www.ibm.com/topics/data-security.

18 Eduardo Berrueta, Daniel Morato, Eduardo Maga na, and Mikel Izal. A survey on detection techniques for cryptographic ransomware. *IEEE Access*, 7:144925–144944, 2019.

19 S. Kok, Azween Abdullah, N. Jhanjhi, and Mahadevan Supramaniam. Ransomware, threat and detection techniques: a review. *International Journal Computing Science Network Security*, 19(2):136, 2019.

20 Fileless-malware. https://www.crowdstrike.com/cybersecurity-101/malware/fileless-malware/#::text=Fileless%20malware%20is%20a%20type,making%20it%20hard%20to%20detect.

21 Sushil Kumar. An emerging threat fileless malware: a survey and research challenges. *Cybersecurity*, 3(1):1–12, 2020.

22 Thomas F. Stafford and Andrew Urbaczewski. Spyware: the ghost in the machine. *The Communications of the Association for Information Systems*, 14(1):49, 2004.

23 Trojan. https://www.avast.com/c-trojan#topic-3.

24 Yier Jin, Nathan Kupp, and Yiorgos Makris. Experiences in hardware Trojan design and implementation. In *Proceedings of the IEEE International Workshop on Hardware-Oriented Security and Trust*, pages 50–57, 2009.

25 Constantinos Patsakis and Anargyros Chrysanthou. Analysing the fall 2020 Emotet campaign. *arXiv preprint arXiv:2011.06479*, 2020.

26 DoS. https://www.paloaltonetworks.com/cyberpedia/what-is-a-denial-of-service-attack-dos3.

27 Tasnuva Mahjabin, Yang Xiao, Guang Sun, and Wangdong Jiang. A survey of distributed denial-of-service attack, prevention, and mitigation techniques. *International Journal of Distributed Sensor Networks*, 13(12), 2017. doi: https://doi.org/10.1177/1550147717741463.

28 Jelena Mirkovic and Peter Reiher. A taxonomy of DDoS attack and DDoS defense mechanisms. *ACM SIGCOMM Computer Communication Review*, 34(2):39–53, 2004.

29 DDoS. https://www.kaspersky.com/resource-center/threats/ddos-attacks.

30 MITM. https://www.imperva.com/learn/application-security/man-in-the-middle-attack-mitm/.

31 Avijit Mallik. Man-in-the-middle-attack: understanding in simple words. *Cyberspace: Jurnal Pendidikan Teknologi Informasi*, 2(2):109–134, 2019.

32 Ryan Heartfield and George Loukas. A taxonomy of attacks and a survey of defence mechanisms for semantic social engineering attacks. *ACM Computing Surveys*, 48(3):1–39, 2015.

33 Social engineering. https://www.cisco.com/c/en/us/products/security/what-is-social-engineering.html.

34 Social engineering_2. https://www.imperva.com/learn/application-security/social-engineering-attack/.

35 Phishing. https://www.imperva.com/learn/application-security/phishing-attack-scam/.

36 SQLi. https://portswigger.net/web-security/sql-injection.

37 Passwordattack. https://crashtest-security.com/password-attack/.

4

Use Cases Data Leakage Attacks

The world is still dealing with a persistent pandemic of COVID-19, and many changes have occurred in work habits, such as working from home and going back to the office, and geopolitical events that have created a broad climate of distrust. These changes increased the attacker chance to launch more attacks over the organizations infrastructure and increased cybercriminals. Security experts use data from billions of sources, including network and endpoint detection tools, incident response (IR) engagements, domain name tracking, and more, to map new trends and attack patterns that they have noticed and evaluated. This chapter reports real-world data leakage and top cybersecurity attacks from 2020 to 2021 in all five continents.

4.1 Most Significant Attacks

This section first defines the attack types and later provides the statistics of the most known attacks that occurred in the recent years. Attacks are categorized/ grouped based on the objective an attacker intends to accomplish after breaking into a victim's network. Each category defines one attack type. For instance, ransomware, data theft, and business email compromise (BEC) are different types of attack which are grouped based on the ultimate goals of the attackers. It is important to note that attack types are different from initial infection vectors. Initial infection vectors refer to the method through which a network is breached and compromised. For example, phishing, stealing credentials, and exploiting vulnerabilities are considered initial infection vectors. Figure 4.1 compares the percentage of the major attack types that occurred in 2021 and 2020 [1].

The following parts provide the 2021s details and statistics of the most prolific attacks revealed by IBM [1]. Other attacks include the followings: Adware, banking Trojan, botnets, cryptominers, defacements, fraud, DDoS, point of sale malware, spam, webscripts, webshells, and worms.

Data Exfiltration Threats and Prevention Techniques: Machine Learning and Memory-Based Data Security, First Edition. Zahir Tari, Nasrin Sohrabi, Yasaman Samadi, and Jakapan Suaboot.
© 2023 John Wiley & Sons, Inc. Published 2023 by John Wiley & Sons, Inc.

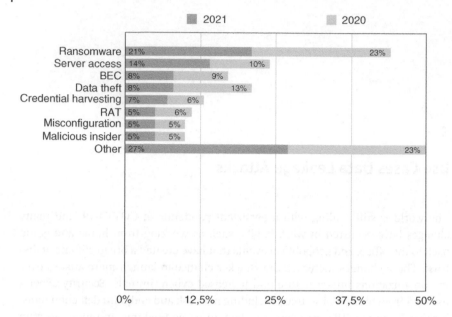

Figure 4.1 Top attack types, 2021 vs. 2020.

4.1.1 Ransomware

This has been the most common attack type for more than three years, and 2021 was no exception, where around 21% of all attacks were Ransomware. Figure 4.2 illustrates the percentage of ransomware's IR occurred during the period of 2020–2021 [1]. According to the figure, despite a slight decline compared to 2020, when ransomware attacks made up 21% of attacks, the numbers have stayed consistent in 2021. However, throughout the year, the frequency of the attacks fluctuated, with May and June typically experiencing greater attack frequencies and January experiencing less. The figures also show that the number of IRs declined in early months of the year and also in the early fall. However, Figure 4.3 shows the majority of the reduction occurred in August and again in November, possibly as a result of many groups' temporary or permanent closures in the months before DarkSide and Babuk in May, Avaddon in June, and REvil in October.

According to IBM research, a ransomware group (ransomware groups are the professionals who create and distribute malware that makes the attacks possible) typically lasts 17 months until rebranding or shutting down. These group often when there is a risk/threat of legal actions such as being caught/arrested change their attack policies. That is, they frequently form and rebrand the attacks. IBM has detected a large number of ransomware actors that have rebranded and

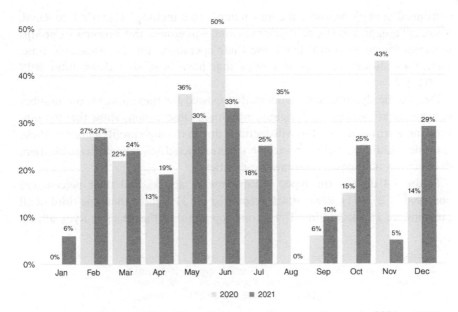

Figure 4.2 Percentage of IR incidents that were ransomware, by month, 2020 vs. 2021.

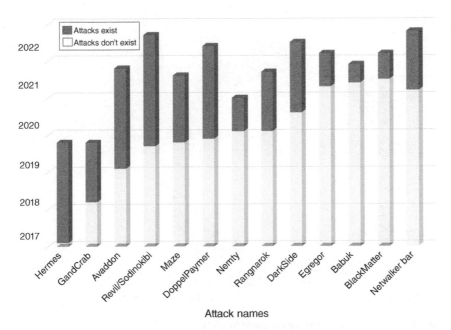

Figure 4.3 Ransomware groups that have shut down, 2017–2021.

continued operations under the new names. This includes: GandCrab to REvil, Maze to Egregor, and DoppelPaymer to Grief. Sometimes, the ransomware groups are even forced to completely cease their operations for a considerable time. Figure 4.3 shows ransomware groups that have been shut down from 2017 to 2021 [1].

Despite the dynamic environment that existed for these attacks, the number of ransomware actors is still significantly high. Observations show that the ransomware's criminal activities will continue due to the high profits gained by these activities. Additionally, law enforcement has restricted abilities which enable them to effectively shut down ransomware activities.

Figure 4.4 depicts the types of ransomware attacks and their percentages observed in 2021 [1]. REvil attack accounted for 37%, more than one-third of all ransomware attacks/strains. The second top strain of the attack is Ryuk attack,

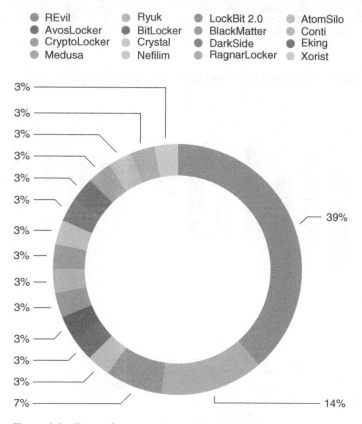

Figure 4.4 Types of ransomware observed in 2021.

which formed 13% of attacks. Figure 4.3 shows that as of mid-October 2021, the evil actors appear to have permanently stopped their operations, most likely due to government enforcement activity. Both Ryuk and REvil attacks constitute two of the longest-running ransomware operations, having emerged in April 2019 and August 2018, respectively.

4.1.2 Server Access

Such an attack occurs when an attacker gains unauthorized access to a server. The attacker, however, does not have clear goals/operations to achieve/perform once gained access to the server. This attack is considered the second most frequent attacks that occurred in 2021, accounting for 11% of all cases. Most of these attacks took place in Asia, where majority of them were successful, i.e. the threat actors were successful in installing malware or using penetration testing tools on servers, such as China Chopper Webshells, Black Orifice malware, Printspoofer, and Mimikatz [1]. In some cases, the threat actors took advantage of a known vulnerability that would have permitted remote code execution on a server. In some occasions, threat actors have used vulnerabilities in Microsoft Exchange servers to break into targeted networks [2], although some of these attacks were unsuccessful in terms of stealing data or using ransomware. Thus, even if the equity of a company prevents attackers from acquiring any level of unauthorized access to their networks, a high number of server access attacks probably mean that businesses are detecting and eradicating attacks before they develop into more harmful activities.

4.1.3 Business Email Compromise (BEC)

These attacks have been experiencing a decline both in 2020 and 2021 years. Hence, it was considered the third most common attack type in 2021. Figure 4.5 depicts the percentage of incidents that were BEC in each region in 2021. The widespread implementation of multifactor authentication (MFA), in 2020, decreased the number of successful attacks that the BEC threat actors were able to execute. Therefore, in 2021, BEC attackers might have realized greater success by shifting their focus to geographies where MFA is not as widely implemented [1, 3].

For example, it appears that BEC attacks were concentrated primarily on Latin American firms. The surge we observed against Latin American organizations suggests that BEC attackers have changed the geographic focus of their operations. While 0% of attacks against Latin American organizations were BEC in 2019, 19% of attacks in 2020 and 20% of attacks in 2021 were BEC ones. North American organizations were still very much in the crosshairs of BEC operations [1].

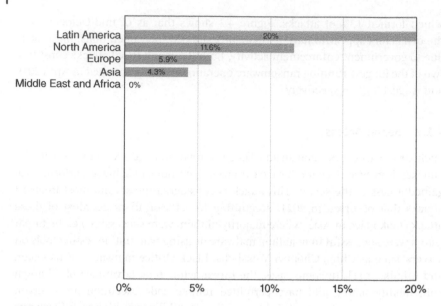

Figure 4.5 Percentage of incidents that were BEC, 2021.

4.2 Top Infection Vectors

Some threat actors first get access to the networks of their victims. Figure 4.6 compares the top breakdown of infection vectors between 2020 and 2021 [1]. The most frequent methods include phishing and vulnerability exploitation which sit on top of the list and rest include the usage of stolen credentials, brute force, remote desktop Protocol (RDP), removable media, and password spraying that account for a smaller percentage of attacks [1].

The famous technology companies and financial institutions have been the most frequently spoofed by phishing kits (i.e. these companies have been the first target for threat actors). Statistics show that the top 11 companies that have been under phishing attack include Microsoft, Apple, Google, BMO Harris Bank (BMO), Chase, Amazon, Dropbox, DHL, CNN, and Facebook [1, 4]. The Anti Phishing Work Group (APWG) reported that the number of phishing attacks in June 2021 alone achieved a high record of 222,127. Organizations can reduce the risk of effect from this attack vector by monitoring for suspicious connections to probably fake organizations. Phishing attack risk can be reduced by using a DNS service devoted to data privacy, such as Quad9 [5].

Table 4.1 depicts the list of top vulnerabilities in 2021 [1]. Another report, shown in Figure 4.7, displays new vulnerabilities identified each year from 2011 to 2021 and cumulative number of vulnerabilities [1]. The figure shows that from 2017 to

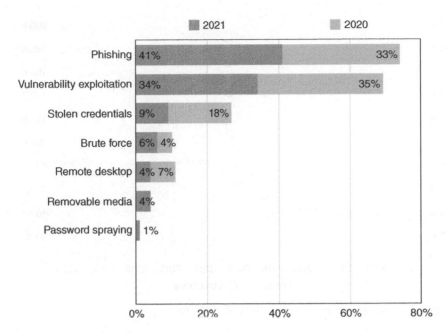

Figure 4.6 Top infection vectors, 2021 vs. 2020.

Table 4.1 Top 10 vulnerabilities of 2021.

Vulnerability type	Attack description
CVE-2021-34523	Microsoft Exchange server flaw enabling malicious actors to bypass authentication and impersonate an administrator. Known generically as ProxyLogon
CVE-2021-44228	Vulnerability in Apache Log4j Library
CVE-2021-26857	Microsoft Exchange Server remote code execution vulnerability
CVE-2020-1472	Netlogon elevation of privilege vulnerability
CVE-2021-27101	Accellion FTA vulnerability susceptible to SQL injection
CVE-2020-7961	Liferay Portal deserialization of untrusted data allows for remote code execution via JSON web services
CVE-2020-15505	Mobile vulnerability allowing for remote code execution
CVE-2018-20062	NoneCMS ThinkPHP remote code execution vulnerability
CVE-2021-35464	ForgeRock AM server Java deserialization vulnerability allows for remote code execution
CVE-2019-19781	Citrix Server path traversal flaw

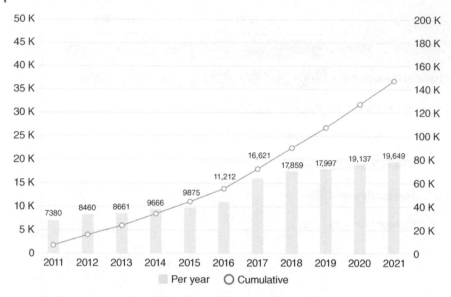

Figure 4.7 Vulnerabilities discovered by year, 2011–2021.

2021, more vulnerabilities and exploits in tools that threat actors can employ to take advantage of security flaws were detected annually [1].

4.3 Top Threats of Recent Years

Reports show that the top threat actors, in 2021, include criminals (account for 97%), nation-state (accounts for 2%), and hacktivist [6] (forms around 1% of actors). The goals of nation-state actors were to conduct espionage and surveillance, and in some cases, they have been laying the groundwork for future sabotage. The work in [1, 6] provides details on some of the most recent interesting and active threats, and these are summarized below.

- *Suspected Iran-based ITG17 uses Aclip backdoor*: In 2021, IBM Security observed a threat actor using a new backdoor, named "Aclip" [7]. More specifically, the attacker used a legitimate messaging and collaboration platform that was probably designed to mask operational interactions, allowing malicious traffic or traffic that had underlying malicious intent to pass unnoticed. Based on the tools, tactics, and infrastructure observed by well-known companies, the threat actor is known as ITG173 (aka MuddyWater) [7].
- *ITG23 – Trickbot Gang – enables Conti ransomware operations*: The cyber-criminal group ITG23, also known as Wizard Spider or Trickbot Gang, is the source of the Trickbot banking trojan, and it has been extensively monitored

by analysts from prestigious firms like IBM. The Trickbot trojan is frequently used in phishing emails to spread Conti ransomware. Hence, the increase in ITG23 Trickbot activity coincided with an uptick in Conti ransomware attacks. The group has mainly relied on two well-known campaigns to achieve their goals, *email campaigns* and *BazarCall campaign*. The former transfers malicious Excel documents and the latter emails themed around subscriptions encourage recipients to call a phony call center where the operator then directs the user to download the BazarLoader malware while pretending to be a service-unsubscriber. The group has also started to recently hijack email threads and "reply all" with malicious attachments [1, 3].

- *Hive0109 active in 2021*: In 2021, Hive0109, also known as LemonDuck, was responsible for a number of hacks, and it has shown its skill at using the ProxyLogon vulnerabilities to infiltrate Microsoft Exchange servers that are not patched. LemonDuck is known for using newsworthy events as phishing baits in its campaigns, and it targets both Linux and Windows systems. The main purpose of the persistent malware known as LemonDuck was to mine cryptocurrencies. It has developed into a large botnet since at least 2018, when it was most likely active. In addition to serving as a first-stage loader for further malware and attacks, LemonDuck spreads rapidly. On infected devices, it continues to mine for cryptocurrency [1].

4.4 Malware Development Trends

Threat actors always coming up with new strategies to increase malware's adaptability across operating systems and difficulty in detection. The work in [1] describe some of the recent trends in malware development and these are summarized below.

- To evade host-based detection measures, ransomware authors used a variety of encryption algorithms. One such is intermittent encryption, which speeds up the encryption process by encrypting individual data blocks rather than the entire system.
- Popular cloud messaging and storage services are increasingly used for command and control (C2) communications to blend in with legitimate traffic. Additionally, DNS tunneling for C2 connections was growing in popularity. To hide C2 activity from network-based sensors, these strategies simulate accurate communications.
- Malware developers were using more complex packaging and code obfuscation methods to hide the malware's true intent and prevent analysis efforts. To make their code harder to reverse engineer, malware developers have also experimented with alternative programming languages, including PureBasic and Nim.

4.4.1 Malware Focus on Docker

Analyzing the influence of malware trends on cloud environments represents that several malware families have shifted their focus of attack from generic Linux systems to Docker containers, which are frequently used in platform-as-a-service cloud environment. The malware families XorDDoS, Groundhog, and Tsunami are a few examples of this change. The nefarious activities of IoT malware (Kaiji), cryptominers (Xanthe, Kinsing), and other malware strains that seek to scale their mining capacity via cloud computing are also highlighted by this Docker-focused campaign, which goes beyond mere bots. In addition to Docker, there are other threat actors that have focused on other container platforms. For example, both the Kubernetes container management system and susceptible Windows containers were compromised by the Siloscape virus. Attackers like TeamTNT, a cybercrime group that has been concentrating on cloud platforms to increase the reach of its cryptojacking botnets, are increasingly incorporating Siloscape into their attacks [8].

4.4.2 Ransomware Focus on ESXi

Analyzing malware trends impacting Linux environments illustrates several ransomware groups are turning their attention to Linux-based VMware ESXi servers. Ransomware developers are learning that it can be more efficient to encrypt the virtual machine (VM) files themselves rather than infect the operating systems running within them as more and more companies rely on virtualization. A Linux variant of the SFile ransomware was released against an ESXi server in 2020, and in 2021 several other ransomware families – including REvil, HelloKitty, Babuk, and BlackMatter – appeared to follow suit. These variations frequently employ ESXi's native command-line administration tool, esxcli, to list and terminate operating VMs before encrypting them [1].

4.4.3 Nim Is In

Golang became the preferred programming language for cross-platform malware developers in 2020 because it could be simultaneously compiled for several operating systems [9]. While Golang is still in use in 2021, additional languages such as Nim are becoming more popular [10]. The system's programming language Nim is statically typed and compiled. It mixes effective ideas from established languages like Modula, Ada, and Python. For example, threat actors created the Nimar backdoor and a version of Zebrocy – a form of malware utilized by the Russian nation-state actor ITG05 – using Nim (aka APT28) [11].

4.4.4 Linux Threats Continue to Evolve

Malware targeting Linux environments has substantially increased over the past year, according to research by IBM Security X-Force Threat Intelligence

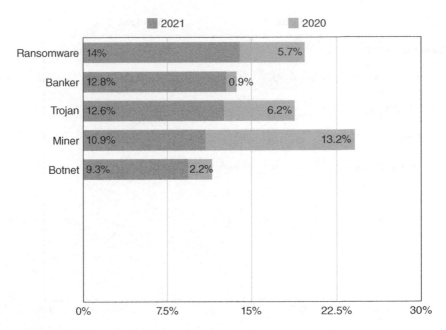

Figure 4.8 Linux malware with unique code, 2021 vs. 2020.

partner Intezer, demonstrating that cybercriminals are still interested in this market [1, 12]. Figure 4.8 shows Linux malware with a unique code in five categories, 2020–2021 and Figure 4.9 compares the new Linux malware and new Windows malware, 2021 [1]. To evaluate innovation, Intezer analyzes the uniqueness of the code in various malware strains. While malware that largely utilizes code has less innovation, malware with more unique variations shows that more innovation has been employed to change the malware. Since 2020, four out of the five categories of Linux malware have seen a rise in unique code, with banking trojans seeing the largest increase – a tenfold increase – in creativity. This rise in Linux targeting may be attributed to businesses' increased use of cloud computing environments, which commonly run on Linux. The level of invention of Linux malware was almost as high as that of Windows-based malware, demonstrating how prevalent Linux malware innovation has become. This trend will undoubtedly continue in 2022.

4.4.5 Threat Actors Target Cloud Environments

Threat actors' ongoing efforts to move targeting into cloud systems were noticed by IBM research on the cloud security threat landscape [1]. Data collected revealed that threat actors employed a number of methods to initially obtain access to the cloud assets of companies, with over a quarter of incidents resulting from threat actors pivoting into the cloud from on-premise networks. In addition,

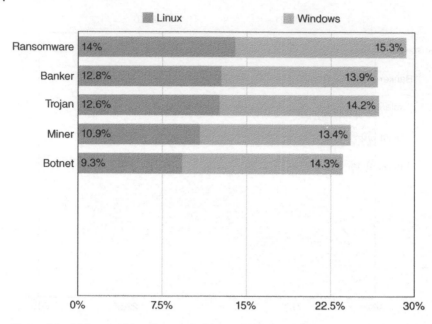

Figure 4.9 Malware with unique code, Linux vs. Windows, 2021.

roughly two-thirds of the cases under study had API misconfiguration problems. Tens of thousands of accounts were available for purchase online in a growing underground market for cloud-related credentials at the same time as this attack/ targeting. Threat actors are following organizations as they migrate to the cloud. A robust cloud security posture requires maintaining sufficiently hardened systems, implementing efficient password procedures, and guaranteeing policy compliance.

4.4.6 Fileless Malware in the Cloud

By using acceptable scripting languages and avoiding the usage of signatures, evasive, fileless malware that hides in memory can get past the detection capabilities of standard security software. Fileless malware attempts to defy standard detection methods by avoiding the use of signatures, evasive which is achieved by taking advantage of some programming languages, such as Golang. Threat actors are now employing Ezuri, an open-source memory loader and crypter developed in Golang, in addition to scripts to launch fileless malware, which makes it much simpler to launch undetected malware [13]. Another example is the Vermillion Strike malicious program which is based on the well-known penetration testing tool Cobalt Strike. However, the Vermillion Strike is created specifically to function on Linux computers, unlike Cobalt Strike [14]. The progression of malware that targets Linux is highlighted by this development, which suggests that operations outside of Windows environments will certainly continue in the future.

4.5 Geographic Trends

Figure 4.10 depicts the breakdown of attacks by region in 2021 and 2020. With 26% of attacks in 2021, Asia[1] has overtaken Europe[2] as the region with the most attacks. This attack pattern appears to have been influenced by a wave of strikes, particularly in Japan, which may have been connected to the 2021 Summer Olympic Games in Japan [15]. The Middle East and Africa[3] and Latin America[4] received 14% and 13% of attacks, respectively, while Europe and North America[5] came in second and third place with 24% and 23% of attacks, respectively.

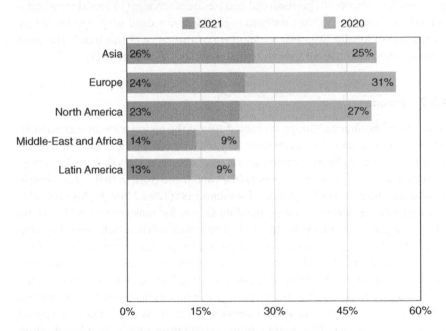

Figure 4.10 Breakdown of attacks by region, 2021 vs. 2020.

1 Asia includes Australia, East and Southeast Asia, India, and the Pacific islands.
2 European organizations include Western Europe, Eastern Europe, and Turkey.
3 The Middle East and Africa to include the Levant, Arabian Peninsula, Egypt, Iran and Iraq, and the entire African continent.
4 Latin America includes Mexico, Central America, and South America.
5 North America includes the United States and Canada.

4.5.1 Asia

The top two attack types affecting Asian organizations in 2021 were server access attacks (20%) and ransomware (11%), closely followed by data theft (10%). The large number of server access attacks in Asia may indicate that Asian businesses are skilled at detecting threats before they develop into more serious attack types. And 9% of attacks are the remote access trojans and adware which are tied for fourth place.

REvil contributed for 33% of ransomware attacks in Asia. The major participants of this attack were Bitlocker, Nefilim, MedusaLocker, and Ragnar Locker. Phishing and vulnerability exploitation shared the top infection vector for Asian organizations in 2021, each responsible for 43% of attacks recorded. To gain initial access to networks, brute force (7%) and the use of stolen credentials (7%) were also sometimes used. The most frequently targeted industries in Asia were those in finance and insurance (30%), closely followed by manufacturing (29%) and then, less frequently, professional and business services (13%) and transportation (10%). From 2015 to 2020, the banking and insurance industry experienced the most attacks globally; Asia saw a long-term continuance of this trend. The most often attacked countries in Asia were Japan, Australia, and India [1].

4.5.2 Europe

With 24% of the attacks, Europe surpassed Asia as the region with the second highest number of attacks. By representing 26% of all attacks in the continent in 2021, ransomware was the most common attack type in Europe. Data theft (10%), configuration errors (8%), malicious insiders (6%), and fraud (6%), in that order, came in second and third, respectively, behind server access (12%). Many highly profitable organizations in Europe could be possible targets for ransomware, which could attract ransomware attackers. In 2021, Ryuk and REvil attacks together contributed to 38% of all ransomware attacks in Europe. Ransomware groups from DarkSide, LockBit 2.0, and Crystal were also reported. These ransomware organizations frequently engage in "big game hunting," which entails concentrating their efforts on large, wealthy firms' enterprise networks to demand a high ransom.

Phishing was the second most common infection vector employed against European companies after vulnerability exploitation (46%). In 12% of cases, violence was utilized by brute force. Manufacturing, which has seen 25% of attacks, was the most frequently attacked industry in Europe in 2021, followed by banking and insurance (18%) and professional and business services (15%). These changes were undoubtedly brought on by ransomware attackers' preference for manufacturing and professional services companies. The most often attacked countries in Europe were Germany, Italy, and the United Kingdom [1].

4.5.3 North America

With 23% of all attacks in 2021, North America was the third most attacked region in the world. In North America, ransomware led all attack types, accounting for 30% of all attacks, much like it performed in Europe. It is likely that the enhanced government enforcement efforts in 2021, including the takedown of botnets and ransomware organizations, are slowing down the attack frequency previously seen in the area. In North America, REvil attacks, along with LockBit 2.0, Conti, CryptoLocker, and Eking accounted for 43% of all ransomware attacks. BEC was the second most frequent attack type in North America, after ransomware, accounting for 12% of attacks, indicating that BEC attackers have resumed their assault on North American businesses to compromise businesses without MFA in place. Attacks on servers (9% of all attacks) came in third for North American companies.

The figures for phishing (47% of the cases), in North America in 2021, suggest that this region's threat actors prefer this attack vector. Second, at 29%, was the use of vulnerability exploitation, followed by portable media (12%), brute force (9%), and stolen credentials (9%). As more North American businesses establish effective patch management procedures in response to multiple significant vulnerabilities reported in 2020 and 2021, threat actors may focus on phishing. Manufacturing was the most often attacked industry in North America, accounting for 28% of all attacks. This attack rate is likely because of the significant supply chain-related strain that the pandemic has placed on manufacturing. Retail and wholesale took the second position with 11%, followed by professional and business services with 15%. Manufacturing, professional services, and wholesale are all appealing targets for ransomware actors. This could be due to the fact that these industries have a low tolerance for downtime and have networks that contain sensitive client data that, if stolen and threatened to be leaked, can put a lot of pressure on a victim to pay a ransom [1].

4.5.4 Middle East and Africa

With 18% of attacks, ransomware and server access attacks both sit at the first place as the most common incident types in the Middle East and Africa. Misconfiguration came in second place with 14%, while DDoS attacks and credential harvesting were also extremely widespread in the area. In these regions, when an initial infection vector was detected, the vulnerability exploitation was resulted in 50% of cases. Access to networks of interest in the Middle East and Africa was frequently gained through the use of stolen credentials, phishing, and other methods. Password spraying and the use of removable media were also occasionally employed to acquire initial access [1].

In 2021, the overwhelming number of targets, in Middle East and Africa, was financial and insurance organizations, accounting for 48% of all attacks. This could potentially be due to the indication of a shift away from nation-state sponsored energy-focused attacks in the region toward cybercriminal attacks targeted at financial organizations. This pattern may also be impacted by Saudi Arabia's decision to diversify its economy away from crude revenues. Around 15% of attacks in the region targeted healthcare businesses, while 10% of attacks targeted energy organizations. The most often attacked countries in the Middle East and Africa were Saudi Arabia, the United Arab Emirates, and South Africa [1].

4.5.5 Latin America

Ransomware accounted for 29% of attacks in Latin America in 2021, which sat in the first place, followed by BEC (21%) and credential harvesting (21%), which tied for the second place. In 2021, the majority of ransomware attacks that were observed in Latin America used the REvil ransomware strain, while Ryuk and AtomSilo were also seen to target businesses in the area. REvil made approximately 50% of all ransomware attacks that were stopped. The rate of BEC attacks against Latin America is higher than for any other areas, as previously described in this publication, and it has sharply increased since 2019. This indicates that BEC attackers are paying more attention to Latin American targets. By accounting for 47% of attacks in this region, phishing was the most frequent infection vector threat actor used against Latin American targets. This pattern is most likely being driven by a large amount of BEC attacks and ransomware attacks that are distributed via phishing. Greater adoption of MFA may help to reduce cases of BEC and stolen credential theft in the region. Around 29% of attacks on firms involved stolen credentials, a significant number when compared to other regions. Only 18% of occurrences at Latin American organizations were caused by vulnerability exploitation, and another 6% were caused via removable media.

In 2021, manufacturing was the industry that was targeted the most, although, with only 22% of the market, it had a small margin. The industries that were closely behind mining (11%) were wholesale and retail (20%), banking and insurance (15%). Energy and professional and commercial services were under moderately strong attack in Latin America. The attack rate for these businesses is likely being driven by ransomware and BEC attackers, which both appear to be interested in attacking these areas. The most often attacked countries in Latin America were Brazil, Mexico, and Peru [1].

4.6 Industry Trends

Finance and insurance were not the most targeted industry from 2017 to 2021 because manufacturing narrowly edged it out. This move may have been

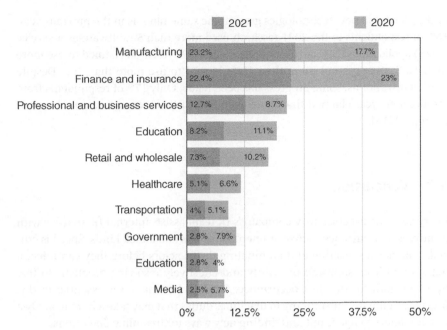

Figure 4.11 Breakdown of attacks on the top 10 industries, 2021 vs. 2020.

influenced by the rash of ransomware and BEC assaults that hit manufacturing companies, which added to the COVID-19 pandemic's impact on the supply chain [1]. In addition to industry and finance, professional and business services were actively targeted by ransomware attackers in 2021. To present a more comprehensive picture of the industry attack environment this year, we are merging professional and business services, as well as retail and wholesale. It is important to note that wholesale, which dominated the list for this industrial group, was significantly more aggressively attacked than retail last year [1]. Figure 4.11 shows a breakdown of attacks on the top 10 industries in 2020 and 2021.

Through the waves of infection variants, the COVID-19 pandemic is changing people's perspectives from taking immediate action to managing a chronic disease. Enterprises continue to see long-lasting changes as a result of the repercussions, and the security community as a whole is also affected. Enterprises are finding that what initially seemed to be a one-time event may persist continuously as a result of the long-lasting shift to remote working, which is changing mindsets. Almost 79% of respondents (to the research) said they are still "somewhat" or "extremely concerned" about the security risks and threats that a significantly larger remote workforce poses, despite another full year of remote work and the use of newer technology.[6] Around 40% of respondents indicated they lacked confidence in the ability of their present security mechanisms to protect remote work [16]. The use

---

6 This research is done by IBM Security X-Force.

of the cloud and new technologies grew at the same rates as in the previous year. 16% of respondents to the 2021 research used more than 50 software-as-a-service (SaaS) applications. 34% of respondents to the 2022 research claimed to use more than 50 SaaS apps, and more than 16% claimed to use more than 100. Despite market disruptions, some progress has been made. Only 17% of respondents from the previous year claimed that more than 50% of their sensitive cloud data was encrypted [16].

4.7 Conclusion

Every year, the cybersecurity company's IR team assists internal IR analysts with hundreds of occurrences across numerous regions and attack kinds. Speed is crucial, whether it's locating and eliminating threat actors before they can infect a network with ransomware or swiftly and effectively resolving problems to free up bandwidth for the next occurrence. Security automation is essential in this fast-paced climate, outsourcing to machines duties that may take a human analyst or team hours to figure out and finding new ways to streamline operations.

Creating a strategy for handling ransomware is essential as this cyberthreat has been the most repetitive in recent years. Every industry and region is susceptible to a ransomware threat, and how your team reacts in the crucial moment will determine how much time and money are lost in the response. On the other hand, during the COVID-19 pandemic, cyberthreat patterns have changed in the world, and it is important for any cybersecurity experts and any business to find new security solutions for the current trends.

References

1 X-Force. X-Force report. https://www.ibm.com/downloads/cas/ADLMYLAZ, 2019.
2 Microsoft. Microsoftreport. https://www.zdnet.com/article/everything-you-need-to-know-about-microsoft-exchange-server-hack/.
3 MZDNET report. https://securityintelligence.com/posts/multifactor-authentication-changing-threat-landscape/.
4 Phishing report. https://apwg.org/trendsreports/.
5 DNS report. https://www.quad9.net.
6 Global reprot. https://cpl.thalesgroup.com.
7 Cyber report. https://securityintelligence.com/posts/nation-state-threat-group-targets-airline-aclip-backdoor/.

8 Malware report. https://www.zdnet.com/article/siloscape-this-new-malware-targets-windows-containers-to-access-kubernetes-clusters/.

9 Dev report. https://go.dev.

10 Nim report. https://nim-lang.org.

11 IBM Cloud report. https://exchange.xforce.ibmcloud.com/malware-analysis/guid:eacc0402f5b07ee440772fcc3b2a7cd9.

12 Intezer report. https://www.intezer.com.

13 Ezuri report. https://www.bleepingcomputer.com/news/security/linux-malware-authors-use-ezuri-golang-crypter-for-zero-detection/.

14 Vermillion Strike report. https://www.securityweek.com/cobalt-strike-beacon-reimplementation-vermilion-strike-targets-windows-linux.

15 Japan Times report. https://www.japantimes.co.jp/article-expired/.

16 Global2020 report. https://www.japantimes.co.jp/article-expired/.

5

Survey on Building Block Technologies

At first glance, one might think the data leakage detection technology is different from technologies used with intrusion detection systems or virus scanners. In fact, they all share the use of machine learning (ML) technologies. In particular, various supervised ML methods have been extensively adopted in anomaly detection and data leakage prevention (DLP) systems for over a decade. This chapter starts looking with technologies that have a high potential to be used as a fundamental building block for DLP methods. Industrial control systems (ICSs), especially Supervisory Control and Data Acquisition (SCADA) systems, are some of the most challenging targets for researchers, as ICSs are vulnerable to cyber-attacks and researchers have put lots of effort to secure such critical systems for over decades.

This chapter is organized as follows. Section 5.1 introduces the consequences of cyber-attacks to various industry sectors, and a useful background for readers on the basics of SCADA systems is provided in Section 5.2. Section 5.3 presents a full taxonomy of SCADA-based IDSs and Section 5.4 provides a taxonomy of supervised-machine learning-based IDSs. Section 5.6 describes an evaluation of SCADA-based IDS supervised learning, and theoretically analyzes the most representative supervised machine learning algorithms for SCADA-based IDSs. Section 5.7 discusses the research gaps, and we conclude the chapter in Section 5.8.

We would like to note that thee work presented in this chapter is extracted from that authors' work that appeared in ACM Computing Surveys in 2020 [1].

5.1 Motivation

SCADA systems have been integrated into our critical infrastructures such as electric power generation, transport systems, water distribution and wastewater collection systems to control and monitor such industrial processes.

Data Exfiltration Threats and Prevention Techniques: Machine Learning and Memory-Based Data Security, First Edition. Zahir Tari, Nasrin Sohrabi, Yasaman Samadi, and Jakapan Suaboot.
© 2023 John Wiley & Sons, Inc. Published 2023 by John Wiley & Sons, Inc.

Since industrial manufacturing and power distribution sites are geographically distant and involve potentially extreme hazards, the integration of SCADA allows operators to maximize cost-effective operations and safety of their personnel [2]. For example, using a Smart Grid application with SCADA technology, power outages can be quickly diagnosed and temporarily fixed remotely and securely from the control center.

A typical SCADA system is operated through a *control center*, consisting of a complex of computers, networks, and databases. The databases store values gathered by Master Terminal Unit (MTU) from sensors e.g. voltage, current, valve pressure, etc. The control center sends control commands to actuators, such as Programmable Logic Controller (PLC), Remote Terminal Unit (RTU), or Intelligent Electronic Device (IED), to control the industrial processes [2]. A SCADA system is pervasive, and its components are interconnected using both wireless and wired communication. On the one hand, SCADA is connected to traditional Information Technology (IT) and networking technologies (e.g. operating systems and Internet protocols). On the other hand, it is also connected to SCADA-based technologies, such as industrial devices and communication protocols such as standard protocols (e.g. IEC 60870-5-101 or 104, and DNP3) and proprietary protocols (i.e. Modbus RTU, RP-570, Profibus, and Conitel) [3]. However, any disruption to SCADA systems can result in significant financial loss or even lead to loss of life. In the past, such systems were secure by virtue of their isolation from corporate networks and the Internet, and due to the use of proprietary hardware and software. In other words, they were self-contained and totally isolated from the public networks. This isolation created the myth that malicious intrusions and attacks from the outside world were not a big concern, and such attacks were expected to only come from the inside. Therefore, when developing SCADA protocols, the security of the information systems and the significance of loss due to Denial of Service (DoS) was given little consideration.

In recent years, SCADA systems have begun to shift away from using proprietary and customized hardware and software in favor of using Commercial-Off-The-Shelf (COTS) solutions [4]. Among the well-known vendors are ABB, Siemens, General Electric (GE), Alstom, SEL, Toshiba, and Schneider Electric [5]. This shift has increased their connectivity to public networks (Internet) using standard protocols, e.g. TCP/IP. In addition, there is a decreased reliance on one vendor. Undoubtedly, this increases productivity and profitability by reducing capital expenditure (Capex). However, this also now exposes such systems to more diverse, intelligent cyber attacks [6]. The convergence of state-of-the-art communication technologies exposes SCADA systems to all the inherent vulnerabilities of these technologies. According to the research result published in 2017 by Kaspersky Lab on the threats landscape for industrial automation systems [7], various industry sectors are affected by serious vulnerabilities that operate remotely using traditional network connectivity, see Figure 5.1.

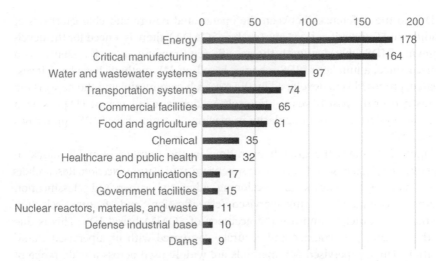

Figure 5.1 The number of vulnerabilities identified in various industries, published in 2017. Reproduced from "Threat landscape for industry automation systems in H2 2017," by Kaspersky Lab ICS CERT, 2018, page 3.

Vulnerabilities targeting SCADA systems have increased significantly since 2009, according to the Open Source Vulnerability Database (OSVDB) [8]. Different actors have different motivations for identifying and exploiting SCADA vulnerabilities. For example, state-based actors are interested in vulnerabilities related to the critical infrastructure, and criminals or hackers are more interested in stealing intellectual property and sabotaging industrial processes. Therefore, the nature of SCADA attacks has shifted from small scale, insider-based attacks to external threat and large-scale attacks. For example, prior to the year 2000, the majority of the reported incidents impacting SCADA networks were either due to accidents or due to disgruntled insiders acting maliciously. Since 2009, there has been a sharp increase in the total number of reported incidents and most of them (above 70%) are attacks originating from the Internet [9].

Numerous malicious attacks pose serious and evolving security threats to SCADA systems. Practically, there is no security countermeasure that can completely protect a target system from potential threats. As mentioned in Chapters 3 and 4, IDS [10] is one of the security solutions that has demonstrated promising results in detecting malicious activities large-scale systems. The source of audit data and the detection methods are the main, salient parts in the development of the IDS. The network traffic, system-level events and application-level activities are the usual sources of audit data. A detection method is categorized either as *signature-based* method and *anomaly-based* one. The former searches for an attack whose signature is already known, while the latter searches for activities that deviate from an expected pattern or from a predefined model of normal behavior of the system.

Due to the differences between the operational nature and characteristics of traditional IT and critical systems (such as SCADA), there is a need for the development of IDSs that deal with the specific requirements of such systems. As a consequence, a number of IDS schemes based on ML methods have been investigated, proposed, and developed by the research community and the networking industry over the past 10 years. Microsoft Academic search engine [11] has been used here to estimate the popularity in machine learning based IDS approaches since 2007.

Figure 5.2 shows the growth over time in the number of publications in *classification/supervised*, *clustering/unsupervised*, and *feature selection*. Researchers have made great efforts in developing advanced supervised classification methods – compared to unsupervised classification and feature selection methods – in order to improve the accuracy of SCADA-based IDS. This is due to their higher performance and accuracy compared with unsupervised classification. Thus, supervised ML methods are widely used across a wide range of SCADA-based IDS approaches.

Many papers have been written that survey IDSs for critical infrastructure systems from different perspectives. For example, Zhu and Sastry [12] emphasize the architectures of IDS for SCADA systems. Mitchell and Chen [13] focus on classifying IDS solutions based on detection methods and audit materials. Holm et al. [14] gather information about the testbeds used for ICSs. In contrast to previous reviews, the focus of this chapter is on *supervised learning* for SCADA-based IDSs. Additionally, this chapter analyzes existing literature based on holistic perspectives, including detection architecture, detection methods, auditing sources, and feasibility of applying IDS to various real SCADA systems.

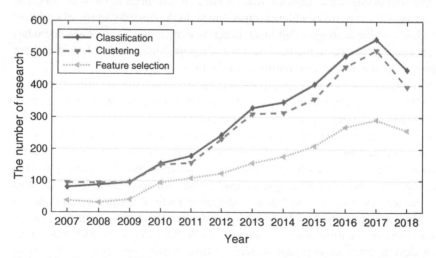

Figure 5.2 Evolution of IDS schemes based on ML methods (between 2007 and 2018 and ongoing).

This survey attempts to review the field of supervised ML methods used for SCADA-based IDS and achieve the following objectives:

- describe a framework that systematically groups a collection of existing SCADA-based IDS methods into appropriate categories and compares their advantages and drawbacks;
- present a comprehensive taxonomy of supervised ML methods specifically used for SCADA-based IDSs;
- describe an evaluation metric to allow theoretical analysis of the most representative supervised ML algorithms from each category, with respect to the requirements of SCADA-based IDSs.

In summary, the described survey presents a taxonomy of supervised ML methods used for SCADA-based IDS and describes a categorizing framework that covers major factors in the selection of a suitable method for SCADA-based IDS.

5.2 Background

This section introduces the key architectural concepts of a SCADA system as well as the classification of SCADA-based IDSs. To distinguish between a SCADA and a generic ICT system, SCADA specific threats and vulnerabilities are also discussed and thus will lead to properly define the specific IDS requirements for SCADA systems.

5.2.1 SCADA System

This is widely used a an industrial system that continuously monitors and controls many different sections of industrial infrastructure. Applications include but are not limited to oil refineries, water treatment and distribution systems, transport systems, manufacturing plants, and electric power generation plants. Hence, a large number of commercial solutions were offered by vendors around the world, including GE Fanuc, Siemens Sianut, and Toshiba, to name a few. Typically, a SCADA system gathers measurements – collects data from the deployed field devices – and sends them to a central site for further processing and analysis. The information and status of the supervised and monitored processes are displayed at the base station or at the utility center. As such industrial systems are large and complex, a central master unit continuously and remotely monitors and controls different sections of the plant to guarantee their proper functioning.

5.2.1.1 SCADA Components

The main components of a typical SCADA system include the following: Master Terminal Unit (MTU), Programmable Logic Controller (PLCs), Remote Terminal Unit (RTU), Intelligent Electronic Device (IED), Human–Machine Interface (HMI), and Communication Media [8].

- *Master Terminal Unit (MTU)*: This is the core of a SCADA system that gathers information from the distributed RTUs and analyzes it to control the various processes [8]. A plant's data is analyzed through histogram generation, standard deviation calculation, and plotting one parameter with respect to another. Based on the performance results, an operator may decide to monitor any channel more frequently, change the limits, or shut down the terminal units. The software can be designed according to the applications and the type of analysis required. The operator may be interested in finding the best operating steps for a plant which will minimize the overall operating cost. To solve this problem, engineers often employ different optimization methods on the collected data to determine the best operating process. The operating process is then converted to appropriate operating signals and then sent to the remote terminal units RTUs through communication pathways (e.g. radio links, leasedline, or fiber optic [15]).
- *Field devices (RTUs, PLCs, and IEDs)*: These are computer-based components deployed at a remote site to gather data from sensors and to control actuators [8]. Each field device may be connected to one or more sensors and actuators that are directly connected to physical equipment (e.g. pumps, valves, motors). The main function of such devices is to convert the electrical signals received by sensors into digital values in order to send them to the MTU for further processing and analysis using some specific communication protocol (e.g. Modbus [16]). On the other hand, they can convert a digital command message received by MTU into an electrical signal in order to control actuators that are controlling some physical aspects of the controlled system. Different field-level devices, e.g. RTUs, PLCs, and IEDs, that are deployed at remote sites perform different functions. RTUs collect data from sensors and send it back to the MTU, and then the MTU takes a decision based on this data and sends commands to different actuators. In addition to the same function of RTUs, PLCs can collect data from sensors and based on the collected data, they can send commands directly to actuators using a local loop. In other words, PLCs can process the data locally and take the decision without contacting MTU. IEDs are part of control systems such as transformers, circuit breakers, sensors, etc., and they can be controlled via PLCs or RTUs.
- *Human–Machine Interface (HMI)*: This provides an efficient human–machine interface through which an operator can monitor/control end devices, such as sensors and actuators. An HMI graphically displays information on the current state of the supervised and controlled process including alerts, warnings, and urgent messages. In addition, the HMI allows the user to interact with the system using switches, buttons, and other controls [8].
- *Historian*: This is a database that stores the different types of data gathered by the SCADA system, such as measurement and control data, events, alarms, and operator activities. This data is used for historical, auditing, analysis, and operational purposes [8].

5.2.1.2 SCADA Architecture

A SCADA network provides the communication infrastructure for different field devices (e.g. PLCs and RTU) of a plant. These field devices are remotely monitored and controlled throughout the SCADA network. To make the network communication more efficient and secure, many modern computing technologies have evolved from a monolithic system to a distributed system and to the current inter-networked systems [8].

(1). Monolithic Systems (1st Generation). The *monolithic* SCADA system is considered to be the first generation SCADA system [8]. At that time, networks were non-existent in general, and therefore a SCADA system was deployed as a stand-alone system, and no connectivity to other systems existed. As can be seen in Figure 5.3, a SCADA master used wide area networks (WANs) to communicate with field devices using communication protocols that were developed by vendors of field devices. In addition, these protocols had limited functionality – they could only do scanning and controlling over points within certain types of RTUs. The communication between the master and field devices (e.g. RTUs) was carried out at the communication bus level using proprietary adapters. To avoid system failures, two identically equipped mainframe systems were used: one as the primary and the other as a backup. The latter was designed to take over when a failure of the primary system was detected. Figure 5.3 illustrates the typical architecture of this type of SCADA architecture.

(2). Distributed Systems (2nd Generation). Figure 5.4 depicts a typical second gen-eration SCADA architecture. With the development of Local Area Networking (LAN) technologies, the second generation of SCADA system distributes the pro-cessing to multiple systems and assigns a specific function for each station [8]. In addition, multiple stations could be connected to a LAN to share information with each other in real time. For instance, the communication server can be set-up to

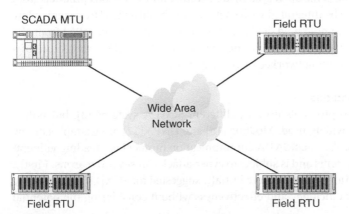

Figure 5.3 The first generation of SCADA architecture.

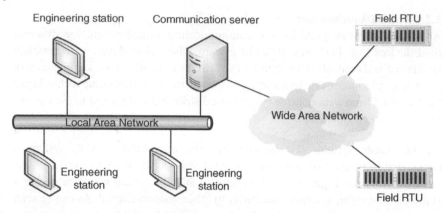

Engineering station   Communication server   Field RTU

Wide Area Network

Local Area Network

Engineering station   Engineering station

Field RTU

Figure 5.4 The second generation of SCADA architecture.

communicate with field devices such as PLCs and RTUs. Some of the distributed stations can be an MTU, a Historian, or an HMI server. The distribution of system's functionalities across the network-connected systems increases the processing power, reduces the redundancy and improves the reliability of the system as a whole. In this generation, system failures are addressed by keeping all stations on the LAN in an online state during the operation time, and if one station (e.g. HMI station) fails, then another HMI station takes over.

(3). Networked Systems (3rd Generation). Unlike the second generation, a third generation SCADA system is based on an open system architecture, rather than vendor controlled, proprietary solutions. One of the major differences is that the third generation can utilize open standard protocols and products. Consequently, the SCADA functionalities can be distributed across a WAN and not just a LAN [8]. For instance, most field devices can be connected directly to the MTU over an Ethernet connection. This open system architecture allows various products from different vendors to be integrated with each other to build a SCADA system at low cost. In addition, a remote field device can be supervised and controlled from any place and at any time using the Internet. Figure 5.5 shows the architecture of a typical third generation networked SCADA system.

5.2.1.3 SCADA Protocols
There are over 150 protocols used by different SCADA systems [3], but only a small number are widely used. Modbus [16] and DNP3 [17] are examples of few well-known protocols. The SCADA communication protocol is a leading vulnerability in SCADA systems and is subject to cyber-attacks for several reasons. Firstly, when communication protocols were initially suggested for SCADA networks, the focus was on their efficiency and effectiveness without considering the potential

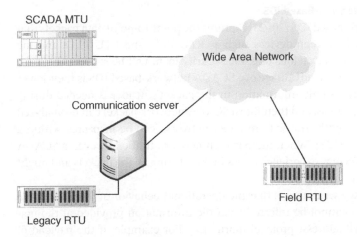

SCADA MTU

Wide Area Network

Communication server

Field RTU

Legacy RTU

Figure 5.5 The third generation of SCADA architecture.

security issues they might encounter in the future. As security concerns became more critical, it was discovered that it was not easy to address such issues, since an upgrade or replacement of a vital SCADA network in an old industrial system can disrupt the production or management of existing critical processes and services. Secondly, most of the original SCADA systems were often separate from other corporate networks. Hence, a large number of communication layers and protocols were designed separately, including GE Fanuc, Siemens Sianut, Toshiba, Modbus RTU/ASCII, Allen Bradley DF1/DH, and other vendor protocols.

Recently, both Modbus and DNP3 have been integrated to work on top of TCP/IP [18]. The Modbus protocol offers a modified version, called Modbus/TCP, that uses the TCP/IP as transport and network protocols. The DNP3 protocol can also work over TCP and UDP. Frames at the link layer are encapsulated into TCP/IP packets so that DNP3 can take full advantage of the Internet technology.

5.2.2 Different Types of SCADA-Based IDSs

An IDS is an autonomous hardware, software, or combination of both system that can detect threats in a SCADA system by monitoring and analyzing network or device activities from both internal and external attackers. In traditional IT systems, IDS can be classified into network-based and host-based IDS [19] depending on the location of the collected data and logs. However, due to the different nature of SCADA systems in terms of architecture, functionalities, and operating devices, SCADA-based IDS, within the scope of this chapter, are categorized based on only based on the source of collected data: *SCADA network-based IDS* and *SCADA application-based IDS*.

5.2.2.1 SCADA Network-Based IDS

A SCADA network-based IDS [20–23] captures the point-to-point data packets that are communicated between devices such as RTU/PLC, and RTU/PLCs and the MTU. If a packet is a suspicious one, the security team will be sent an alarm for further investigation. An advantage of a SCADA network-based IDS is their lower computation costs, as only information in the packet's header is needed during the investigation process, and therefore a SCADA network packet can be analyzed on-the-fly. Consequently, traffic from larger networks can be inspected within a short period of time [23]. When there is high network traffic however, a SCADA network-based IDS may experience issues in monitoring all the packets and might miss some attacks.

However, the key weakness is that the operational behavior of the underlying SCADA processes cannot be inferred from the information provided at the network level (e.g. IP address, protocol, port, etc.). For example, if the payload of the SCADA network packet contains a malicious message, which is crafted at the application level, the SCADA network-based IDS cannot detect it, particularly when this is not violating the specifications of the protocol being used, or the communication pattern between SCADA networked devices [8, 24–26].

5.2.2.2 SCADA Application-Based IDS

SCADA data, which comprises the measurements and control data generated by sensors and actuators, represents the majority of the information. Using this data the operational behavior of a given SCADA system can be inferred [25–29]. In contrast to SCADA network-based IDSs that only inspect network level information, a SCADA application-based IDS can inspect high level data (i.e. SCADA data) to detect the presence of unusual behavior. For example, SCADA network-based IDSs are often unable to detect high-level control attacks [30] from packet headers; which can be detected by analyzing SCADA data [28].

Since the information source of a SCADA application-based IDS can be gathered from different remote field devices, following are the various ways to deploy a SCADA application-based IDS [8]. (i) It can be deployed in the historian server, as this server is periodically updated by the MTU server which acquires, through field devices, such as PLC and RTU, the information and status of the monitored system for each time period. However, this type of deployment raises a security issue when the information and status stored in the historian differ from the realtime data in the field. This could occur when the MTU server has been compromised or the data has been changed using False Data Injection attacks [31–33]. (ii) It can also be deployed in an independent security hardened server, which from time to time acquires information and statuses from the monitored field devices [24]. Consequently, the large number of requests from this server might increase the network overheads resulting in degraded performance of the IDS. (iii) Each adjacent field device can be connected with a server running a SCADA application-based IDS, which is similar to the work proposed by Igor et al. [34]. However, the key issue is that SCADA data is directly/indirectly correlated, and therefore sometimes there is an abnormality in a parameter not because of itself, but due to anomalous value in another parameter [25, 26]. Therefore, it would be appropriate to identify and monitor correlated parameters, such as sensor readings related to a single process.

5.2.2.3 Signature-Based vs. Anomaly-Based SCADA IDS Methods

Many types of SCADA-based IDS have been proposed in the literature, and these fall into two broad categories in terms of the detection strategy [8]: *signature-based detection* [35, 36] and *anomaly-based detection* [20–23, 37–39].

A signature-based IDS detects malicious activities in a SCADA system's network traffic or in its application events. It does this by using pattern matching methods to detect telltale events against a database of signatures [35] or fingerprints [36] of known attacks. The false positive rate (i.e. incorrectly identifying a normal event as an attack) in this type of IDS is very low and can approach zero. Moreover, the detection time can be fast because it is based only on the use of a matching process during the detection phase. Despite the aforementioned advantages of signature-based IDSs, they typically fail to detect new attacks (e.g. zero-day) whose signatures are not known, or which do not exist in its database. Therefore, the database must be constantly updated with patterns of new attacks.

An anomaly-based IDS assumes that the behaviors of intrusive activities are noticeably distinguishable from normal behavior [19]. The "normal model" is created using a realistic training set using advanced mathematical/statistical methods. Any significant deviation from this model is flagged as an anomaly or potential attack. For example, normal SCADA network traffic can be obtained over a period of *normal* operations, and then a modeling method is applied to build the normal SCADA network profiles. During the detection phase, the deviation degree between the current network traffic and the created normal network profile is computed: if the deviation exceeds the predefined threshold, the current network traffic will be flagged as an intrusive activity. The primary advantage of anomaly-based IDSs compared to signature-based ones is that new or unknown attacks can be detected, although it generally suffers from higher false positive rate (i.e. detecting normal behavior as malicious).

5.2.3 SCADA Threats and Vulnerabilities

When SCADA was initially suggested, the focus was on efficiency and effectiveness without considering the potential security issues it might encounter in the future. As security concerns became more critical, it was discovered that it was not easy to address such issues, since an upgrade or replacement of a vital SCADA network in an old industrial system can disrupt the production or management of existing critical processes and services [3]. SCADA was also originally developed for *isolated* systems. Modern critical infrastructure has since been inter-connected via the Internet network to increase scope and capability and we have thus seen various new attacks on the systems. An example is the Havex malware that allows attackers to remote access and controls the system using a backdoor channel. Such malware affected victims in numerous industries, including sections of energy, aviation, and defense to name a few. The Stuxnet worm that targets PLC devices and gives unexpected commands to the infected control device [40]. This threat primarily targets Iran's nuclear program. The SQL Slammer worm that exploits buffer overflow vulnerability and performs DoS on the infected system (i.e. Davis-Besse – the American nuclear power plan). We categorize vulnerabilities of the SCADA into three aspects as follows:

5.2.3.1 Hardware

A SCADA system is geographically distributed (i.e. covering regions of cities), and many low-level controllers/sensors are wirelessly inter-connected. As a result, it is hard to prevent attackers from accessing SCADA components, wirelessly or even physically. For instance, attackers could intercept the wireless communication signal using tools like Aircrack-NG [41] to gain access to the network. In the field, it is even possible that attackers intrude into the station and direct access to the control device (e.g. using the USB drive malware).

The physical component also has a tight relationship with its software counterpart. Hence, an attack with a series of malicious commands could severely affect the hardware. An example is the Aurora Generator Test showing the destruction of the electric generator by remotely attack from the network [42]. Furthermore, the inclination to use COTS devices in SCADA system makes the system more vulnerable. Since the COTS equipment has a generic design and protocol standards, it has become a target of exploitation [3].

5.2.3.2 Software

SCADA-based protocols use plaintext messages to communicate between sensors and actuators (e.g. Modbus, DNP-3, IEC 60870-5-101 and IEC 60870-5-104). These simple communications can be easily manipulated by false data injection attacks [31, 43–45]. Here attackers inject (e.g. using man-in-the-middle [MITM] method) a fake measurement into a closed loop control system. This can disrupt or even stop the critical system.

Patching the newly discovered vulnerability can be complicated for a SCADA system. Since the distributed control components are mostly Windows or Linux based computers, inherited vulnerabilities are inevitable. Unfortunately, with the availability requirement and diversity of system components, appropriate security patches might take several months to arrive [8]. This is because system components might come from different manufacturers, using various standards or proprietary protocols. In some cases, software/hardware is being used for the extended period of time after the end of manufacturer supported warranty [46].

5.2.3.3 Security Administration and Insider Attacks

Apart from the security technology, attackers could harvest information using social engineering to attack employees of the targeted organization. A bad security practice, such as weak passwords or bad configurations, could make the SCADA system vulnerable. On the other hand, an angry former employee could hack into the system cause devastating damages to the system. For instance, the incident in Queensland Australia that the former staff flood millions liters of sewage water into parks and rivers by using a radio transmitter and computer from his car [47].

5.2.4 Requirements of SCADA-Based IDSs

SCADA is distinguished from a traditional IT system by key characteristics such as availability and reliability are critical. It also includes a wide range of proprietary COTS components, i.e. the cyber-physical components are tightly coupled. Hence, the key requirements for a SCADA-based IDS can be listed as follows:

- *Availability and robustness*: According to the availability constraint, the IDS technology does not only require anomaly detection that covers both known and unknown attacks, but it also requires support for a model updating mechanism that minimizes downtime. With regard to robustness, the IDS has to be compatible with incomplete features gathered from different platforms to allow components from diverse manufacturers to be used. Furthermore, the security system has to deal with training/detecting data that contains a little portion of attacks event and lots of noises [48].
- *Scalability and resilience*: Despite a large number of logs that are continuously generated from a number of sensors/controllers, the detection module should not slow down the manufacturing or control process. Conversely, it should give timely automated protection and alarms. Since a decentralized or distributed IDS could be an answer to the scalability issue, the design of algorithms should also account for the possibility that detection devices may themselves be compromised or fail [49]. To extend scalability without scarifying availability, resilience is also an important requirement.
- *Information aggregation and correlation*: Since a SCADA system has a tight cyber-physical relationship [8], the IDS should be able to make use of multiple attributes in detecting anomalies. The SCADA system integrates Operational Technology (OT), such as sensors and actuators, as well as IT, such as databases, servers, firewalls, and routers. As a result, a SCADA-based IDS has to support

aggregation and correlation of variables from multiple sources. Besides, manipulation of either cyber or physical world could affect one another. For instance, false-data injection attack [31] that infiltrates fake measurement data into the system to cause physical disruption. Hence, it is important to monitor anomaly from a holistic perspective, including cyber perspective (i.e. network communication, application behavior) and physical perspective (e.g. signals from sensors/controllers).

- *Feasibility*: As the nature of the SCADA system can be different depending on the application (e.g. electric power distribution, water supply system and manufacturing process control system), the practicality study of the proposed system is crucial. In addition, the completeness of assessing the proposed model is also important for the critical infrastructure system. Despite the limited research and development cost, the same system can act differently on different evaluation environment (e.g. tested on a simulator, SCADA test-bed and implementing the real system).

5.3 Taxonomy

Protecting a SCADA system from intrusion is a challenging task because it not only inherits many of the existing ICT vulnerabilities but also includes vulnerabilities from the OT field components. In addition, the implementation of countermeasures suffers due to the limited computational resources on the OT side. Thus, there is a need to study IDS systems used for SCADA. Motivated by the work proposed in [12, 13, 50–52], the existing approaches can be classified using three different categorizations based on the requirements of SCADA-based IDSs. Figure 5.6 shows our taxonomy of SCADA-based IDSs.

- *Function-centric*: As part of its operations, a SCADA system generates alarms for processes that go beyond their operating parameters, e.g. due to an expected or unexpected change in the underlying physical processes. While this may not always correspond to an attack, alert-based responses address inherent problems in SCADA operations, which are otherwise not possible to capture using traditional IT-based IDS. Based on the requirements of the strict availability, the IDS can respond immediately to unusual situations, e.g. [23, 40, 53–62], or provide a delayed notification summarizing similar alarms [63–70].
- *Information-centric*: If we examine the information used for the detection, then IDS systems can be further categorized into Host-based Intrusion Detection (HID) and Network-based Intrusion Detection (NID). Host-based methods detect intrusions by examining data gathered from hosts, such as device memory, application logs [40, 53, 57, 63, 71–73], the change of system configuration [65], Network-based methods collect data from either a network, a

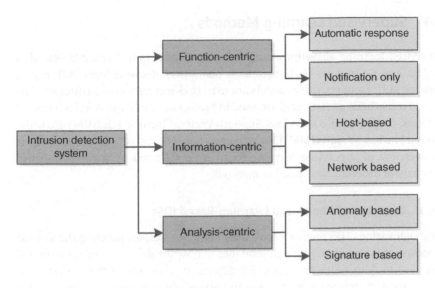

Figure 5.6 A taxonomy of IDSs for SCADA systems.

hub or a router and detect anomalies at the source, destination, protocol, and payload from network data [55, 64, 67, 74–79].

- *Analysis-centric*: This category focuses on different analysis methods for detecting outliers. As discussed in Section 5.2.2, this has two subgroups, namely *signature-based* and *anomaly-based* approaches. The scope of this review is *anomaly-based approach*, which employs various kinds of machine learning methods.

As three previously discussed categories classify existing work from different perspectives, a single publication can be included into three categories. For instance, [40, 53, 57] are grouped as *automatic response, host-based*, and *anomaly-based* according to their functions, detecting sources and analysis methods.

However, since this chapter/review focuses on supervised learning algorithm, the number of reviewing literature mostly consists of *anomaly based* approaches. This is because the anomaly-based detection focuses on finding deviations (outliers) from the trained normal or abnormal models rather than using the pre-defined patterns of attacks to detect abnormal events, e.g. patterns of spoof Address Resolution Protocol (ARP) messages or sequence of Application Programming Interface (API) called by known malicious programs. A few numbers of signature-based approaches were included as they employed supervised learning algorithms to dynamically generate sets of signatures for detecting suspicious incidents.

5.4 Supervised Learning Methods

Supervised learning algorithms use labeled training data to formulate detection models, e.g. set of rules [80], separation plane [81], decision trees [82], neural network [83]. Later on, these models are used to detect anomalies. Different classification methods or classifiers are used to predict anomaly, e.g. Artificial Neural Network (ANN) [83], One Class Support Vector Machine (OCSVM) [61], the Hidden Markov Model (HMM) [53], to name a few. The rest of this section presents an overview of supervised learning-based IDSs followed by a comprehensive summary of different classification methods.

5.4.1 Overview of Supervised Learning-Based IDSs

Although various IDS methods have different processes, we describe the generic process in this section to give a general idea of how the detection model is trained and used to detect attacks. Figure 5.7 depicts an overview of the implementation of the IDS approach in practice. In particular, such systems consist of five main processes: (A) data collection, (B) feature extraction and selection, (C) tagging, (D) training, and (E) anomaly detection. Data collection (see Figure 5.7A) represents the measurement step, where the input data is collected, e.g. logs of events or system states, traffic trace or Net-flow data from a network monitor and so on. Figure 5.7B.1 shows the feature extraction and feature selection processes, discriminating features are extracted and selected into a form that is usable in the classification process. The feature selection step might not be required for some machine learning approaches (i.e. ANN [83], that include network pruning and contrasting procedures which automatically select the discriminant features).

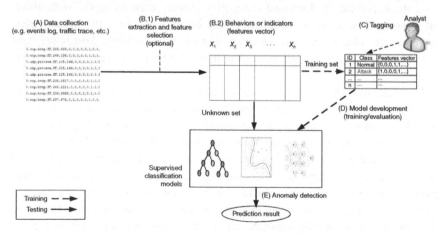

Figure 5.7 The process of the supervised learning-based IDS approach.

In the Figure 5.7B.2, each data point (i.e. record) is represented using a feature vector which consists of attributes $x_1, x_2, \ldots, x_n$ (e.g. behaviors or indicators). Sometimes values of features require to be normalized at this stage to prevent feature with a large range (e.g. payload size) to overweight feature with a relatively small range (e.g. binary). For instance, Min–Max normalization [84] can be used to transform the numeric value v of feature x to v' that ranges between [0, 1] as follows,

$$v' = \frac{v - min_x}{max_x - min_x},\tag{5.1}$$

where min_x and max_x are the minimum and the maximum value of the feature x. Note that, each data point may not always be a tuple with a specific number of features, some instances of a sample could also be a sequence of features. We elaborate this in more detail in Section 5.4.2. In Figure 5.7C, each training record must be labeled to identify the class (i.e. *normal* or *attack* in the context of the IDS) that the data instance belongs to, either manually or automatically, using input from an analyst or expert. In several cases, the attack incident is hard to simulate or collect from the field. For these scenarios, IDS designers use only *normal* dataset to train the model (e.g. [61, 63, 85–87]). Figure 5.7D shows the model development process. The labeled dataset is used to train and evaluate the classification model. In order to improve the detection accuracy, parameters of the model could be adjusted, and the training/evaluation process is repeated until the anticipating efficiency is satisfied.

Once model training is complete, the model can be used to classify new instances of data. Figure 5.7E shows the process of detecting an anomaly using the classification model. Each unknown data item is labeled as either benign or malicious (most systems will provide lower-level detail for malicious points). Finally, the output of this module will be presented to the administrator to notify or take a response action.

5.4.2 Taxonomy of Supervised Learning Methods

Even though there exist several ML classification methods/algorithms to detect anomalies [88], there is a lack of a taxonomy of these methods in the literature. A proper taxonomy is not only important to develop the evaluation matrix, but this also helps to separate between computational and architectural complexity of SCADA IDS systems. Hence, this section will present a structured view of classification methods based on nine categories (see Figure 5.8). Each category is described in detail below.

5.4.2.1 Probabilistic Method
This category predicts a class of unseen data based on probabilities. During the training phase, the presence of certain features of each class is used to calculate the

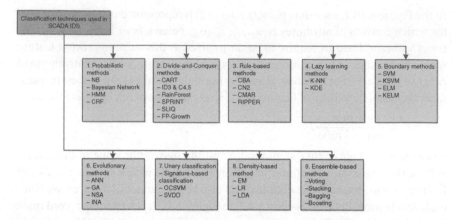

Figure 5.8 Categories of classification algorithms used in SCADA-based IDSs.

distribution of joint or conditional possibility [89]. This number reflects the probability that a particular input falls into one of the predefined classes of objects to be classified. Examples of method in this category are Naïve Bayes (NB), Bayesian Network, Hidden Markov Model (HMM), and Conditional Random Field (CRF).

A basic probabilistic method like NB [90] learns conditional probability of each feature from the training data based on the assumption that every feature can be seen independently (i.e. conditionally independent). NB predicts the class of the input based on the highest joint likelihood. Bayesian Network method [91] generalizes NB classifier by combining Bayesian variables with directed acyclic graph structure. The vertex in the graph depicts variable (i.e. features and class), whereas the edge represents a probabilistic relationship between these variables. The graph is used to compute posterior probability of each class given all evidence.

On the other hand, some probabilistic models work on a sequence of features instead of the fixed number of features. For instance, HMM [78] inherits concept of NB to predict the class of data point based on a series of observable features over time. The assumption of HMM is that an observable feature is generated by the particular hidden system states. That is explained as a Markov process. The hidden state at time t depends on the previous state $t - 1$. Once the joint probability of the future state is calculated, the likelihood of the observable sequence is determined using knowledge of the predicted hidden states. HMM is used to classify labels of events based on sequences of features that are traced over the monitoring period. For instance, messages from a log of communication are considered a sequence of features.

CRF is similar to HMM but more complicated. Instead of relying on a joint probability, the CRF works based on conditional probability [92]. As a result, CRF is more flexible. In other words, it includes a wide variety of overlapping features. However, this makes CRF less efficient in terms of computational complexity issue compared to HMM. Apart from that, when the newer data becomes available, CRF model does not support re-training of the model. Therefore, it is not suitable for attacks that change over time.

5.4.2.2 Divide and Conquer Method

This includes (but is not limited to) a broad category of algorithms known as the *decision tree*. It formulates a tree-like data structure from a set of attributes of each training tuple. Using a decision tree a rule set is easily derived, which can be used to classify the input into a particular group [65, 73, 80]. There are several algorithms in the group, such as Classification and Regression Tree (CART), Iterative Dichotomiser (ID3), C4.5 (an improved ID3), Frequent Pattern Growth (FPG), Supervised Learning in Quest (SLIQ), SPRINT, and Random Forest (RF).

CART consists of a set of decision rules, which is described using a set of if-else rules using a structure of *binary tree* [93]. The *node* of the tree represents a feature that is used to classify data points, while the *edge* represents decision paths. The path that connects more than one class is called a sub-tree. The path that yields only one class is called the *leaf* node and represents the final outcome. In reality, the classification node gives a mixture of instances from different categories; hence the feature that best discriminates the input data is chosen (so-called *splitter*). After that, the recursive process repeats at the next level of the tree until the classification reaches a leaf node. Since method finding the best splitter is based on the greedy approach (non-backtracking), the output decision tree might not be optimized. Tree pruning method is the most commonly used [88] to reduce the size of the tree.

The advanced decision tree methods like ID3 and C4.5 build decision tree the same way, but C4.5 has been improved over ID3 in various aspects. Specifically, C4.5 handles both continuous and discrete attributes. If the attribute $X \in \mathbb{R}$, the *splitting threshold* will be used to divide the data into two groups instead of the exact value of the discrete X. Apart from that, C4.5 allows the training data with some missing attribute values, and it supports tree pruning after creation. According to the research [65], C4.5 is faster and more flexible compared to its precedent ID3; therefore, it is a better choice for the context of the SCADA IDS that produces variety and a large amount of the monitoring inputs data. Scalability is an important issue of tree based classifiers as the size of tree is growing when the training data is larger [94]. Advanced decision tree methods improve scalability and accuracy compared to the classic methods. For instance, IBM proposes SLIQ [94] and SPRINT [95] algorithms, which are based on a scalable method that splits parts of the tree from memory to the database on a hard drive to address the scalability issue.

Aside from the decision tree methods, divide, and conquer approach also includes a method that works based on a frequent pattern, for example, FP-Growth algorithm. The researchers [73] use FP-Growth to discovers common communication patterns of the smart grid system. Then, the infrequently seen pattern is identified as an anomaly. The FP-Growth uses *FP-Tree* data structure to summarize patterns of events (i.e. nodes) that frequently occur together (i.e. edges of the tree). Although the FP-Growth method is efficient, the data structure might be too large to fit in the main memory.

5.4.2.3 Rule-Based Method

This uses a set of rules to determine classes of inputs. Undeniable, the rule is easier for a human to understand the reason behind a decision, compared to the probabilistic and numerical models. A rule generally contains condition and conclusion parts. The *conclusion* is the output of the classification, whereas the *condition* is the features of particular object that are being classified. The efficiency of rule-based method is measured by *coverage* and *accuracy*. Coverage shows how many tuples in the dataset satisfy by the *condition*. The *accuracy* determines the number of tuples that apply the *conclusion*. A definition of rules set is either specified by specialists of the particular system or mined from the training data using various supervised learning methods.

With respect to automate rules discovery approach, a set of rules can be extracted from the training data. This process can be done by *sequential covering* algorithms or *decision tree* methods [88]. The sequential covering approach extracts rules from training data one-by-one in sequence, whereas the decision tree formulates a multiple tree-like structure of decision rules. There are many different rules mining approaches, such as Classification Based on Associations (CBA) [96], CN2 [97], Multiple Association Rules (CMAR) [98], and Repeated Incremental Pruning to Produce Error Reduction (RIPPER) [99].

The simple method like CBA [96] selects the most effective rules that identify a class of each tuple from the training set. The CBA algorithm learns a Class Association Rule (CAR) from the training set D, defined as $x_i \rightarrow C_i$, where the feature x_i implies a class C_i. The rule holds support $sup\% = |x_i|/|D|$ and confident $conf\% = |x_i \rightarrow C_i|/|D|$, where $|x_i|$ depicts total number of tuples with the attribute x_i, $|x_i \rightarrow C_i|$ means total number of attribute value x_i that implies the class value C_i, and $|D|$ denotes total number of tuples in the training set. These are minimum thresholds (i.e. $sup\%$ and $conf\%$) that determine if the rule should be selected for the classification. Although the selected rules are the most effective, they might not be the best discrimination. In addition, a scalability issue is an important limitation. That is, the rule-based method scales poorly with the large training data, especially when outliers cannot be avoided compared to the decision tree method (i.e. C4.5) [99].

The more sophisticated approaches like CMAR and RIPPER, on the other hand, aim to increase the robustness of the approach by eliminating impurities from the training data and reducing the number of rules generated from the training phase. CMAR [98] extends FP-Growth method [73] to formulate a CAR-Tree and minimizes memory space requirement (e.g. by using tree pruning method); hence,

CMAR has a better classification accuracy and scalability compared to the classic CBA and C4.5 algorithms. RIPPER [58] aims to address the impurity issue by proposing an iterative pruning method for reducing error and allow a large and noisy training dataset to be used. More specifically, the training data is divided into *growing* and *pruning* sets. The growing part is used to formulate a rule-set, whereas the new set of rules is pruned immediately with the pruning data set until there is no improvement from the pruning step. The new set of rules is integrated with a rule-set from the previous iteration.

5.4.2.4 Lazy Learning Method

This method differs from others in terms of the learning process. The main idea behind the method is to update the training model as late (hence lazy) as possible. For example, the training data is stored in the memory without building the prediction model like another method. The prediction model is only built during the classification step. It offers both advantages and disadvantages. Even though the lazy learning method offers the best performance at learning step, this advantage is a trade-off of computational complexity when it is making a prediction or classification. However, it is more flexible than others because the trained model can be incrementally improved [66, 101].

The commonly used lazy learning method is k-Nearest-Neighbor (k-NN) [102]. It compares the input with k data points using Euclidean distance function. The advanced method like kernel density estimation (KDE) implements k-NN based approach (e.g. nearest neighbors, reverse neighbors, and shared neighbors [103]) as a kernel function that is used to formulate the density function (i.e. multivariate Gaussian [66]) of the *normal* data; hence, the boundary of the *normal* can be described using parameters of the density function. Given one data point contains n features, the anomaly is detected by projecting the data point into n-dimension space of features. The data point that resides beyond the *normal* boundary is considered anomaly.

5.4.2.5 Boundary Method

Unlike the lazy learning method, this method considered an eager learner. Support Vector Machine (SVM) [104] is the most common method in this category. It transforms the training data into a decision boundary (so-called hyperplane). The idea of hyperplane is that the training data with *non-linear mapping* is transformed into an adequate higher dimension, where two classes can be linearly separated by the hyperplane. Also, the algorithm aims to maximize the width of the separation plane. Despite the training time being very long, this approach dominates other methods by having less prone to over-fitting on the training data. The SVM-based solution is quite common for SCADA-IDS, in practice, it is combined with other methods (such as *pruning* and *kernel-trick*) to archive a higher detection accuracy [81], lower false positive and negative alarm [60], minimize an offline learning phase [59], or to apply with environment where input features are limited [67].

Another example of the boundary method includes method in the research [68]. The proposed method is used to identify anomaly for proprietary communication (e.g. vehicle CAN bus protocol). Since the communication protocol is not disclosed by manufacturer, it is challenging to detect attacks on those critical system. The researchers [68] identify field boundaries based on the pre-defined knowledge of control variables and the actual control signals from various operations situations. After that, they are able to train a classifier, which is used to detect anomaly. Although the proposed method is specific to the particular control system, the same principle could be applied when communication specification is unknown.

5.4.2.6 Evolutionary Method

The evolution of living organism inspires the development of artificial intelligent methods. Various methods have been proposed for SCADA-IDS (e.g. [23, 69, 83, 105]). There are two well-known methods namely, Artificial Neural Network (ANN) and Genetic Algorithm (GA). ANN uses a brain-like structure (i.e. a network of neural cells) for classification. The neural network consists of three different layers of nodes, namely *input layer*, *hidden layer(s)*, and *output layer*. The input layer can contain several nodes depending on the input data (e.g. number of features of each tuple). Every input node has connections with every node in the hidden layer. The connections have different weight values; these weights are fitted during the training period in order to provide the most accurate output according to the supervised knowledge. There can be more than one hidden layer of the neural network. Even though ANN gives a high prediction accuracy in various applications (e.g. image/voice recognition, misuse behavior and anomaly detection), the explanation of how ANN works is still controversial [106]. Researchers do not fully understand how the ANN classifies the input data, and designing of the ANN topology (i.e. number of nodes and hidden layers) is still trial and error. The output layer could be only one node in case of a binary classification problem. That is, giving output between 0 and 1, which serves as a likelihood of being a particular class. For multi-class classification problem, the number of outputs could be k nodes, represent the prediction of k-classes. Each output node indicates likelihood of each class. Important limitations of ANN method are the requirement of a large training dataset and the trained model might be over-fitted to the training set; hence, it is not applicable in some contexts. For example, recording all possible attack data from the real SCADA system.

GA algorithm [107], on the other hand, simulates the process of selective survival in evolution theory. It assumes that the knowledge (e.g. anomaly detection rules) can be represented as a *chromosome* of the living things. These chromosome can be optimized according to *evaluation objectives*. In context of IDS, design of *evaluation function* is crucial to optimize the *fitness* of the outcome. GA is well known for minimizing the effect of erroneous training sets and sometimes overcomes the problem of multiple local optima. Other aspects of nature are also applied in anomaly detection. Negative Selection Algorithm (NSA) or Immune Network Algorithm (INA) [105] formulates the detector module for the classification between normal and abnormal data. The idea was initially derived from the organic process where immune cells detect harmful agents in our body.

5.4.2.7 Unary Classification

Unary or one-class classification (OCC) solves the binary or multi-class classification problem by primarily learning from a training set of one class only (i.e. *normal* system states); hence, the anomaly can be detected as the class of *others*. This approach advantages other solution when one class of the training data can be clearly observed, while information of other classes is severely hard to record.

The most common algorithm in this category is OCSVM (so-called Support Vector Data Description [SVDD]), e.g. [61, 63, 85–87, 108, 109]. Therefore, basic principle of SVDD is similar to the SVM method. discussed previously. Instead of separating between two classes using a linear hyperplane. In higher dimensional space of the data, SVDD formulates boundary function of a spherically shaped that minimally covers the complete population of the target class [110]. Let the sphere is described by the center a and radius $R \geq 0$, SVDD aims to minimize volume of the sphere by minimizing value of R^2 described in the *error function* as,

$$\text{minimize} \quad F(R, a) = R^2,$$
$$\text{subject to} \quad \|x_i - a\|^2 \leq R^2, \ \forall i, \tag{5.2}$$

where x_i denotes distance between the data point i and the center a. However, the perfect spherical shape could also include outliers from the training set (hence not optimized). According to [110], the separation plane is formulated by resolving the following optimization problem:

$$\text{minimize} \quad \frac{1}{2}\|\omega\|^2 + \frac{1}{vr}\sum_{i=1}^{r}\xi_i - \rho,$$
$$\text{subject to} \quad (\omega \cdot \Phi(x_i)) \geq \rho - \xi_i, \ \xi_i \geq 0, \ i = 1 \cdots r, \tag{5.3}$$

where $x_i \in X$ is a data point out of total r samples in the training set X, and $\Phi : X \to H$ denotes the mapping function from raw to the high dimensional space. The normal vector and compensation parameter of the hyperplane H is denoted by ω and ρ respectively; $v = (0 \cdots 1)$ is a trade-off parameter that controls proportion of support vectors in the training set. Lastly, ξ_i represents the slack variable that allows some training samples to be incorrectly classified. This optimization problem is solved using Lagrange multiplier, which can find detail in the further reading [110].

5.4.2.8 Density-Based Method

This method builds an estimate function from statistical data based on the training set. It can be used for both clustering and classification problems. Examples of algorithms in this group are expectation maximization (EM), logistic regression (LR), and linear discriminant analysis (LDA). EM is an iterative approach, and it works well on incomplete training data [111]. In the training period, it adjusts parameters of *likelihood function* based on the data point from the previous round. The aim is to optimize settings of the likelihood function. This process repeats on the next round until the stopping criteria are met (e.g. difference of output is zero or remain unchanged). Since EM method maximizes accuracy of classification function, the advanced IDS solution [62] incorporates EM method into one-class classifier to reduce the outlier from the training data set in the pre-processing phase to get the more accurate classification model.

LR [112], on the other hand, is mainly used for binary classification problem. It maps value of each feature, e.g. payload size $x = (1 \cdots 100)$ of the network traffic, with likelihood of the predicting class (say *malicious* and *benign*). Basically, the method tries to fit all data points in the sigmoid curve by shifting the line and re-calculate the likelihood till the maximum likelihood value is found. An important limitation of LR method is when classes have a *complete separation*. That is, some features can separate two classes; hence, the binary function cannot be used to classify the input.

The more advanced method like LDA [113] is suitable for classifying data with multiple classes and multiple features (so-called dimension). Data point x with n features can be plotted on a n-dimensional space to find a separation point, separation line, or separation plane, when $n = 1, 2, 3$ respectively. In reality, data might have more than three dimensions. Hence, it is complicated to calculate the separation plane directly. LDA resolves this problem by reducing complexity of data dimensions. In case of binary classification, it creates a new axis and projects all data points onto the new axis. Regardless of the feature dimension, data points of two classes can be separated on the new axis. The new axis is formulated from the training data by maximizing the combination of *means* of data points in each class and minimizing combination of *between and within scatters*. The density based method, however, performs well only if a larger number of training data points are available.

5.4.2.9 Ensemble-Based Method

The idea behind this method is to combine two or more methods to improve the accuracy of individual methods. The most popular methods are *Voting*, *Stacking*, *Bagging*, and *Boosting*. This method requires other methods to be used as base methods. These can be any of the aforementioned approaches, different algorithms or their variations.

To begin with, *Voting* is the simplest method to decide a final prediction result from multiple voters. Majority of the votes will be chosen as a final decision. Votes are gathered from a collection of classifiers. *Stacking* is the more advance voting.

Instead of taking the majority vote, it uses a meta-learner to justify the best result based on the supervised knowledge. In other words, outputs from a collection of first-level classifiers are fed to a second-level learning algorithm. The meta-learner is trained to optimize the final prediction [114].

Take the research in [115] as an example, decision tree based classifier and rule based classifier are stacked to efficiently detect anomaly from a large network traffic log. Firstly, the C4.5 decision tree is used to detect known network attack events from all communication traffic. The attack events are classified using C4.5 method, meanwhile, the normal traffic is further examined by CBA classifier, which is trained with normal data. Therefore, the well-known anomaly is quickly filtered out and the unknown log is examined at the second stage using the different classifier.

On the other hand, *Bagging* and *Boosting* focus on distribution of the training data. This is because the combination of independent bases can dramatically improve the efficiency of final prediction. *Bagging* (so-called Bootstrap Aggregating) obtains data subset for different baselines by using bootstrap sampling method [116]. The different base classifiers are aggregated using *voting* and *averaging* method to improve prediction accuracy. *Boosting* [117] improves accuracy by building the stronger classifier from an existing weak classifier. Suppose a distribution of data D consists of three parts X_1, X_2, and X_3, and we only have a weak classifier that correctly predicts only X_1 and X_2. Let the wrong classification X_3 denoted by h_1. In order to correct the mistake made by h_1, boosting method derive a new distribution D' from D. For example, focus more on instances in X_3. Then, train a classifier h_2 from D'. Suppose that the new classifier has correct classification in X_1 and X_3. We can now combine classifiers h_1 and h_2 to get a stronger classifier. The process is repeated by adjusting the distribution's parameters until no improvement can be made.

Despite the complexity of incorporating several methods, this method has been used by a large number of works (e.g. [55, 71, 72, 75, 76, 82, 118, 119]). The algorithms included not only classification-based but also clustering-based methods. The selected paper in each category is evaluated in Section 5.6 based on the proposed holistic-analytical evaluation method.

5.5 Systematic Literature Review

As SCADA systems are deployed for critical infrastructures and cyber-physical systems, a holistic view of their security design is important. This section explains the approach we used in systematically searching and selecting papers for our review based on the guideline proposed by Kitchenham [120]. It also introduces the criterion used for the evaluation of SCADA-based IDS supervised learning.

Research questions: This review aims to address the following research questions:

- How can we best categorize the existing corpus of literature for SCADA-based supervised learning based intrusion detection systems?
- What are the limitations of these current research approaches?
  In order to include holistic views of limitations in the second questions, the current literature is combined from the following aspects:
  (*) What architectural design approaches have been used in existing research?
  (*) What data sources have been used for anomaly detection?
  (*) How has aggregate attack data been used in existing research to improve system security?
  (*) How feasible are the methods for application to the area studied?
- How can we further improve supervised SCADA-IDS approaches?

5.6 Evaluation of Supervised Learning Methods

This section provides a detailed review of SCADA-based IDSs in each of the categories presented in Section 5.4.2. We describe the paper selection process, followed by the evaluation criteria of each selection. We collected information of proposed solutions with regard to quantity (i.e. the number of publications that used a similar approach) and quality (e.g. benefits, drawbacks, and constraints). This information is used to evaluate supervised learning approaches with respect to holistic perspectives from each criterion.

5.6.1 Paper Selection Process

In order to select the relevant and important papers from SCADA-based IDS research, we followed the literature review protocol illustrated in Figure 5.9. In step 1, we chose key databases in information technology publications to find papers, namely Association for Computing Machinery (ACM) Digital Library, IEEEXplore (IEE/IEEE), SCOPUS (Elsevier), and Web of Science. Then we defined keywords in three topics to locate potential papers in each database as follows:

- *SCADA*: SCADA, Smart grid, Critical Infrastructure, Industrial Control System, ICS.
- *Intrusion detection*: Intrusion Detection, IDS, Anomaly Detection.
- *Machine learning method*: Machine learning, ML, classification, classifier.

For each database in steps 2 and 3, we searched and selected the papers using the snowball sampling method [127], which starts with a small set of highly relevant papers, and then follows its references to build a larger pool of papers to review. The snowball sampling approach was chosen because some important

Figure 5.9 Paper selection process.

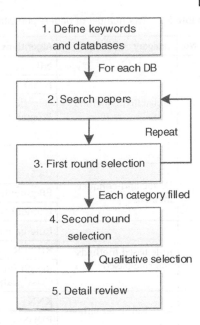

and relevant research might not be indexed by the databases or the search engines that were used. As illustrated earlier in Figure 5.2, the number of publications on SCADA-based IDS based on supervised learning solution has risen significantly since 2007 which reflects the renewed and increasing public interest in the protection of critical infrastructure. Hence, we limited the time range from 2007 to present. We formulated search strings suitable for each database based on the keywords above. Next, we ran the queries, assembled the located papers, and removed the duplicate papers. The paper abstract and keywords in the located papers were chosen to be related to the three main topics defined above. We then sorted the located papers by main supervised learning algorithms described in Section 5.4.2.

In step 4, the papers were examined more closely for categorization. Key inclusion criteria were relationship to SCADA security; use of IDS; use of supervised learning to train IDS; and quality threshold – clear methodology described; method was implemented and evaluated; and paper was published in journal or conference that we were able to access the full text. If there were several papers in a particular category, the journal publications were considered with a higher priority compared to conference proceedings. This was because the journals have less restriction on the number of pages and multiple revision cycles, hence they discussed the proposed approaches more comprehensively. The conference papers were also selected based on the relevancy and ranks of the conferences suggested by the Computing Research and Education Association of Australasia (CORE) [128]. The number of papers published in each category are summarized in Table 5.1.

Table 5.1 The number of papers published in each category.

No.	Category	Algorithms	# of paper	Total	References
1	Probabilistic method	NB	1	7	[90]
		HMM	3		[53, 57, 78]
		Genetic Programming	1		[77]
		CRF	1		[64]
		MLE	1		[74]
2	Divide-and-conquer methods	C4.5	2	4	[65, 80]
		FP-growth	1		[73]
		Random Forests	1		[80]
3	Rule-based methods and rule-based	Rule-based	1	3	[56]
		RIPPER	1		[58]
		Rough Sets Classification	1		[100]
4	Lazy learning methods	KNN	1	2	[101]
		RDOS	1		[66]
5	Boundary methods	SVM	4	5	[59, 60, 67, 81]
		Field Boundary	1		[68]
6	Evolution methods	IDS-NNM	1	4	[23]
		NSA	1		[105]
		ANN	1		[83]
		IWP-CSO with HNA-NN	1		[69]
7	Unary classification	Signature-based	2	13	[121, 122]
		Rules-based	3		[40, 61, 123]
		SVDD	1		[108]
		OCSVM	6		[61, 63, 85–87, 109]
		Single Windows Classification	1		[124]
8	Density-based method	ML	1	1	[62]
9	Ensemble-based method	Multiples methods	6	8	[55, 71, 72, 75, 76, 82, 118, 119]
10	Benchmarking paper	Multiples methods	5	5	[64, 70, 79, 125, 126]
				52	

5.6.2 Evaluation Criteria

SCADA-based IDSs differ in their design (i.e. auditing sources and monitoring attacks) and targeted application (i.e. topology and components), therefore, we cannot solely justify the compatibility of IDSs based on the statistical metrics (i.e. accuracy, specificity, sensitivity). For this reason, we have used a qualitative comparison instead.

In order to understand the challenges of SCADA-based IDS with supervised learning methods, we propose some evaluation criteria to measure the effectiveness and efficiency of the proposed algorithms with respect to the requirements of SCADA-based IDSs discussed in Section 5.2.4. Table 5.2 summarizes the key criterion of each measure and the reason behind its selection.

5.6.3 Categories of SCADA-Based IDS Systems

5.6.3.1 Rule-Based Method

As shown in Table 5.3, the rule-based method is one of the most common method among all categories from the selected set of publications in this survey. With respect to the detection approach (see Table 5.3 column *Approach*), more than half of the proposed solutions in the literature use signature-based approach. In most

Table 5.2 Evaluation criteria for SCADA-based IDSs.

Criterion	Reasons
Algorithm	Review the most and least popular classification methods for SCADA-based IDSs studied in the literature with associated benefits, drawbacks, and constraints
Approach	Compare the literature from accuracy and flexibility point of view. Although the signature-based method precisely detects attacks, the anomaly-based approach is more flexible in detecting future attacks such as the zero-day exploits
Architectural properties	The architecture design directly reflects how well it is tailored for SCADA systems. To be specific, we examine the system based on scalability, availability, distribution capability, and robustness of the systems
Auditing sources	Show how far IDS can cover the different types of attacks on the resource constrained environment. Some work detects the anomaly based on the communication behavior only, while others consider the physical state or multiple variables in combination
Application domain	Indicate holistic design of security system that ranges from anomaly detection, supported decision making to investigation support
Feasibility	Show the distance between simulation and reality. As SCADA is deployed on the critical infrastructure, the simulation and the actual environment are different. Therefore, testing on the real world situation or the SCADA-based simulator is crucial

Table 5.3 Comparison of methods for SCADA-based IDS groups by classification methods.

Category	Authors	Algorithms	Signature-based	Anomaly-based	Hybrid approach	Scalable	Real time detection	Decentralized/distributed	Resilient	Network traffic	SCADA specific protocol	Application behavior	Physical state	Unified cyber-physical	Detection	Prevention	Investigation	Simulation/testbed	SCADA-testbed	Prototype	Real-world deployment	Open source	Portable
Probabilistic	Tylman [90]	NB		✓			✓			✓	✓				✓			✓				✓	
	Zhou et al. [53]	HMM		✓			✓			✓					✓	✓		✓					
	Hosic et al. [77]	Genetic Programming		✓			✓			✓					✓			✓					
	Zohrevand et al. [57]	HMM		✓	✓			✓					✓	✓	✓	✓		✓					
	Stefanidis and Voyiatzis [78]	HMM					✓			✓					✓			✓			✓		
	Andrysiak et al. [74]	MLE		✓			✓			✓					✓								
Divide and conquer	Pan et al. [73]	FP-growth			✓	✓				✓			✓		✓			✓					
	Samdarshi et al. [80]	C4.5,RandomForests			✓					✓			✓		✓			✓					✓
	Moon et al. [65]	C4.5		✓						✓		✓			✓					✓			

Category	Reference	Method
	Coutinho et al. [100]	Rough Sets Classification
Rule-based	Premaratne et al. [54]	Rules enumeration
	Yang et al. [121]	IEC 60870-5-104 Signature
	Asif and Al-Harthi [122]	Signature-based
	Yang et al. [123]	If-then rules
	Erez and Wool [124]	Single Window Classification
	Yang et al.[40]	Rule-based
	Pan et al. [58]	RIPPER
	Jamei et al. [56]	Rule-based
Lazy learners	Silva and Schukat [101]	K-NN
	Tang and He [66]	RDOS
Boundary	Masduki et al. [81]	SVM
	Patrascu and Patriciu [59]	SVM
	Vijayanand et al. [67]	SVM
	Patel et al. [60]	SVM
	Markovitz and Wool [68]	Field Boundary
Evolutionary	Linda et al. [23]	IDS-NNM
	Lima et al. [105]	NSA
	Kosek [83]	ANN
	Shitharth and Prince Winston [69]	IWP-CSO with HNA-NN

(Continued)

Table 5.3 (Continued)

Category	Authors	Algorithms	Approach			Architecture				Auditing					Application			Feasibility					
			Signature-based	Anomaly-based	Hybrid approach	Scalable	Real time detection	Decentralized/distributed	Resilient	Network traffic	SCADA specific protocol	Application behavior	Physical state	Unified cyber-physical	Detection	Prevention	Investigation	Simulation/testbed	SCADA-testbed	Prototype	Real-world deployment	Open source	Portable
Unary based	Yasakethu et al. [61]	OCSVM		✓			✓			✓					✓	✓					✓		
	Nader et al. [85]	OCSVM		✓			✓						✓		✓				✓				
	Nader et al. [108]	SVDD		✓									✓		✓			✓					
	Maglaras and Jiang [86]	OCSVM		✓			✓								✓			✓					
	Nader et al. [109]	OCSVM		✓						✓	✓				✓			✓					
	da Silva et al. [87]	OCSVM		✓		✓	✓	✓		✓	✓				✓					✓			
	Wan et al. [63]	OCSVM		✓			✓			✓	✓	✓			✓			✓					
Density based	Yoo and Shon [62]	EM		✓			✓			✓	✓				✓			✓					

Category	Reference	Methods
Ensemble	Mustafa et al. [82]	HoeffdingTreeNB, LimAttHoeffdingTreeNBAdaptive, HoeffdingTreeNB, and HoeffdingTreeNBAdaptive
	Branisavljevic et al. [119]	PCA, ANN, OCSVM, others (six methods)
	Shahir et al. [118]	HMM, SVM
	Ponomarev and Atkison [71]	REPTree,NB,Simple Logistic, Ripple-Down Rule, Decision Stump, C4.5
	Maglaras et al. [75]	IT-OCSVM and SNA
	Cruz et al. [76]	OCSVM, SNA, and K-means clustering
	Kosek and Gehrke [72]	RM-AD
	Krishnan and Balasubramanian [55]	FCM clustering and RBA
Benchmarking	Özgür abd Erdem [125]	SVM, NB, DT
	Hurst et al. [70]	LDC, UDC, QDC, PARZENC, and TREEC
	Swetha and Meena [79]	DT, K-NN, SVM
	Junejo and Goh [126]	Multiple
	Onoda [64]	HMM,CRF, OCSVM, SVDD, Rule-based

cases, experts are required to establish a set of detection rules, especially, to learn about the known normal/abnormal states associated with SCADA-based hardware, e.g. IED [54, 121], Generic Object Oriented Substation Events (GOOSE), Sampled Measured Value (SMV) protocols [40], and behavior of automated process [124].

In general, the predefined rules are functions of normal states rather than fixed constants. Take the research in [54] as an example, they define misuse detection rules using multiple alert functions, namely correlation between switching devices, alarms from relay protection function, time-related constraints of critical control commands, and payload length detector. We observed fewer papers in this group (e.g. Rough Sets Classification [56] and RIPPER [58] methods) that used automated rules set discovery method compared to the signature-based approach. Apart from that, special "honey" tokens can also be applied to detect tampers with the communication traffic [122].

Since Rule-based method is the easiest method to understand and customize manually by a human, this method is suitable for specific environments like building automation control network (i.e. fire alarm system) [58], SCADA RTUs [100], and micro-phasor measurement units (μPMUs) [56]. These systems require specialists or engineers to define associated rules that describe normal states of the system; therefore, rule-based method is more efficient compared to methods in the other categories. Additionally, the automated detection approaches can also be integrated into the rule-based solution to improve flexibility in detecting unknown malicious incidents.

5.6.3.2 Ensemble-Based Method

This method also commonly appears in the literature. As ensemble approaches build the classification model by selecting the best result from multiple classifiers. Despite the complexity of this method, a number of works [55, 72, 75, 76, 82, 118, 119] have successfully used it to obtain better detection rate accuracy. Apart from accuracy, ensemble method also has the advantage of prediction models that are robust and resistant to false from the malicious cyber event [129]. Also, the research [72] overcomes insufficient training data issue by combining result from OCSVM and k-means clustering method to increase the detection speed and achieve real time performance. In [71], the network telemetry (e.g. packet size and time of arrival) is used instead of the actual network data. Various telemetry features are taken into account. The boosting method creates a strong classifier out of several weak ones. On the other hand, multi-class classifiers (e.g. HMM and SVM) favor big and small class differently. Hence, the bagging method can be used to find the most effective classifier for the particular class, which is chosen to give a label to the detecting event [118].

5.6.3.3 Unary Classifier

In some cases [63, 86, 87, 109], unary classifiers, such as the OCSVM, have outperformed other classification methods in terms of accuracy. Unary classifiers work well when there is only one class of data available. Since there is a lack of datasets containing real SCADA attacks, the OCSVM classifier can be used to train only using the normal data [130]. Hence, OCSVM is more popular than the original SVM, which requires both normal and abnormal training set [87]. However, a constraint of unary classifier is that the training dataset must not contain attack instances. It is possible in a real-life scenario that, there could be some 0-day attacks that remain undetected [131].

5.6.3.4 Probabilistic Method

Probabilistic classifiers are useful to provide an estimate a probability distribution over a set of classes, rather than a single class that the observation should belong to. HMM is the most popular option in this group. Although HMM is computationally efficient and flexible to retrain the model when the updated data is available, it cannot capture higher order correlation of the data. This is because of a strict states dependency assumption of HMM. For instance, the same sequence of features could indicate different states depending on different contexts or intentions. This issue is known by researchers [53, 57, 64]. A method like N-gram is used to preserve contextual meaning by grouping N sequence of observations together. Apart from that, multiple independent factors (e.g. *Task and resource models*, *Control data flow models*, and *Critical state of critical processes*) are correlated to increase prediction accuracy and decrease the false alerts.

5.6.3.5 Other Methods

The remaining methods proposed in the literature are across various categories of algorithms, such as divide-and-conquer (i.e. [65, 73, 80]) and boundary methods (e.g. SVM [59, 60, 67, 81] and Field Boundary [68]). However, lazy learning (i.e. [66, 101]) and density-based (i.e. EM [62]) are occasionally used for supervised SCADA IDS. Some constraints have been learned from applying these solutions. For example, the lazy learning method does not scale enough for the large network [101] and the density method still lacks accuracy to be used in the real field [62].

5.6.4 Approaches Used to Detect Anomalies

Based on the *approach* column in Table 5.3, published works are categorized into three types: *signature-based*, *anomaly-based*, and *hybrid*. A **signature-based solution** is specifically designed for a particular system or protocol, as discussed in Section 5.6.3. Due to the constraint of using the rules, only known attacks, such as MITM attack and ARP cache poisoning, are analyzed to evaluate the detection efficiency [123]. Even though these tasks require the knowledge in system protocols, operations, and specific characteristic of attacks, it usually offers a low false alarm rate compared to machine learning solution, hence more practical for industry. Besides, the signature based method requires footprint of attacks to be updated regularly and cannot guarantee the new intrusion threats such as zero-day exploits [48]. Therefore, we observed most of the proposed works are anomaly-based detection.

It is hard to keep the detection rules up-to-date as the new vulnerability is emerging regularly. The **anomaly-based approach** focuses on building a model of normal/abnormal behaviors instead of defining rules. In constructing the model, various machine learning algorithms were used (see column *Algorithms* in Table 5.3). However, the decision of what algorithm should be used not only depends on characteristic of auditing sources (e.g. network traffic, application usage behavior or physical state of the actuator; see column *Auditing*) but also vary by the character of data and constraints of applications. With network traffic dataset from Defense Advanced Research Projects Agency (DARPA) [130], different algorithms are applied. For instance, [64] used HMM algorithm to focus on characteristic of sequential behaviors, whereas SVM is used in [60, 81] with selected features of network communication data (considered as data-point) to build the optimal separation plane between the center of two classes, which is used to distinguish between benign and anomaly incidents. Meanwhile, the author in [55] aims to develop an adaptive IDS, which can keep update attack information over time. The proposed work fuses Anomaly Detection Agent (ADA) and Rule-Based Agent (RBA) to detect misuse from the network traffic data. Based on the same dataset, an ensemble method is considered [82] to eliminate noises from training or testing dataset. With more than one classifier, the boosting method selects the best prediction results from classifiers, hence accuracy is improved.

The **hybrid method** combines both system specific signature and behavior based detection model. For example, a defense-in-depth strategy in [78]. The IDS system consists of "Header subsystem" and "Data subsystem," where the signature of abnormal Modbus protocol header is defined in the first module, and the HMM is used to detect (in depth) attacks from traffic data in the second module. Combination of signature and behaviors model helps to speed up the detection and highlight the specific type of attacks. Similarly, Distributed Intrusion Detection System (DIDS) system in [76] handles known exploitations with signature definition while using anomaly-based approach to prevent the emerging threats. Despite tight coupling to the system and complexity of combining two detection systems, the number of hybrid-method is quite small compared to other approaches.

5.6.5 Architectural Design Properties

The decision between centralized and decentralized architecture is always controversial. On one hand, the centralized IDS is easy to monitor and make a decision from the central location without limitations of resources; hence, the more complicated detection or classification tasks can be done. On the other hand, the decentralized or distributed IDS architecture is more scalable and resilient compared to the centralized scheme [10]. According to the requirement of SCADA-IDS in Section 5.2.4, here, the architectural perspective is discussed based on four key aspects: (i) scalability of the algorithm, (ii) real-time performance, (iii) decentralization, and (iv) resilience as follows:

Scalability of algorithm: We observed not many papers that explicitly state scalability property of their work. For instance, the work in [87] proposes the OCSVM based algorithm, where the sub-model learns heterogeneous normal training sets to detect outliers of the large and diverse system. Apart from that, the cost of maintenance is important for scalability design. Authors in [73] developed a scalable stateful IDS to prevent temporal attacks. Besides, enlarging the existing complex system is costly and difficult tasks. The scalable system helps to save lots of money and time for maintenance tasks. Hence, the hybrid approach was used. Firstly, the signature is used to reduce irrelevant events. Secondly, the anomaly detection model examines more closely on the suspect events. The proposed common paths algorithms mines data from both physical (synchrophasor) and logical (system logs) to formulate signatures of attacks (common paths). This fusion method identifies attacks from abnormal states which shared in the common paths.

Real-time performance: This is a crucial property. Based on Table 5.3: column *Architecture*, it is clear that most of the literature focuses on real-time detection characteristics to avoid reduction of a system's availability. For instance, the critical infrastructure like railway traffic control. This system needs to be monitored at real-time. In [74], the traffic control data gathered from Wireless Sensor Network (WSN) is modeled using Autoregressive Fractional Integrated Moving Average (ARFIMA) method, which analyzes the deviation between parameters of the network traffic and creates a statistical model for the system. The Maximum Likelihood Estimation (MLE) algorithm is used to detect the anomaly in this control system.

Parallel processing is needed to archive real-time performance. Network Intrusion Detection System (NIDS) in [63] has been tested on the simulated Modbus/TCP system. Two OCSVM based algorithms were proposed to analyze both control and process data simultaneously. The detection process consumed less than 27 seconds to detect attacks with small, medium, and large number of abnormal function control behavior. On the other hand, as parts of the CockpitCI project, the Domain-specific IDS for SCADA ICS (Industrial Control System) [76] focuses on decreasing the false positives of OCSVM by proposing IT-OCSVM algorithm. By running several OCSVMs in parallel, the final outcome is chosen using the mean value method and social network analysis (SNA). They monitored three layers, data-link, network, and transport protocols, to detect attacks, e.g. MITM and DoS.

Decentralization: The design of distributed IDS is arbitrary and specialized for particular system. For instance, the IDS for Advanced Metering Infrastructure (AMI) in [82] distributes IDS modules into three components: Meter-IDS, Data Concentrator-IDS, and Headend-IDS, from small to a large stream of information respectively. The IDS filters attacks from the smallest unit (Meter-IDS) to the largest (Headend-IDS) serially. However, the proposed system requires the whole network to be isolated and free from noise (i.e. communication between other devices in the network) to achieve the best detection accuracy, hence, it is suitable for Software Defined Network (SDN) SCADA. On the other hand, the Distributed IDS has been used in [76]. With several IDS distributed through the wide network, they are not only able to identify attacks from different parts of the system but also increase system robustness in case of failure that causes sub-networks to be disconnected from the central server. The DIDS breaks the whole network traffic data down to subsets of the disjoint dataset. By using the IT-OCSVM method and weighting method (i.e. voting between results from the classifiers to get the best prediction outcome), the proposed DIDS is able to increase detection accuracy while minimizing the rate of false alarms.

From a different angle, the work [87] points out that the distributed NIDS processes the detection in parallel and is suitable for a large scale SDN SCADA. The proposed NIDS consists of five components SDN controller, historian server, feature selector, one-class classifier, and NIDS management interface. Each component is responsible for different tasks. For example, the SDN controller monitors anomalous flows in network switches, while the historian server stores snapshots of networks to be able to apply the parallel MapReduce operation. The proposed OCC works well with a large dataset, it uses only one set of normal network data to detect the DoS attack on Modbus protocol.

Resilience: A formal definition of resilience is the ability of a system to recover from faults and return to its original state or other working states. Interestingly enough, only a limited number of works discussed resiliency of IDS systems. In [59] the time-out has been used to discard unresponsive classifier workers. The proposed work integrates Game theory and data streaming classifiers (which work in parallel) to heuristically detect various type of attacks. The IDS feeds abnormal events into the game model to determine win conditions between attacker and defender, hence, the IDS can detect the unknown threats by learning for the existing data. The result shows detection accuracy is better than using KNN and decision trees methods. Another example has not explicitly specified the resilient characteristic in the paper. We assume that the distributed IDS with parallel detection components like [82] resists to failures. Since a number of IDS components are duplicated and work independently, some faulty nodes would not affect the whole system.

5.6.6 Data Sources Used for Anomaly Detection

Several sources of information can be inspected to identify misuse or abnormal events in a SCADA system. Literature in this review is categorized into four groups for auditing data: (i) Network traffic, (ii) Physical state, (iii) Application usage behavior, and (iv) Unification of cyber-physical state. Since most works chose to monitor network traffic, we separate out *SCADA specific protocol* to check if the IDS uses generic communication features or SCADA specific protocols' features. This is shown in column *Auditing* in Table 5.3.

Most network-based IDS solutions were tested with **SCADA-based datasets** or a **combination of generic and SCADA-based** datasets. In [55], both types of communication data are used to train various functionalities detection agents (namely Sniffer Agent, Filter Agent, Rule Mining Agent, Anomaly Detection Agent, and Rule-Based Agent). The proposed multiagents IDS shows a better detection performance on the SCADA-based dataset [132] compared to the generic KDD CUP 99 dataset [129]. Meanwhile, instead of extracting features from contents of packets (e.g. TCP/IP or Modbus), the researchers [71] make use of *telemetry* characteristic. By capturing flows of the transmitting packets between clients and servers, they are able to differentiate between PLC machine of attacker and engineer. This approach makes senses when considering contexts of ICS network since nodes are resource-constrained and connected wirelessly. They claimed the accuracy of telemetry method is closed to other IDS approach yet harder to evade using encryption methods [71].

On the other hand, since the SCADA protocol is based on existing Internet standards, some approaches (e.g. [59, 64] and [81]) used **generic traffic data** to evaluate the proposed IDS solutions. In [59], the pre-recorded *pcap* dataset, which contains various network attacks, has been used to verify the game-based multi-agents IDS solution. This dataset has also been used in the Capture The Flag contest at DEFCON event. The work [81] focuses on the particular Remote to Local (R2L) attack. The generic KDD 99 Dataset [129] has been used to evaluate the detection accuracy. The probabilistic-based IDS in [64] randomly chose 10,000 normal packets from DARPA dataset [130] to train the proposed model, and they selected another 10,000 random normal and unauthorized connection data for testing.

Physical control states data can be complicated to model and to detect misuse incidents. Some researchers [85] gathered datasets from a Gas Pipeline testbed [132] to develop and test their solution. Various fault injection exploits on the control/sensing signals (e.g. negative pressure value injection, fast change response injection, bust response injection, wave pressure injection, and single packet injection) have been studied. The proposed model was trained by using normal control states, and by properly tuned free parameters for the kernel function (bandwidth of the kernel and the number of eigenvectors), they were able to detect both slow and burst response injection attacks. The IDS solution for water treatment system [126] was evaluated by injecting 10 types of attack into their proposed Secure Water Treatment (SWaT) testbed. The attack disturbed PLC with fault sensor and actuator signals (e.g. data of inflow/outflow rate or level of water in tanks). In their work, various classic classifiers have been compared in detecting the false signals (e.g. SVM, RF, NB, BRTree, BayesNet, and IBK).

Software behavior-based IDSs have a less significant number of published works compared to the network-based approach. The work [65] monitors both software and network-based behavior. They defined software behavior using sets of API calls. For instance, *file copying* action is described using API Copy-File, CopyFileA, and MoveFileA, whereas *file deletion* is defined by calling DeleteFileA and RemoveDirectoryA functions. On the other hand, network behaviors (e.g. excessive network access, changes of packet delivery on ARP/MAC/IP protocols) also been fused with software activities to formulate decision tree for normal and malicious behaviors. In [63], the behavior of control functions has been model to detect misuse incident. Although the researcher extracted control commands from SCADA control packets, the detection model only focuses on behavior of software usage (commands issued) instead of network protocol properties. In this case, the models of normal behavior are learned by using numbers of commands issued per minute. In the experiment, they injected 280 malicious and 720 normal commands to the simulated Modbus/TCP system. The OCSVM and RE-KPCA (Reconstruction Error based on Kernel Principal Component Analysis) classifiers are trained and used to classify anomaly in a series of control commands.

The **cyber-physical** IDS [83] correlates digital data and physical signal to disclose anomaly. Take Distributed Energy Resources (DER) IDS as an example, the proposed IDS detects anomaly based on context. Variables from photovoltaic (PV) and meteorological data (e.g. solar, wind, and temperature properties) are aggregated with contextual variable (i.e. timestamp of each measurement). The ANN classifier is used to detect cyber or physical attacks. The research [83] is extended by incorporating with variables of distance between adjacent nodes in [72]. Furthermore, the holistically monitoring solution in [40] combined knowledge from three sources: (i) physical states, e.g. critical switching signal correlation and key analog signal comparison, (ii) protocol specifications, e.g. parameters from GOOSE and SMV protocols, and (iii) behaviors, such as, Substation Configuration Description (SCD) files and IEC 61850 packet contents. The research [40] aims to detect exploits from malware, namely Havex and Stuxnet.

Table 5.4 summarizes available datasets referred to by literature in this survey. Various data types are included, namely network traffic, location, physical states, sensors/actuator logs, and states of control devices.

Table 5.4 Description of dataset.

Dataset	Data type	Description	References
DARPA	Raw TCP/ IP dump files	The dataset published by Defense Advanced Research Projects Agency (DARPA) initiative for evaluation of network-based intrusion detection system	[130]
KDDCup99	The feature extracted from DARPA raw network data dump	The dataset based on network communication data has been widely used to test the network intrusion detection system. It originally used for the Data Mining Tools competition	[129]
NSL-KDD	The improve version of KDDCup99	The improved version of KDDCup99 which removes a number of duplicated records	[133]
A control system testbed to validate critical infrastructure protection concepts	TCP/IP data communication in various control system	Data is measured from a laboratory-scale gas pipeline, a laboratory-scale water tower, and a laboratory-scale electric transmission system. It is a pre-processed network transaction from 100,000 to 5,000,000 records	[132]
AIS dataset	Marine vessel movement characteristics	The kinematic and non-kinematic vessel characteristics dataset is a location-based marine movements information collected by U.S. Coast Guard Services. The example of features is latitude, longitude, ground speed, course over ground, rate of turn and vessel type	[134]
Behavior-based attack detection and classification in cyber physical systems using machine learning	Physical state of sensors and actuators	The states are collected from the physical state of sensors and actuators every second for 28,800 records in total. The state can be used to analyze the effects of cyber-attacks on the physical states	[126]
Water supply system dataset	Water supply control system status	It contains log files of multiple features such as inflow, outflow, water level, temperature, and running status of water stations. The data was collected from 2011 to 2014 at city of Surrey in BC, Canada	[57]
BOCISS dataset	Physical state of control system	Physical state of critical control system is simulated from the Siemens Tecnomatix Plant Simulator	[70]

Table 5.5 Description of testbed.

Name	SCADA-based?	Approach	Description	References
Fire Alarm System testbed	Y	Physical	Building Automation and Control (BAC) networks or BACnet testbed simulate the operation of fire alarm system using BACnet protocol monitoring module	[58]
SCADA testbed	Y	Physical	It simulates a small SCADA system which composed of Human–Machine Interface (HMI) Station, managed switch and two PLCs. This can be used to simulate the network attack such as TCP port scanning, ARP cache spoofing and denial of service attack	[75]
CSIT SCADA IDS	Y	Simulated	The testbed consists of SCADA nodes (e.g. HMI, historian, IED), protocols (i.e. IEC 60870-5-103) and malicious host to simulate attacks incident, such as MITM attacks. However, details of the software used in the simulate is undisclosed for security purposes	[123]
Gas pipeline testbed	Y	Physical	This testbed simulates typical SCADA control units, namely Master Terminal Unit (MTU), Remote Terminal Units (RTU) and Human–Machine Interface (HMI)	[85]
Secure Water Treatment (SWaT)	Y	Simulated	This testbed scales down water treatment system. It is designed to develop a security solution for cyber physical system (CPS), such as water treatment, electric power generation and distribution. It is composed of networking layers, PLCs, HMIs, SCADA workstation and Historian unit	[126]
SCADAsim	Y	Simulated	Based on OMNET++, it emulates the network communication of simulated and real devices to analyze the impact of attacks on the devices on SCADA network	[131]
Cyber-physical testbed	Y	Simulated	This is based on Cyber-physical build for IEC 61850 based smart substations. The testbed consists of six layers from simulation to substation layer. It supports a number of network-based attacks, such as malformed packet, MITM, address resolution protocol (ARP) spoofing	[135]
Accord Framework	N	Simulated	Accord provides a well-tested and documented library for constructing various types of algorithms	[139]
CONPOT ICS/ SCADA Honeypot	Y	Simulated	It can be used to simulate the network of programmable logic controllers (PLC) units to analyze network telemetry of honeypots and the packages generated by intruders	[140]

5.6.7 The Feasibility of the Proposed Work

Table 5.3 column *Application* compares coverage of IDS design from perspective of security suited, i.e. Security Information and Event Management (SIEM) tools [136, 137]. Despite system's availability being crucial, only a few researchers included information about their decision support strategies to help system administrator preventing the system from being attacked [138]. Most of the work offers only feature detection in their design.

On the other hand, from aspect of practicality, researchers used various methods to verify feasibility to deploy the system in the reality range from simulation to physical testbed. Indeed, the simulated software could lack fidelity, especially the physical signal, which is hard to simulate the actual signal from different hardware devices [14]. However, the physical testbed does not scale enough to verify the system, as the physical testbed scale down the real control system. According to Table 5.3 column *feasibility*, only 4 out of 50 approaches have deployed in the field [61, 68, 74, 118]. Twelve papers are tested on SCADA-based testbed or implemented as a testing prototype, whereas the rest are evaluated using various machine learning framework (e.g. MATLAB [69], WEKA [80], ACCORD [78]) or a generic network simulator (e.g. hardware in the loop testbed [73]).

Table 5.5 lists available testbeds that were used by the literature surveyed in this review including both physical and simulated testbed. As referred to by the papers in this survey, the evaluation testbed includes both SCADA-based and general purpose systems.

5.7 Key Open Problems

This section presents key research gaps and future research directions of SCADA-based IDSs that use supervised machine learning approaches.

5.7.1 Testbeds and Test Datasets Need Further Research and Development

Since it is not practical to train and evaluate a supervised IDS system on a real SCADA system, testbeds, and test datasets are crucial for developing a security solution. However, SCADA is widely applied on various control systems, and each of them has the different constraints (e.g. power/water/gas distribution system, manufacturing processes, or railway control system). This makes the construction of high fidelity testbeds costly. Furthermore, some of them are unable to reuse in different contexts of applications. We found that some testbed solutions/datasets in Tables 5.4 and 5.5 either are for general IT system (e.g. [129, 130, 133, 139]) or too specific (such as [126, 134]). Thus, the fidelity can be low compared to the real-world system or not reliable to be used with different settings and scale. With respect to the development cost, the direction of research should focus on developing a high fidelity simulation testbed and not the more expensive hardware-based solution.

5.7.2 Resilience and Validation of the Security Design Have Not Yet Been Sufficiently Explored

Since SCADA is designed for critical control systems, system availability is crucial. Although several articles focused on real-time performance in detecting threats and scalability of the system, *resilience* – which allows the recovery of the security system after the faults (e.g. attacks or natural disaster) to its original or useful state – is often ignored. Besides, most of the research detects anomalies solely based on network traffic from a single source only. Thus, a single point of failure could easily stop the whole security system. For distributed solutions – SCADA DIDS, e.g. [55, 57, 59, 72, 74–76, 79, 82, 87, 123], the validation of security and system resilience is a complex task. The formal method, which is used to design the critical system, could also be used to verify the security system (e.g. using the recovery model [141]) and further develop an optimization solution from security and resilience perspectives.

5.7.3 Prevention and Investigation Are Not Yet Well Studied

Although the proposed IDS solutions serve as parts of an overall security system, an active SCADA system should rely on a more holistic solution. Some of the research work [23, 40, 53–62] covers both detection and prevention by including automatic critical incident response. However, there is only one work [60] that includes forensic solution in the selected literature, which helps to record and reconstruct the attack event to identify system vulnerability. It is still an open question, how to incorporate these three areas of security measures to deliver the resilience and robustness to the SCADA system.

5.7.4 Distributed IDS Collaboration for SCADA Systems Is Still in an Early Age of Development

DIDS collaborates multiple IDSs to enable scalability to the large network as well as mitigating with the massive parallel attacks. The research [143, 144] shows that aggregation and correlation between various data sources have potential to detect distributions of malware or exploit. However, the more challenging problem of collaborative IDS is how can the distributed network of IDSs share their knowledge and efficiently improve the detection efficiency. The result from the new research [142] illustrates a potential of improving DIDS efficiency by introducing a distributed learning model. That is, multiple learners (or IDSs) share information about malicious events to improve their own detection models. However, this is still in an early stage of the distributed learners and need further study.

5.8 Summary

This chapter looked at emerging research into the application of supervised-learning-based approaches to implementing anomaly detection systems (i.e. DLP and IDS). We have reviewed over a 100 of the peer-review literature. Our study illustrates the development of such systems from industry perspectives and provided a comprehensive study of Supervised-ML approaches for SCADA-based IDS systems using specific criteria and properties. We have proposed a framework to categorize various Supervised-ML methodologies as well as qualitative and quantitative comparisons between various state-of-the-art research to identify the directions of research that target different data auditing sources and attacking methods. We have discussed additional issues and challenges for industrial-based IDS systems using supervised-learning methods and illustrated the trends to develop such systems. To identify the future directions in developing new algorithms and to guide the selection of algorithms for industrial-based IDS systems.

References

1 Jakapan Suaboot, Adil Alharthi, Zahir Tari, John Grundy, Abdulmohsen Almalawi, and Khalil Drira. A taxonomy of supervised learning for IDSs in SCADA environments. *ACM Computing Surveys*, 53(2):1–40, 2020. http://dx.doi.org/10.1145/3379499.

2 Stuart A. Boyer. *SCADA: Supervisory Control And Data Acquisition*. International Society of Automation, USA, 4th edition, 2009.

3 Vinay M. Igure, Sean A. Laughter, and Ronald D. Williams. Security issues in scada networks. *Elsevier Journal of Computers & Security*, 25(7):498–506, 2006.

4 Andrew Nicholson, Helge Janicke, and Tim Watson. An initial investigation into attribution in SCADA systems. In *Proceedings of the 1st ACM International Symposium on ICS & SCADA Cyber Security Research*, pages 56–65, 2013.

5 Hossein Zeynal, Mostafa Eidiani, and Dariush Yazdanpanah. Intelligent substation automation systems for robust operation of smart grids. In *Proceedings of the IEEE Innovative Smart Grid Technologies-Asia (ISGT ASIA)*, pages 786–790, Kuala Lumpur, Malaysia, 2014.

6 Paul Oman, Edmund Schweitzer, and Deborah Frincke. Concerns about intrusions into remotely accessible substation controllers and SCADA systems. In *Proceedings of the 27th Annual Western Protective Relay Conference*, volume 160, pages 1–16, 2000.

7 Kaspersky Lab ICS CERT. Threat landscape for industrial automation systems in H2 2017, 2018.

8 Abdul Mohsen Afaf Almalawi. *Designing unsupervised intrusion detection for SCADA systems*. PhD thesis, RMIT University, School of Computer Science, November 2014.

9 Abdul Mohsen Afaf Almalawi, Xinghuo Yu, Zahir Tari, Adil Alharthi Fahad, and Ibrahim Khalil. An unsupervised anomaly-based detection approach for integrity attacks on SCADA systems. *Elsevier Journal on Computers & Security*, 46:94–110, 2014.

10 Terry Escamilla. *Intrusion Detection: Network Security Beyond the Firewall*, volume 8. John Wiley & Sons, 1998.

11 Arnab Sinha, Zhihong Shen, Yang Song, Hao Ma, Darrin Eide, Bo-june Paul Hsu, and Kuansan Wang. An overview of microsoft academic service (MAS) and applications. In *Proceedings of the 24th ACM International Conference on World Wide Web (WWW)*, pages 243–246, 2015.

12 Bonnie Zhu and Shankar S. Sastry. SCADA-specific intrusion detection/ prevention systems: a survey and taxonomy. In *Proceedings of the 1st Workshop on Secure Control Systems (SCS)*, volume 11. Berkeley University of California, 2010.

13 Robert Mitchell and Ing-Ray Chen. A survey of intrusion detection techniques for cyber-physical systems. *ACM Computing Surveys*, 46(4):55, 2014.

14 Hannes Holm, Martin Karresand, Arne Vidström, and Erik Westring. A survey of industrial control system testbeds. In *Proceedings of the 20th Nordic Conference on Secure IT Systems (NordSec 2015)*, pages 11–26. Springer International Publishing, October 2015.

15 Jingcheng Gao, Jing Liu, Bharat Rajan, Rahul Nori, Bo Fu, Yang Xiao, Wei Liang, and C. L. Philip Chen. SCADA communication and security issues. *Wiley Journal of Security and Communication Networks*, 7(1):175–194, 2014.

16 Modbus IDA. Modbus messaging on TCP/IP implementation guide v1. 0a. http://www.modbus.org/docs/Modbus_Messaging_Implementation_Guide_V1_0a.pdf, 2004.

17 Munir Majdalawieh, Francesco Parisi-Presicce, and Duminda Wijesekera. DNPSec: Distributed network protocol version 3 (DNP3) security framework. In *Advances in Computer, Information, and Systems Sciences, and Engineering*, pages 227–234, Dordrecht, 2007. Springer Netherlands.

18 Eric Knapp and Joel Langill. *Industrial Network Security: Securing Critical Infrastructure Networks for Smart Grid, SCADA, and Other Industrial Control Systems*. Elsevier, MA, USA, 2011.

19 Dorothy E. Denning. An intrusion-detection model. *IEEE Transactions on Software Engineering*, SE-13(2):222–232, 1987.

20 Alfonso Valdes and Steven Cheung. Communication pattern anomaly detection in process control systems. In *Proceedings of the IEEE Conference on Technologies for Homeland Security (HST)*, pages 22–29, 2009.

21 Philip Gross, Janak Parekh, and Gail Kaiser. Secure selecticast for collaborative intrusion detection systems. In *Proceedings of the 3rd International Workshop on Distributed Event-Based Systems (DEBS)*, pages 50–55, Edinburgh, UK, 2004. Institution of Engineering and Technology.

22 Peng Ning, Yun Cui, and Douglas S. Reeves. Constructing attack scenarios through correlation of intrusion alerts. In *Proceedings of the 9th ACM Conference on Computer and Communications Security (CCS)*, pages 245–254, New York, USA, 2002.

23 Ondrej Linda, Todd Vollmer, and Milos Manic. Proceedings of the IEEE conference on neural network based intrusion detection system for critical infrastructures. In *International Joint Conference on Neural Networks (IJCNN)*, pages 1827–1834, Atlanta, GA, USA, June 2009.

24 Igor Nai Fovino, Andrea Carcano, Thibault De Lacheze Murel, Alberto Trombetta, and Marcelo Masera. Modbus/DNP3 state-based intrusion detection system. In *Proceedings of the 24th IEEE International Conference on Advanced Information Networking and Applications (AINA)*, pages 729–736, Perth, WA, Australia, April 2010.

25 Andrea Carcano, Alessio Coletta, Michele Guglielmi, Marcelo Masera, Igor Nai Fovino, and Alberto Trombetta. A multidimensional critical state analysis for detecting intrusions in SCADA systems. *IEEE Transactions Industrial Informatics (TII)*, 7(2):179–186, 2011.

26 Igor Nai Fovino, Alessio Coletta, Andrea Carcano, and Marcelo Masera. Critical state-based filtering system for securing SCADA network protocols. *IEEE Transactions on Industrial Electronics*, 59(10):3943–3950, 2012.

27 Yang Wenxian and Jiang Jiesheng. Wind turbine condition monitoring and reliability analysis by SCADA information. In *Proceedings of the 2nd IEEE International Conference Mechanic Automation and Control Engineering (MACE)*, pages 1872–1875, Hohhot, China, July 2011.

28 Julian L. Rrushi. *Composite Intrusion Detection in Process Control Networks*. PhD thesis, Università degli Studi di Milano, Milano, Italy, January 2009.

29 A. Zaher, S. D. J. McArthur, D. G. Infield, and Y. Patel. Online wind turbine fault detection through automated SCADA data analysis. *Wind Energy*, 12(6):574–593, 2009.

30 Dong Wei, Yan Lu, Mohsen Jafari, Paul M. Skare, and Kenneth Rohde. Protecting smart grid automation systems against cyberattacks. *IEEE Transactions on Smart Grid*, 2(4):782–795, 2011.

31 Adnan Anwar, Abdun Naser Mahmood, and Mohiuddin Ahmed. False data injection attack targeting the LTC transformers to disrupt smart grid operation. In *Springer International Conference on Security and Privacy in Communication Systems*, pages 252–266, Cham, 2014.

32 Adnan Anwar, Abdun N. Mahmood, and Zahir Tari. Ensuring data integrity of OPF module and energy database by detecting changes in power flow patterns in smart grids. *IEEE Transactions on Industrial Informatics (TII)*, 13(6):3299–3311, 2017.

33 Jared Verba and Michael Milvich. Idaho national laboratory supervisory control and data acquisition intrusion detection system (SCADA IDS). In *Proceedings of the IEEE Conference on Technologies for Homeland Security*, pages 469–473, 2008.

34 Igor Nai Fovino, Alessio Coletta, Andrea Carcano, and Marcelo Masera. "Critical state-based filtering system for securing SCADA network protocols," IEEE Transactions on Industrial Electronics, 59(10):3943–3950, October 2012. doi:https://doi.org/10.1109/TIE.2011.2181132.

35 Digitalbond.com. IDS-signatures/Modbus-tcp. http://www.digitalbond.com/index.php/research/ids-signatures/modbus-tcp-ids-signatures/, July 2013.

36 Zhongqiang Chen, Yuan Zhang, Zhongrong Chen, and Alex Delis. A digest and pattern matching-based intrusion detection engine. *The Computer Journal*, 52(6):699–723, 2009.

37 Sathish Alampalayam P. Kumar, Anup Kumar, and S. Srinivasan. Statistical based intrusion detection framework using six sigma technique. *International Journal of Computer Science and Network Security*, 7(10):333–342, 2007.

38 Dayu Yang, Alexander Usynin, and J. Wesley Hines. Anomaly-based intrusion detection for SCADA systems. In *Proceedings of the 5th International Topical Meeting on Nuclear Plant Instrumentation, Control and Human Machine Interface Technologies (NPIC&HMIT)*, pages 12–16, Albuquerque, NM, USA, 2006.

39 Mohiuddin Ahmed, Adnan Anwar, Abdun Naser Mahmood, Zubair Shah, and Michael J. Maher. An investigation of performance analysis of anomaly detection techniques for big data in SCADA systems. *EAI Endorsed Transactions on Industrial Networks And Intelligent Systems*, 2:1–16, 2015.

40 Yi Yang, Hai-Qing Xu, Lei Gao, Yu-Bo Yuan, Kieran McLaughlin, and Sakir Sezer. Multidimensional intrusion detection system for IEC 61850-based SCADA networks. *IEEE Transactions on Power Delivery*, 32(2):1068–1078, 2017.

41 Thomas d'Otreppe de Bouvette. Aircrack-ng - main documentation. https://www.aircrack-ng.org/documentation.html, 2009.

42 Joe Weiss. Aurora generator test. In *Handbook of SCADA/Control Systems Security*, pages 107–114. CRC Press, Boca Raton, FL, USA, 2016.

43 Adnan Anwar and Abdun Naser Mahmood. Vulnerabilities of smart grid state estimation against false data injection attack. In J. Hossain and A. Mahmud, editors *Springer Journal on Renewable Energy Integration*, pages 411–428. Springer, Singapore, 2014.

44 Adnan Anwar, Abdun Naser Mahmood, and Zahir Tari. Identification of vulnerable node clusters against false data injection attack in an AMI based smart grid. *Elsevier Journal on Information Systems*, 53:201–212, 2015.

45 Adnan Anwar, Abdun Naser Mahmood, and Mark Pickering. Modeling and performance evaluation of stealthy false data injection attacks on smart grid in the presence of corrupted measurements. *Elsevier Journal of Computer and System Sciences*, 83(1):58–72, 2017.

46 Sajid Nazir, Shushma Patel, and Dilip Patel. Assessing and augmenting SCADA cyber security: a survey of techniques. *Elsevier Journal of Computers & Security*, 70:436–454, 2017.

47 Marshall D. Abrams and Joe Weiss. Malicious control system cyber security attack case study–Maroochy Water Services, Australia, 2008.

48 Abdun Naser Mahmood, Christopher Leckie, Jiankun Hu, Zahir Tari, and Mohammed Atiquzzaman. *Network traffic analysis and SCADA security*. 2010.

49 Bela Genge, Piroska Haller, and Istvan Kiss. A framework for designing resilient distributed intrusion detection systems for critical infrastructures. *Elsevier International Journal of Critical Infrastructure Protection*, 15:3–11, 2016.

50 I naki Garitano, Roberto Uribeetxeberria, and Urko Zurutuza. A review of SCADA anomaly detection systems. In *Proceedings of the 6th Springer International Conference on Soft Computing Models in Industrial and Environmental Applications*, pages 357–366, 2011.

51 V. Jaiganesh, S. Mangayarkarasi, and P. Sumathi. Intrusion detection systems: a survey and analysis of classification techniques. *International Journal of Advanced Research in Computer and Communication Engineering*, 2(4):1629–1635, 2013.

52 Jan Vávra and Martin Hromada. Evaluation of anomaly detection based on classification in relation to SCADA. In *IEEE International Conference on Military Technologies (ICMT)*, pages 330–334, Brno, Czech Republic, 2017. IEEE.

53 Chunjie Zhou, Shuang Huang, Naixue Xiong, Shuang-Hua Yang, Huiyun Li, Yuanqing Qin, and Xuan Li. Design and analysis of multimodel-based anomaly intrusion detection systems in industrial process automation. *IEEE Transactions on Systems, Man, and Cybernetics: Systems*, 45(10):1345–1360, 2015.

54 Upeka Kanchana Premaratne, Jagath Samarabandu, Tarlochan S. Sidhu, Robert Beresh, and Jian-Cheng Tan. An intrusion detection system for IEC61850 automated substations. *IEEE Transactions on Power Delivery*, 25(4):2376–2383, 2010.

55 Krishnan Dhanalakshmi Krishnan and Kannapiran Balasubramanian. A fusion of multiagent functionalities for effective intrusion detection system. *Security and Communication Networks*, 2017:6216078, 2017.

56 Mahdi Jamei, Emma Stewart, Sean Peisert, Anna Scaglione, Chuck McParland, Ciaran Roberts, and Alex McEachern. Micro synchrophasor-based intrusion detection in automated distribution systems: toward critical infrastructure security. *IEEE Internet Computing*, 20(5):18–27, 2016.

57 Zahra Zohrevand, Uwe Glasser, Hamed Yaghoubi Shahir, Moham-mad A. Tayebi, and Robert Costanzo. Hidden Markov based anomaly detection for water supply systems. In *IEEE International Conference on Big Data*, pages 1551–1560, WA, USA, 2016. IEEE. http://dx.doi.org/10.1109/BigData.2016.7840763.

58 Zhiwen Pan, Salim Hariri, and Youssif Al-Nashif. Anomaly based intrusion detection for building automation and control networks. In *Proceedings of the 11th IEEE/ACS International Conference on Computer Systems and Applications (AICCSA)*, pages 72–77, 2014.

59 Alecsandru Patrascu and Victor-Valeriu Patriciu. Cyber protection of critical infrastructures using supervised learning. In *Proceedings of the 20th IEEE International Conference on Control Systems and Computer Science (CSCS)*, pages 461–468, 2015.

60 Ahmed Patel, Hitham Alhussian, Jens Myrup Pedersen, Bouchaib Bounabat, Joaquim Celestino Júnior, and Sokratis Katsikas. A nifty collaborative intrusion detection and prevention architecture for smart grid ecosystems. *Elsevier Journal of Computers & Security*, 64:92–109, 2017.

61 S. L. P. Yasakethu, J. Jiang, and A. Graziano. Intelligent risk detection and analysis tools for critical infrastructure protection. In *Proceedings of the IEEE EUROCON Conference*, pages 52–59, 2013.

62 Hyunguk Yoo and Taeshik Shon. Novel approach for detecting network anomalies for substation automation based on IEC 61850. *Springer Journal of Multimedia Tools and Applications*, 74(1):303–318, 2015.

63 Ming Wan, Wenli Shang, and Peng Zeng. Double behavior characteristics for one-class classification anomaly detection in networked control systems. *IEEE Transactions on Information Forensics and Security (TIFS)*, 12(12):3011–3023, 2017.

64 Takashi Onoda. Probabilistic models-based intrusion detection using sequence characteristics in control system communication. *Springer Journal on Neural Computing and Applications*, 27(5):1119–1127, 2016. http://dx.doi.org/10.1007/s00521-015-1984-y.

65 Daesung Moon, Hyungjin Im, Ikkyun Kim, and Jong Hyuk Park. DTB-IDS: an intrusion detection system based on decision tree using behavior analysis for preventing APT attacks. *Springer Journal of Supercomputing*, 73(7):2881–2895, 2015.

66 Bo Tang and Haibo He. A local density-based approach for outlier detection. *Elsevier Journal of Neurocomputing*, 241:171–180, 2017.

67 R. Vijayanand, D. Devaraj, and B. Kannapiran. Support vector machine based intrusion detection system with reduced input features for advanced metering infrastructure of smart grid. In *Proceedings of the 4th IEEE International Conference on Advanced Computing and Communication Systems (ICACCS)*, pages 1–7, 2017.

68 Moti Markovitz and Avishai Wool. Field classification, modeling and anomaly detection in unknown can bus networks. *Elsevier Journal on Vehicular Communications*, 9:43–52, 2017.

69 S. Shitharth and D. Prince Winston. An enhanced optimization based algorithm for intrusion detection in SCADA network. *Elsevier Journal on Computers & Security*, 70:16–26, 2017.

70 William Hurst, Madjid Merabti, and Paul Fergus. Big data analysis techniques for cyber-threat detection in critical infrastructures. In *Proceedings of the 28th IEEE International Conference on Advanced Information Networking and Applications Workshops (WAINA)*, pages 916–921, Victoria, BC, Canada, 2014.

71 Stanislav Ponomarev and Travis Atkison. Industrial control system network intrusion detection by telemetry analysis. *IEEE Transactions on Dependable and Secure Computing (TDSC)*, 13(2):252–260, 2016.

72 Anna Magdalena Kosek and Oliver Gehrke. Ensemble regression model-based anomaly detection for cyber-physical intrusion detection in smart grids. In *IEEE Electrical Power and Energy Conference (EPEC)*, pages 1–7, Ottawa, Canada, 2016.

73 Shengyi Pan, Thomas Morris, and Uttam Adhikari. Developing a hybrid intrusion detection system using data mining for power systems. *IEEE Transactions on Smart Grid (TSG)*, 6(6):3104–3113, 2015.

74 Tomasz Andrysiak, Łukasz Saganowski, and Wojciech Mazurczyk. Network anomaly detection for railway critical infrastructure based on autoregressive fractional integrated moving average. *Springer Journal on Wireless Communications and Networking*, 2016(1):245, 2016.

75 Leandros A. Maglaras, Jianmin Jiang, and Tiago J. Cruz. Combining ensemble methods and social network metrics for improving accuracy of OCSVM on intrusion detection in SCADA systems. *Elsevier Journal of Information Security and Applications*, 30:15–26, 2016.

76 Tiago Cruz, Luis Rosa, Jorge Proença, Leandros Maglaras, Matthieu Aubigny, Leonid Lev, Jianmin Jiang, and Paulo Sim oes. A cybersecurity detection framework for supervisory control and data acquisition systems. *IEEE Transactions on Industrial Informatics (TII)*, 12(6):2236–2246, 2016.

77 Jasenko Hosic, Jereme Lamps, and Derek H. Hart. Evolving decision trees to detect anomalies in recurrent ICS networks. In *IEEE World Congress on Industrial Control Systems Security (WCICSS)*, pages 50–57, London, UK, 2015. IEEE. https://doi.org/10.1109/WCICSS.2015.7420323.

78 Kyriakos Stefanidis and Artemios G. Voyiatzis. An HMM-based anomaly detection approach for SCADA systems. In *Proceedings of the IFIP International Conference on Information Security Theory and Practice*, pages 85–99, 2016.

79 R. Bala Sri Swetha and K. Goklia Meena. Smart grid – a network based intrusion detection system. In *Proceedings of the International Conference on Innovations in Computing Techniques (ICICT)*, pages 29–36, Coimbatore, India, 2015. Semantic Scholar.

80 Rishabh Samdarshi, Nidul Sinha, and Paritosh Tripathi. A triple layer intrusion detection system for SCADA security of electric utility. In *Proceedings of the IEEE Annual India Conference (INDICON)*, pages 1–5, 2015.

81 Bisyron Wahyudi Masduki, Kalamullah Ramli, Ferry Astika Saputra, and Dedy Sugiarto. Study on implementation of machine learning methods combination for improving attacks detection accuracy on intrusion detection system (IDS). In *Proceedings of the IEEE International Conference on Quality in Research (QiR)*, pages 56–64, 2015.

82 Mustafa Amir Faisal, Zeyar Aung, John R. Williams, and Abel Sanchez. Securing advanced metering infrastructure using intrusion detection system with data stream mining. *Springer Journal on Intelligence and Security Informatics*, 7299:96–111, 2012.

83 Anna Magdalena Kosek. Contextual anomaly detection for cyber-physical security in smart grids based on an artificial neural network model. In *IEEE Joint Workshop on Cyber-Physical Security and Resilience in Smart Grids (CPSR-SG)*, pages 1–6, 2016.

84 Selim Aksoy and Robert M. Haralick. Feature normalization and likelihood-based similarity measures for image retrieval. *Elsevier Journal of Pattern Recognition Letters*, 22(5):563–582, 2001.

85 Patric Nader, Paul Honeine, and Pierre Beauseroy. Intrusion detection in SCADA systems using one-class classification. In *Proceedings of the 21st IEEE Signal Processing Conference (EUSIPCO)*, pages 1–5, Marrakech, Morocco, 2013.

86 Leandros A. Maglaras and Jianmin Jiang. Intrusion detection in SCADA systems using machine learning techniques. In *Proceedings of the IEEE Science and Information Conference (SAI)*, pages 626–631, 2014.

87 Eduardo Germano da Silva, Anderson Santos da Silva, Juliano Araujo Wickboldt, Paul Smith, Lisandro Zambenedetti Granville, and Alberto Schaeffer-Filho. A one-class NIDS for SDN-based SCADA systems. In *Proceedings of the 40th IEEE Annual Computer Software and Applications Conference (COMPSAC)*, volume 1, pages 303–312, 2016.

88 Jiawei Han, Micheline Kamber, and Jian Pei. *Data Mining: Concepts and Techniques*. Elsevier, MA, USA, 3rd edition, 2012.

89 Charles Sutton and Andrew McCallum. An introduction to conditional random fields. *Foundations and Trends® in Machine Learning*, 4(4):267–373, 2012.

90 Wojciech Tylman. SCADA intrusion detection based on modelling of allowed communication patterns. In *New Results in Dependability and Computer Systems*, pages 489–500, 2013.

91 Nir Friedman, Dan Geiger, and Moises Goldszmidt. Bayesian network classifiers. *Springer Journal of Machine learning*, 29(2-3):131–163, 1997.

92 Roman Klinger and Katrin Tomanek. *Classical Probabilistic Models and Conditional Random Fields*. Dortmund University of Technology, Dortmund, Germany, 2007.

93 Roger J. Lewis. An introduction to classification and regression tree (CART) analysis. In *Annual Meeting of the Society for Academic Emergency Medicine*, pages 1–14, San Francisco, CA, 2000. The Pennsylvania State University.

94 Manish Mehta, Rakesh Agrawal, and Jorma Rissanen. SLIQ: a fast scalable classifier for data mining. In *Springer International Conference on Extending Database Technology (EDBT)*, pages 18–32, 1996.

95 John Shafer, Rakeeh Agrawal, and Manish Mehta. SPRINT: A scalable parallel classifier for data mining. In *Proceedings of the 22nd International Conference on Very Large Data Bases (VLDB)*, pages 544–555, Mumbai, India, 1996.

96 Bing Liu, Wynne Hsu, and Yiming Ma. Integrating classification and association rule mining. In *Proceedings of the 4th ACM International Conference on Knowledge Discovery and Data Mining*, pages 80–86, 1998.

97 Peter Clark and Tim Niblett. The CN2 induction algorithm. *Springer Journal of Machine Learning*, 3(4):261–283, 1989.

98 Wenmin Li, Jiawei Han, and Jian Pei. CMAR: accurate and efficient classification based on multiple class-association rules. In *Proceedings of the IEEE International Conference on Data Mining*, pages 369–376, 2001.

99 William W. Cohen and Yoram Singer. A simple, fast, and effective rule learner. In *Proceedings of the 16th National Conference on Artificial Intelligence and the 11th Innovative Applications of Artificial Intelligence Conference Innovative Applications of Artificial Intelligence*, pages 335–342, 1999.

100 Maurilio Pereira Coutinho, Germano Lambert-Torres, Luiz Eduardo Borges da Silva, Jonas Guedes Borges da Silva, Jose Cabral Neto, and Horst Lazarek. Improving a methodology to extract rules to identify attacks in power system critical infrastructure: new results. In *Proceedings of the IEEE Conference on Transmission, Distribution and Exposition*, pages 1–6, 2008.

101 Pedro Silva. *On the Use of K-NN in Intrusion Detection for Industrial Control Systems*. Master's thesis, Department of Information Technology, Galway, Ireland, 2014.

102 Zubair Shah, Abdun Naser Mahmood, Mehmet A. Orgun, and M. Hadi Mashinchi. Subset selection classifier (SSC): a training set reduction method. In *Proceedings of the 16th IEEE International Conference on Computational Science and Engineering (CSE)*, pages 862–869, Sydney, NSW, Australia, 2013.

103 M. F. Schilling. Mutual and shared neighbor probabilities: finite-and infinite-dimensional results. *Advances in Applied Probability*, 18(2):388–405, 1986.

104 Corinna Cortes and Vladimir Vapnik. Support-vector networks. *Springer Journal of Machine Learning*, 20(3):273–297, 1995.

105 Anna D. P. Lima, P. A. Fernando, and Lotufo and Carlos R. Minussi. Disturbance detection for optimal database storage in electrical distribution systems using artificial immune systems with negative selection. *Elsevier Journal on Electric Power Systems Research*, 109:54–62, 2014.

106 Christopher M. Bishop. *Neural Networks for Pattern Recognition*. Oxford University Press, 1995.

107 Wei Li. Using Genetic Algorithm for network intrusion detection. In *Proceedings of the United States Department of Energy Cyber Security Group Training Conference*, pages 24–27, 2004.

108 Patric Nader, Paul Honeine, and Pierre Beauseroy. l_p-norms in one-class classification for intrusion detection in SCADA systems. *IEEE Transactions on Industrial Informatics (TII)*, 10(4):2308–2317, 2014.

109 Patric Nader, Paul Honeine, and Pierre Beauseroy. Detection of cyberattacks in a water distribution system using machine learning techniques. In *Proceedings of the 6th IEEE International Conference on Digital Information Processing and Communications (ICDIPC)*, pages 25–30, Beirut, Lebanon, 2016.

110 David M. J. Tax and Robert P. W. Duin. Support vector data description. *Elsevier Journal of Machine Learning*, 54(1):45–66, 2004.

111 Arthur P. Dempster, Nan M. Laird, and Donald B. Rubin. Maximum likelihood from incomplete data via the EM algorithm. *Journal of the Royal Statistical Society: Series B (Methodological)*, 39(1):1–22, 1977.

112 David G. Kleinbaum, Lawrence L. Kupper, Keith E. Muller, and Azhar Nizam. *Applied regression analysis and other multivariable methods*, volume 601. 1988.

113 Sebastian Mika, Gunnar Ratsch, Jason Weston, Bernhard Scholkopf, and Klaus-Robert Mullers. Fisher discriminant analysis with kernels. In *Proceedings of the 1999 IEEE Signal Processing Society Workshop*, pages 41–48, 1999.

114 Joseph Sill, Gábor Takács, Lester Mackey, and David Lin. Feature-weighted linear stacking, 2009.

115 Radhika Goel, Anjali Sardana, and Ramesh C. Joshi. Parallel misuse and anomaly detection model. *Internation Journal of Network Security*, 14(4):211–222, 2012.

116 Bradley Efron and Robert J Tibshirani. *An Introduction to the Bootstrap*. CRC Press, New York, WA, USA, 1994.

117 Zhi-Hua Zhou. *Ensemble Methods: Foundations and Algorithms*. Chapman and Hall/CRC, New York, WA, USA, 2012.

118 Hamed Yaghoubi Shahir, Uwe Glasser, Amir Yaghoubi Shahir, and Hans Wehn. Maritime situation analysis framework: vessel interaction classification and anomaly detection. In *Proceedings of the IEEE International Conference on Big Data (Big Data)*, pages 1279–1289, Santa Clara, USA, 2015.

119 Nemanja Branisavljević, Zoran Kapelan, and Dušan Prodanović. Improved real-time data anomaly detection using context classification. *IWA Journal of Hydroinformatics*, 13(3):307–323, 2011.

120 Barbara Kitchenham. Procedures for performing systematic reviews. Technical report, Keele University, Keele, UK, 2004.

121 Yi Yang, Kieran McLaughlin, Tim Littler, Sakir Sezer, and Haifeng Wang. Rule-based intrusion detection system for SCADA networks. In *Proceedings of the 2nd IET Renewable Power Generation Conference (RPG)*, pages 1–4. Institution of Engineering and Technology (IET), 2013.

122 Muhammad Kamran Asif and Yahya Subhi Al-Harthi. Intrusion detection system using Honey Token based Encrypted Pointers to mitigate cyber threats for critical infrastructure networks. In *Proceedings of the IEEE International Conference on Systems, Man, and Cybernetics (SMC)*, pages 1266–1270, 2014.

123 Yi Yang, Kieran McLaughlin, Sakir Sezer, Tim Littler, Eul Gyu Im, Bernardi Pranggono, and Haifeng Wang. Multiattribute SCADA-specific intrusion detection system for power networks. *IEEE Transactions on Power Delivery*, 29(3):1092–1102, 2014.

124 Noam Erez and Avishai Wool. Control variable classification, modeling and anomaly detection in modbus/tcp scada systems. *Elsevier International Journal of Critical Infrastructure Protection*, 10:59–70, 2015.

125 Atilla Özgür and Hamit Erdem. Intrusion detection classifiers comparison in different operating environments. In V. Kiray, R. Ozcan, and T. Malas, editors, *Proceedings of the 9th International Conference on Electronics Computer and Computation (ICECCO)*, pages 24–27, Turkey, 2012. Turgut Ozal Univ. ISBN 978-605-87394-6-8.

126 Khurum Nazir Junejo and Jonathan Goh. Behaviour-based attack detection and classification in cyber physical systems using machine learning. In *Proceedings of the 2nd ACM International Workshop on Cyber-Physical System Security (CPSS)*, pages 34–43, New York, WA, USA, 2016.

127 Patrick Biernacki and Dan Waldorf. Snowball sampling: problems and techniques of chain referral sampling. *Sociological Methods & Research*, 10(2):141–163, 1981.

128 The Computing Research and Education Association of Australasia (CORE). CORE Conference Portal. http://portal.core.edu.au/conf-ranks/, 2018.

129 Aditya Ashok, Manimaran Govindarasu, and Jianhui Wang. Cyber-physical attack-resilient wide-area monitoring, protection, and control for the power grid. *Proceedings of the IEEE*, 105(7):1389–1407, 2017.

130 Shen Yin, Xiangping Zhu, and Chen Jing. Fault detection based on a robust one class support vector machine. *Elsevier Journal of Neurocomputing*, 145:263–268, 2014.

131 Carlos Queiroz, Abdun Naser Mahmood, and Zahir Tari. SCADASim-A framework for building SCADA simulations. *IEEE Transactions on Smart Grid (TSG)*, 2(4):589–597, 2011.

132 Thomas Morris, Anurag Srivastava, Bradley Reaves, Wei Gao, Kalyan Pavurapu, and Ram Reddi. A control system testbed to validate critical infrastructure protection concepts. *Elsevier International Journal of Critical Infrastructure Protection*, 4(2):88–103, 2011.

133 Aditya Ashok, Siddharth Sridhar, A. David McKinnon, Wang Pengyuan, and Manimaran Govindarasu. Testbed-based performance evaluation of attack resilient control for AGC. In *Proceedings of the Resilience Week (RWS)*, pages 125–129, Chicago, IL, USA, August 2016. IEEE.

134 U.S. Coast Guard Navigation Center. Automatic identification system overview. http://www.navcen.uscg.gov/?pageName=AISmain, 2015.

135 Yi Yang, H. T. Jiang, Kieran McLaughlin, L. Gao, Y. B. Yuan, W. Huang, and Sakir Sezer. Cybersecurity test-bed for IEC 61850 based smart substations. In *Proceedings of the IEEE Power & Energy Society General Meeting*, pages 1–5, Denver, CO, USA, 2015.

136 Kavita Agrawal and Hemant Makwana. A study on critical capabilities for security information and event management. *International Journal of Science and Research*, 4(7):1893–1896, 2015.

137 S. Sandeep Sekharan and Kamalanathan Kandasamy. Profiling SIEM tools and correlation engines for security analytics. In *IEEE International Conference on Wireless Communications, Signal Processing and Networking (WiSPNET)*, pages 717–721, Chennai, India, 2017.

138 Carlos Queiroz, Abdun Mahmood, and Zahir Tari. A probabilistic model to predict the survivability of SCADA systems. *IEEE Transactions on Industrial Informatics (TII)*, 9(4):1975–1985, 2013.

139 Cézar Roberto Souza. The accord.net framework. http://accord-framework .net, 2014.

140 Lukas Rift, Johnny Vastergaard, Daniel Haslinger, Andrea Pasquale, and John Smith. Conpot ICS/SCADA honeypot. http://conpot.org, 2013.

141 Guillaume Babin, Yamine Aït-Ameur, Neeraj Kumar Singh, and Marc Pantel. A system substitution mechanism for hybrid systems in Event-B. In *Proceedings of the International Conference on Formal Engineering Methods*, pages 106–121, Cham, 2016. Springer International Publishing.

142 Rongjun Xie, Ibrahim Khalil, Shahriar Badsha, and Mohammed Atiquzzaman. Fast and peer-to-peer vital signal learning system for cloud-based healthcare. *Wlsevier Journal of Future Generation Computer Systems (FGCS)*, 88:220–233, 2018.

143 Zhongqiang Chen, Mema Roussopoulos, Zhanyan Liang, Yuan Zhang, Zhongrong Chen, and Alex Delis. Malware characteristics and threats on the internet ecosystem. *Elsevier Journal of Systems and Software*, 85(7):1650–1672, 2012.

144 Ivo Friedberg, Florian Skopik, Giuseppe Settanni, and Roman Fiedler. Combating advanced persistent threats: from network event correlation to incident detection. *Elsevier Journal of Computers & Security*, 48:35–57, 2015.

6

Behavior-Based Data Exfiltration Detection Methods

Although an intrusion detection system (IDS) is an important impediment for attackers, this could not guarantee that a target system is fully protected. Various advanced, clandestine, and sophisticated penetration methods are used by hackers to gain access to systems, including critical systems such as supervisory control and data acquisition (SCADA) and Smart Grid systems. Once they compromise and install a malicious software on a user's machine, the use of a host-based protection system will play a critical role to thwart the threat and will alert the security team.

This chapter aims to present an effective data exfiltration detection method, called Sub-Curve HMM, which is essentially based on the abnormal behavior of processes running on various servers or terminal machines. This chapter shows step by step how to detect a malicious software that is involved in the data exfiltration. The problems related to the detection of data-stealing behaviors are first discussed in Section 6.1, and a summary of existing solutions for such problems are discussed in Section 6.2. Section 6.3 provides details of the Sub-Curve hidden Markov model (HMM) method, and Section 6.4 illustrates the experimental setup and the experimental results are given in Section 6.5. A summary about Sub-Curve HMM is given in Section 6.6, and concluding remarks are provide in Section 6.7.

6.1 Motivation

The high penetration of data-centric services, such as critical infrastructure, mobile computing, or online transactions, has markedly increased the risk of exposing the sensitive data of legitimate users to sophisticated malware and tools [1]. The main purpose of this malware and tools is to access and steal sensitive data from the users. Consequently, detecting malicious software is a crucial topic to prevent user's privacy. This is even more critical for specific organizational targets, such as government bodies or military authorities (e.g. leakage

Data Exfiltration Threats and Prevention Techniques: Machine Learning and Memory-Based Data Security, First Edition. Zahir Tari, Nasrin Sohrabi, Yasaman Samadi, and Jakapan Suaboot.
© 2023 John Wiley & Sons, Inc. Published 2023 by John Wiley & Sons, Inc.

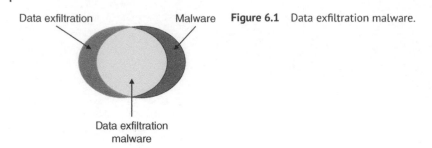

Data exfiltration   Malware   **Figure 6.1**   Data exfiltration malware.

Data exfiltration
malware

of subcontractor database [2]). Recent outbreaks of ransomware malware are good examples of devastating consequences. These advanced persistent threats (APTs) are often lying dormant in our devices (i.e. workstation and/or portable) and remain undetected by the antivirus software.

Figure 6.1 depicts the relationship between a malicious software and a data exfiltration threat. Even though not all malware aim to steal sensitive data nor all data breaches were carried out through the use of malware, it is undeniable that a malicious software is one of the most crucial tools for attackers to search through millions of users machines and automatically gather invaluable sensitive information. The intuition is that a malware is a very effective hacking tool. Despite the struggle of millions users around the world to keep their computer software up to date with the security patch, the manufacturers themselves still could not release a timely update software when the new venerability is discovered. Hence, malware is considered as one of the most serious threats in the modern time.

Some important limitations of existing malware detection methods are as follows: (i) the signature of the malware is new to the antivirus software, and (ii) the anomaly-based systems cannot detect variations in the malware behavior; and they therefore cannot differentiate between legitimate and malignant activities. Intuitively, attackers develop malicious programs using various common methods, which are performed using similar series of application programming interface (API) calls. Hence, observing the behavior of all running processes (to identify potential malware) is the key to detecting data breaches.

Existing work [3–5] have shown that HMM can accurately discriminate between the behavior of a malware and a benign software. HMM models a program's activities as probabilities of sequences of API calls. Although previous studies (e.g. [4, 6]) show promising accuracy in detecting malware, experiments however were carried on *short* API sequences (i.e. around 280 instructions on average). Dynamic behavior analysis of a malware can generate though very long sequences of API calls. Indeed, our experiments on Keylogger malware (MD5 hash value `d4259130a53dae8ddce89 ebc8e80b560`) generated more than 300,000 series of API calls in less than two minutes (see Figure 6.2). This study found that HMM performs poorly with *long* API sequences. This is because the

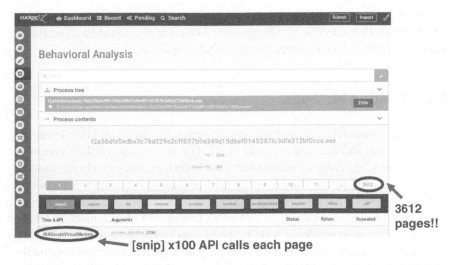

Figure 6.2 Cuckoo sandbox's API calls monitoring report of the sample program MD5 hash value `d4259130a53dae8ddce89ebc8e80b560` (around two minutes observation).

HMM only gives a matching probability $P(O|\lambda)$ between the model λ and all data in the testing sequence O for a whole API sequence. Since the matching score is computed using joint probabilities of each API instruction (INS) in a given sequence, malware could evade the detection by posing as a benign software for the majority of the time and only performs malicious activities for a brief period of time to make the final matching score smaller and indistinguishable from benign software. Nevertheless, to the best of our knowledge, existing work has not properly addressed the impact of the length of API sequences on the detection accuracy. Hence, this work focuses on improving the detection accuracy of long API sequences, where API calls datasets vary from around 5000 to nearly 80,000 instructions per API sequence on average.

This chapter describes Sub-Curve HMM as an effective method that addresses the HMM limitations by focusing on *subsets* of API calls sequences. It is indeed focusing on finding *subsets* of matching patterns rather than the average probabilities from the whole sequence. Specifically, Sub-Curve HMM observes *subsets* of a sequence from API INS, which looks for high matching probabilities with the training sequences. These probabilities (i.e. likelihood) scores are converted to a *curve*. Sub-Curve HMM also uses changing trends (or slope) of the curve to detect discontinuities in the series of probability scores, called Sub-Curve. These curves are selected as features, and they are used by classifiers to detect fragments of malware's suspicious behaviors. The experimental results show that Sub-Curve HMM outperforms existing ones in malware detection accuracy, especially for the

Keylogger family that had the longest average API sequence length in this study (76,101 INS). The detection accuracy is over 94% compared to the baseline HMM accuracy of 83%, which includes the whole API sequence.

6.2 Existing Methods

Existing malware detection methods can be generally categorized into *investigative*, *preventive*, and *detective* methods [1, 7]. The *investigative* method identifies security flaws by trying to reconstruct data breach events – which are used to develop a security patch. The *preventive* method uses access control mechanisms to prevent sensitive data from being acquired by an unauthorized party. However, these measures cannot guarantee end-user's computer to be completely secure from intruders who employ a wide range of attacks vector (so-called APT) [1]. Various investigative solutions have been proposed, such as watermarking methods [8] and activities tracking [9]. This is a passive solution and useful for auditing and forensic purposes. As a result, according to the report [10], the industry spends less money on investigation compared to detection and prevention measures.

The *preventive* method, on the other hand, affects normal usage of legitimate user. For instance, forced user to enable multiple factors access control or restricting them from using external storage [11] or accessing workstations from external network. Furthermore, those measures cannot guarantee end-user's computer to be completely secure from intruders who employ a wide range of attacks vector (so-called APT) [1]. For instance, vulnerability of email client that allows attackers to access the encrypted message without a key (known as EFAIL attack [12]). That is, attackers create a three-part email, which contains an encrypted message in the middle of head and tail. In the head element, they add enclosed HTML image tag just before the encrypted element in the middle, and the close tag is added afterward in the tail to make the secret as a part of the tag. As a result, the receiver is deceived to decipher the secret message in the middle of email using their own secret key and sends the plain text to attackers via the HTTP request (i.e. as a parameter of image URL). This security flaw allows hacktivists to steal sensitive data without having a secret key. Hence, detection solution has been the most important security measure for the industry [10].

The *detective* method includes network-based monitoring (e.g. analyzing covert network traffic [1, 13] or the use of data hiding methods [13]) and host-based monitoring, such as malicious dataflows detection [14, 15] and detecting malicious program behavior [3–5]. However, the aforementioned solutions are considered a supplementary to the host-based solution. This is because the target of malware is the sensitive data, and the data usually located in a host, according to the reports [16, 17]. Hence, the host-based malware detection method is one of the

Table 6.1 Malware detection sources used by existing methods and their limitations.

Paper	Detection source	Method	Limitations
Wong and Stamp [18]	Detect malware using *opcodes*	Hidden Markov model (HMM)	Require the executable binary to be decompiled; static analysis
Reff et al. [19]	Detect malware using *strings* contained in executable files	*n*-gram	String is updated frequently; not efficient
Wei et al. [20]	Detect malware by analyzing *dataflow patterns*	Taint analysis	Computationally expensive algorithm
Fan et al. [21]	Mining *discriminate features* from malware and benign software	All Nearest Neighbor (ANN)	Require both malware and benign software in the training
Kolosnjaji et al. [22]	Detect malware using *dynamic API calls*	Deep neural network	Require a large-scale training data
Confora et al. [5]	Detect malware using *dynamic API calls*	HMM and structural entropy	Support only limited length of API call sequence (<2000 API calls)

most promising solutions to prevent the data exfiltration. There are two crucial aspects of the malware detection problem: (i) the signature of the malware is new to antivirus software; and (ii) the anomaly-based systems cannot detect variations in the malware behavior, and they therefore cannot differentiate between legitimate and exfiltration activities. Intuitively, if a Trojan horse software accesses sensitive data, it is highly likely to cause data leakage.

Table 6.1 depicts different detection sources used by related research to detect malicious programs. As well as the different machine learning (ML) methods, the limitations have been described. It is clear that the static detection sources, namely opcodes, strings, dataflow, and static features of the executable binary, can be easily evaded by separating the malicious payload from the malware itself and dynamically downloading the data-stealing code from the remote server later on. Hence, the dynamic API calls are more suitable for dealing with this obfuscation method. From the aspect of detection source, the state-of-the-art heuristic methods for detecting malware are categorized into static and dynamic methods.

6.2.1 Static Methods

This extracts features of a specimen by looking at its file structures, including the binary object, opcode (Operation Code), text, and the API sequence. These characters are extracted from the executable or archive objects for training and testing samples.

Many solutions offer methods to converse binary code into IR (Intermediate Representation) code. For example, in research [23], DroidNative framework detects Android-based malwares. They extract MAIL (Malware Analysis Intermediate Language) from native bytecode of applications and generate the innovative control-flow graph (CFG) patterns to represent application features. This method can mitigate with polymorphic malwares that use the code obfuscation method. On the other hand, the whole analysis platform (DECAF) is proposed by Henderson et al. [24]. The binary sample from any platform is tracked using taint analysis method to reveal the relationships of low-level information flows. A series of special shadow commands are inserted into low-level instruction to track data propagation at the register level. This method gives highly granular information on how sensitive data is processed; however, the problem is the high resource consumption and the semantic gaps between low-level operations and the application-level context. Furthermore, such a method allows developers to install plugins used to detect specific characteristics of programs such as function hooking feature or key logging behavior.

ML-based methods show their ability to detect new variants of malware. Work in [21] proposed a malicious sequential pattern extraction method and a neural-network-based classifier to predict unseen malicious software. The pattern of opcodes is extracted using an algorithm based on generalized sequential pattern (GSP) to find a set of discriminating features. Then a set of data with feature vector is classified using an *All Nearest Neighbor* classifier. In contrast, work in [25] focuses on reduction of computational complexity in selecting features rather than improvement of detection accuracy. Information from API calls is extracted from binary files and then converted to meta-data. They proposed a combination of multi-linear and binary logistic regression methods to reduce dimensions of features from the API information. After that, a tree classifier is trained to detect malware. However, Fan et al. [21] and [25] mine features from the whole sequence of samples. Hence, these methods could be useful for static analysis only, and it requires training data from both malicious and legitimate software.

Scanning for specific string of messages could be useful to detect malware, e.g. the specific names of files or registry values that a program wants to access. However, many studies on *n*-gram solutions may lead to overfitting and performance limitations [19].

A limitation of extracting static information from binary sources is that attackers can hide the malicious code as encrypted binaries or download it from a remote location during runtime [26]. By using simple encryption and compression methods, the malicious code can be decrypted and unpacked into the memory at runtime [27]. Furthermore, malware might be used only to check whether the running platform is its target or not. The actual malicious code could be downloaded later or never, depending on the findings of the first-stage malware. Kotler and Klein [26] reports a malware that can deceive antivirus's sandbox and use it to pass on sensitive data stolen from users without them noticing it.

6.2.2 Dynamic Methods

This method tries to address the limitations of the static method by observing the execution behavior of a program by running it in a controlled environment or a sandbox. This method is promising as it can achieve a higher detection accuracy compared to the static and hybrid methods [3].

A sandbox-based method has been proposed in UNVEIL framework [28] to analyze ransomware. It focuses on finding suspected malware by using artificial user files as a bait. UNVEIL tracks changes in files to identify ransomware behavior. This work adds a malicious detection layer between the operating system I/O scheduler and the driver of the file system. It identifies an attack by monitoring abnormal write and delete operations that could lead to encryption, overwriting, or deletion of user files. On the other hand, the Peeper framework [29] detects data leakage by monitoring all operations related to sensitive files. It extracts suspicious activities by checking anomalous activities and comparing them to the user's profile for file creation, duplication, and modification. This work is designed for the cloud-based environment. In [30], the CBM sandbox is designed to extract API call sequences for a large-scale malware database. Their results have shown a high precision in clustering suspicious samples. However, our work does not focus on extracting behavior from binary programs; instead, the proposed method uses API sequence extracted from the existing sandbox system [31] to develop data leakage detection system.

Clustering methods are also used to find classes of unknown variants. The work in [32] proposed *Malware Instruction Set* (MIST), a multilevel representation of API call sequence. They successfully clustered unknown malware into classes of malware. This work has been extended to resolve malware labeling problems in the *AutoMal and MalLabel* (AMAL) system [33]. They extended the analysis to include file systems, memory, network, and registry. The system can group unknown files precisely by using multiple clustering algorithms. On the other hand, Annachhatre et al. [4] uses HMM method to score API call sequence of imitated variants generated from different malware toolboxes. These scores are used to create clusters of malware, which are used to detect unknown variants.

HMM-based methods have been found to be efficient in malware detection. For instance, authors in [3] compared different analysis methods (i.e. static, dynamic, and hybrid) to extract sequences of API calls. The output is used in training and testing based on HMM. Their evaluation shows that HMM-based detection on dynamic API call sequence outperforms static or hybrid analysis. In [5], HMM and structural entropy have been compared for the detection and classification of Android malware. In this study, HMM is found better in discriminating between malicious and benign samples; however, it is not as efficient in classifying the malware into families compared to the entropy-based method. Indeed, it does not make sense to compare different programs using HMM scores directly without considering the length of input sequences. As suggested by Annachhatre et al. [4], the score needs to be converted into a length-independent value before it can be used by a classifier.

On the other hand, Kolosnjaji et al. [22] proposed a complex deep neural network method that combines both sequential and n-grams characteristics. Their results show the best performance among classical neural networks, HMM and SVM (support vector machine) methods. However, since it requires a large-scale training data, it would be too complicated for detecting a small and specific set of behavior. To the best of authors' knowledge, this proposed work is probably the first attempt to identify short sequences of data breach activities that might be hidden in a long sequence of legitimate activities.

6.3 Sub-Curve HMM Method

This section describes the Sub-Curve HMM method that aims to effectively extract shorter sequences of API calls as features to improve the accuracy and efficiency of dynamic malware detection method using HMM.

Figure 6.3 depicts the architecture of the Sub-Curve HMM method. It consists of components for feature extraction and classification. The executable binaries of malware and benign programs are used for training and testing. There are three steps in selecting discriminating feature vectors: API feature extraction, HMM training, and Sub-curve extraction. The feature vectors are then used to train a binary classifier and used for malware detection. The API feature extraction and HMM training steps are discussed in Sections 6.3.1 and 6.3.2, while the Sub-curve feature extraction is presented in Section 6.3.3. Section 6.3.4 describes the malware detection phase which requires training classifiers and malware classification. The solid line represents the training steps. The training dataset is separated into two subsets, one for the training of HMMs and the other for the training of a binary classifier. Since an HMM is a one-class model, it does not need benign samples for the HMM training. In contrast, both malware and benign programs are used during the training of the selected binary classifier. Specifically, HMMs are modeled from the sequence of API calls, whereas the classifier uses feature vectors extracted from HMMs. For the testing, unknown data is extracted with its features using the trained HMMs. Then it is classified to being a malware or benign using the trained a classifier (depicted using dotted lines in Figure 6.3).

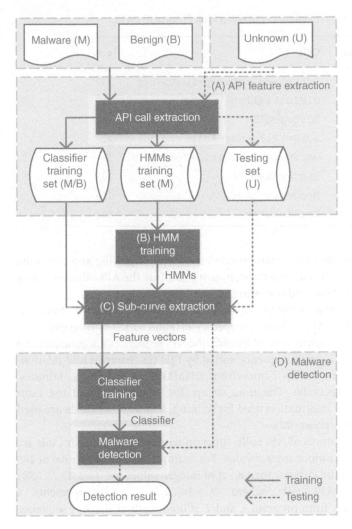

Figure 6.3 Architecture of Sub-Curve HMM.

6.3.1 API Feature Extraction

During this step, the program execution behavior is translated into a numerical representation. Based on a sequence of API calls, function names are mapped to series of integers, which can be modeled in the second step using HMM. Software and malware samples are executed inside a sandbox to capture their dynamic behavior, and the API call sequences have been extracted for experiments. In a production environment, this will be done by monitoring the dynamic API calls in real time.

Table 6.2 Example of first eight INS observed from Process ID 2428.

PID	Time stamp	Calls	o
2428	5451567	SetUnhandledExceptionFilter	149
2428	5451577	OleInitialize	117
2428	5451577	LdrLoadDll	73
2428	5451577	LdrGetProcedureAddress	72
2428	5451577	GetSystemTimeAsFileTime	56
2428	5451577	RegOpenKeyExA	133
2428	5451587	RegQueryValueExA	136
2428	5451587	RegCloseKey	124

The API call sequence extraction process starts with importing and executing software and malware in a testing environment to capture the API calls, including a mix of both application- and operating-system-level calls.

Table 6.2 illustrates an example of API call sequences extracted from PID (process ID) 2428. The API calls are grouped by PID and sorted by time executed. That is, if one process spawns several threads, the API sequences are concatenated from all threads into a single sequence sorted by PID (i.e. parent–child relationship). The value *Time Stamp* comes from HHMMSSmmm (Hours, Minutes, Seconds, and Milli-seconds). The time stamp (for sequencing) and the *Calls* columns are the only information used for training, and all other fields are used for cross-checking purposes only.

To represent the features of API calls, function names under column *Calls* are replaced with a set of unique integer value. For example, if there are a total of 288 distinct API calls in the dataset, then a set of integer values $o \in \{1, 2, 3, \ldots, 288\}$ represents unique API calls, where $O_i = \{o_1, o_2, o_3, \ldots, o_T\}$ represents a sequence of API calls from program i, and T is the length of the API sequence observed.

The collected dataset consisted of six malware families that have been identified as by Symantec [16] and Checkpoint [17] as topmost significant threats with data-stealing behaviors. A feature vector of a program i is generated from the API sequence O_i and HMMs $\lambda_1 - \lambda_6$ (i.e. models trained by six selected malware families). Every unknown sample i is tested against each of the HMMs, and their matching scores are used to extract features (Section 6.3.3) and then kept in the feature vector $V_i = \{S_{i\lambda_1}, \ldots, S_{i\lambda_6}\}$, where $S_{i\lambda_1}, \ldots, S_{i\lambda_6}$ are feature scores between the testing sample i and HMMs $\lambda_1, \ldots, \lambda_6$.

6.3.2 HMM Training

Figure 6.4 depicts the relationship between the hidden states and the observations in the context of the HMM. The Markov process is a random process in which future is independent of the past, given the present. Likelihood of observing outputs depends on the underlying states of the system. HMM assumes system is a Markov process with hidden states. In the context of this research, API calls are the observable event, whereas the hidden states relate to behaviors of the executing process, and the sequence of API calls indicates the state of the software.

Based on the extracted API sequences of known malware, HMMs are trained to assign feature scores for testing samples. The training process follows the Baum–Welch algorithm [34]. The training parameters $\{\lambda, O, \tau\}$ consist of HMM λ, API sequence O, and coverage threshold τ. An HMM $\lambda = (A, B, \pi)$ has three components: a transition matrix A $(N \times N)$; an emission probability matrix B $(N \times M)$; and a probabilities vector of an initial state π, which sets the same value for every state. The number of observable values M is equal to the number of unique API calls. The HMM training parameters are defined as follows:

- N is set to four hidden states.
- M is set to 288.
- $A(N \times N)$ is randomized, where $\sum_j a_{ij} = 1$.
- $B(N \times M)$ is randomized, where $\sum_k b_i(o_k) = 1$.
- π is set to 0.25 for all states ($1/N$).

Unlike other applications of HMM (e.g. speech [35], object recognition [36]), the number of hidden states N to identify malware behavior using API calls is unknown. The result from existing work [5] suggests that higher number of hidden states results in better matching scores. However, when carrying out the experiments using our own scoring system (see Section 6.3.3 **Step 5**: *Compute the feature score*), the differences between scores from 4, 6, 8, or higher number of hidden states were negligible. To keep the training to a minimum, four hidden

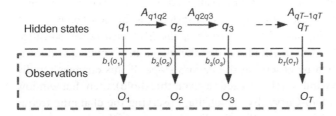

Figure 6.4 Hidden Markov model: states and observations.

states were chosen, as the training time increases dramatically with increase in the number of states.

Since the API sequence could start at any state, all states were assumed to be equally probable, including the initial state ($\pi_1, \ldots, \pi_4 = 0.25$).

In training the HMM, the training data consists of API sequences $O = \{O^{Fj_1}, \ldots, O^{Fj_k}\}$, where F_j denotes malware family $i \in \{1, \ldots, 6\}$ and k is the total number of training samples for a particular malware family (i.e. k differs for each malware family). The API sequences O are extracted from separated HMM training set described in Section 6.3.1. To build a single HMM for each family of malware, API sequences of malware belonging to the same family were concatenated and used to train the HMM. Finally, the convergence threshold τ is set to 1×10^{-4}, meaning that the training process will stop when the log-likelihood that O is generated from the current model λ is less than or equal to 1×10^{-4}. Since several malware instances were combined into a single training sequence, in some cases, the model did not converge if the threshold τ was smaller than 1×10^{-4}.

6.3.3 Sub-Curve Extraction

Features from API call sequences are extracted using Sub-Curve HMM. Particularly, such a method focuses on detecting fragments of matching behavior instead of using the whole sequence. The standard forward algorithm or α-pass [37] estimates the likelihood of an API calls sequence being matched with a HMM using the data from the whole sequence. Take the API sequence matching using the log-likelihood in Figure 6.5 as an example, the forward algorithm uses $T1$ to compare two API call sequences, which will detect program A and B as benign (i.e. less likely match to the malware model). However, if we consider a shorter period $T2$ or $T3$, both program A and B partially act like a malicious software (i.e. has a higher matching likelihood). Consequently, the short malicious activities are difficult to detect, since the matching probability is averaged with a larger portion of non-matching instructions.

In principle, Sub-Curve HMM keeps track of α-pass testing output for every single API INS. All the data points are visualized as curves (i.e. curves on a line graph). After the whole API sequence is tested, the hidden behavior can be identified by checking for *abrupt changes of the likelihood curve*, so-called *Sub-Curve*. Specifically, this method divides the curve into smaller windows. The change is identified by observing the curve's slope. If this changes rapidly compared to previous windows (i.e. exceeds a given threshold), then that window will be identified as a Sub-Curve. By visualizing observing the changing trends of the curve, it is interesting to note that the discontinuities of the slope represent the change in the log-likelihood values, which indicates a behavioral change of the program or malware.

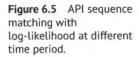

Figure 6.5 API sequence matching with log-likelihood at different time period.

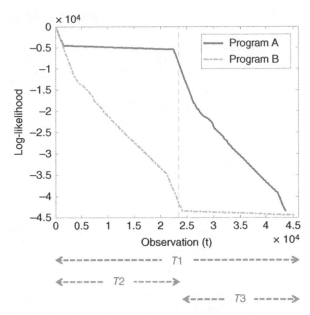

Figure 6.6 shows the flowchart of Sub-Curve HMM extraction. The details of the various steps involved in extracting numerical features can be summarized as follows:

Step 1 [Generate a log-likelihood curve]: Here, the α-pass [37] algorithm was extended to collect data points of a curve. For the ease of understanding, details of the modified HMM α-pass function is given first, followed by a definition of the curve.

Given HMM $\lambda = (A, B, \pi)$ with N hidden states and an observation sequence $O = \{o_1, o_2, \ldots, o_T\}$, where T is the length of API sequence observed, a matching probability $P(O|\lambda)$ is computed using the generic α-pass function defined as $\alpha_t(1) = \pi_i b_i(o_1)$ and $\alpha_{t+1}(j) = b_j(o_{t+1})\sum_i \alpha_t(i)a_{ij}$ when $t > 1$. The matching probability between HMM λ and the given API sequence $P(O|\lambda)$ is described using α-pass functions as $\sum_i \alpha_T(i)$, defined in Eq. (6.1):

$$\alpha_t(i) = \begin{cases} \alpha_1(i) = \pi_i b_i(o_1) & t = 1, \\ \alpha_{t+1}(j) = b_j(o_{t+1})\left[\sum_{i=1}^{N}\alpha_t(i)a_{ij}\right] & t > 1, \end{cases}$$

$$P(O|\lambda) = \sum_{i=1}^{N}\alpha_T(i). \tag{6.1}$$

Unfortunately, this method has an underflow problem when the length T is large. The likelihood value will shrink too quickly to zero, since the output is a

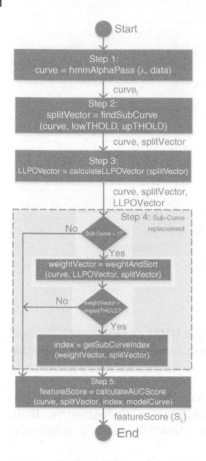

Figure 6.6   Flowchart of Sub-Curve extraction.

multiplication of several small values between 0 and 1. Thus, the likelihood is normalized and transformed into a logarithm domain to prevent an occurrence of the exception output (i.e. $-\infty$).

The modified α-pass algorithm keeps track of the log-likelihood value of each instruction in O from o_1 to o_T. These data points will be used to find discontinuities of the trend of log-likelihood score (i.e. explained in Step 2).

Let ρ_{uv} is a likelihood of API sequence O being matched with the model λ from data points o_u to o_v $(u < v)$, defined as:

$$\rho_{uv} = \sum_{t=1}^{v} \log \left[\sum_{i=1}^{N} \alpha_t(i) \right] - \sum_{t=1}^{u} \log \left[\sum_{i=1}^{N} \alpha_t(i) \right]$$

$$= \sum_{t=u}^{v} \log \left[\sum_{i=1}^{N} \alpha_t(i) \right],$$ (6.2)

$$2 \leq u, v \leq (T - 1).$$

Given that curve C is an array of log-likelihood from o_1 to all data point o_t, denoted as $C = \{\rho_{12}, \rho_{13}, \rho_{14}, \ldots, \rho_{1t}, \ldots, \rho_{1T}\}$, where $2 \leq t \leq T$.

A sub-curve $C_{uv} \in C$ is a log-likelihood from data point o_u to o_v that has a log-likelihood score of p_{uv}, as described in [37]. One curve consists of one or more non-overlapping sub-curve(s) with respect to discontinuities of log-likelihood curves.

Step 2 [Find sub-curve C_{uv}]: The curve C is passed on to Algorithm 6.1 (Find Sub-Curve algorithm), which uses log-likelihood trends to find discontinuities and splits the curve C into sub-curve C_{uv}. From reverse engineering perspective, each iteration of finding matching probability between λ and API call o_t yields a similar likelihood value to its neighbor INS (e.g. o_{t+1}, o_{t+2}, and so on). This makes a smooth curve when visualized as a line graph of likelihood-API sequence. The area of the smooth curve is termed as *locality*. The instructions sequence within the same locality will give a similar likelihood score, whereas the different localities might have different trends. The trend of locality indicates how likely the sequence O matched with HMM λ. Since the training data contains more malicious actions than the generic activities, the series with higher similarity score is assumed to be more suspicious. Finding discontinuities aims to separate the period of harmful acts from normal program's executions.

As shown in Algorithm 6.1, the curve is divided into small segments with a fixed window size of 500 data points. The size indicates the number of instructions that could be included in the same set of activities. During our experiments, the window size was varied to find the approximate value that is suitable for detecting suspicious activities. Then, for each window, the trend of matching scores (i.e. slope of the Sub-Curve C_{uv}) is computed using a fraction of log-likelihood change per the number of instructions. The trend value of the previous connecting window is compared with the current. The algorithm decides whether the trends are not to be continued by using the lower and upper thresholds (*lowTHOLD* and *upTHOLD* in Algorithm 6.1). These two thresholds provide an indication of a rapid increase or decrease in the trend.

By varying the window size, if the size is too small then the prediction accuracy will be worse since the curve is split into several small pieces. These insignificant fluctuations of the curve occur too frequently; hence, the small window size does not help to create differentiable categories of programs. On the other hand, if the window size is too large, the result becomes closer to the baseline method without the Sub-Curve method because the trend covers too many localities. Also, the

---

Algorithm 6.1 Find Sub-Curve.

Input: *curve, lowTHOLD, upTHOLD*
Output: *splitVector, numSubCurve*
   Initialisation:
1: *numSubCurve* = 1
2: *len* = *size(curve)*
3: *splitVector* = [1, *len*]
4: *window* = 500
5: *maxItr* = *len/window*
6: *from* = 1, *to* = *window*
   For each window find sub-curve:
7: **for** *i* = 1 to *maxItr* **do**
8:    *slope* = *calSlope(curve, from, to)*
    Set first block as a baseline:
9:    **if** (*i* ≠ 1) **then**
10:    *prevSlope* = *slope*
11:    **else**
12:    *change* = *slope/prevSlope*
    Compare the change to the lower/upper thresholds:
13:    **if** (*change* < *lowTHOLD*)
    OR (*change* > *upTHOLD*) **then**
14:      *split* = *from* + *window/2*
      Add a split point at the end of vector:
15:      *splitVector* = [*splitVector*(1 to *end* − 1), *split*,
      splitVector(*end*)]
16:      *numSubCurve* = *numSubCurve* + 1
17:    **end if**
18:    *prevSlope* = *slope*
19: **end if**
20: *from* = *to*, *to* = *to* + *window*
21: **end for**
22: **return** *splitVector*

---

number of sub-curves will be closer to 1, which gives original score of the whole sequence (ρ_{1T}).

Step 3 [Compute LLPO vector]: This step calculates similarity vector for all Sub-Curve(s). Since program's API calls vary in length, the longer sequence has lesser accumulative likelihood compared to the short one, i.e. as shown in Eq. (6.2), the final result is an accumulation of negative values. Hence, to avoid *length dependent* issue, the log-likelihood scores need to be converted to a length-independent feature value. This problem is addressed using log-likelihood per line of code (LLPO) score [4] that uses the length to normalize differences between API sequences. Equation (6.3) shows function δ used to compute LLPO score from the Sub-Curve C_{uv}:

$$\delta(C_{uv}) = \frac{\rho_{uv}}{v - u}. \tag{6.3}$$

The LLPO vector collects scores of Sub-Curve C_{uv} from the same curve C. These scores are used to determine the most suspicious Sub-Curve in the Sub-Curve replacement process.

Step 4 [Sub-Curve replacement]: If two or more Sub-Curves C_{uv} are found in Step 2, the curve replacement candidate C^{rc} is determined based on weight and impact factors. The weight W of a Sub-Curve C is computed using the length of the API sequence. Given T as the total length of the curve C, the weight of the replacement candidate C^{rc}, denoted as $W(C^{rc})$, is defined as follows:

$$W(C^{rc}) = \frac{length(C^{rc})}{T}. \tag{6.4}$$

The candidate Sub-Curves are sorted descending using the LLPO vector from the curve with highest LLPO score to the lowest one. Hence, the top of the list is the most suspicious Sub-Curve. Since the sequence is broken down into small parts, several incomplete series of API calls that are too short will be picked up easily (considered as noise). In order to eliminate the noise, the threshold of impact factor *impactTHOLD* is used to determine the significance of the Sub-Curve by comparing with the weight $W(C^{rc})$:

$$W(C^{rc}) \geq impactTHOLD. \tag{6.5}$$

If the condition in Eq. (6.5) is satisfied, then the replacement Sub-Curve C^r is chosen as the representation of the whole program's behavior ($C^r \leftarrow C^{rc}$). Otherwise, the next candidate in the list is determined. Finally, if there is no candidature Sub-Curve C^{rc} chosen, the original curve is selected ($C^r \leftarrow C^{rc}$). The selected curve is then used to compute the feature scores.

Step 5 [Compute the feature score]: After removing irrelevant period of API sequence using the Sub-Curve method, this step generates the feature vector from the selected curve by comparing with a model's curve, which comes from testing the particular HMM with its training data.

Although testing the trained HMM with the training data should give the best matching result, the matching possibility does not guarantee to be 100% because the training process is terminated when the tolerance threshold is reached. The idea is to compare how close the trend of the selected curve C^r compared to the ideal that is self-tested model's curve (C^λ). Intuitively, the two area values between C^λ and C^r are used to extract characters of malware and benign program, namely area under curve (AUC) and area over curve (AOC). For ease of referencing, AUC and AOC are grouped together and referred to as *ABCScore* (area between curves score).

Algorithm 6.2 computes *ABCScore* based on idea of finding average area under and over model's curve. Data points from both curves are graphically compared to formulate average area under and over curve C^λ (referred to as `areaUC` and `areaOC`). If the data point of C^r has lower value than C^λ, the absolute value from data points difference is accumulated in `areaUC`. Otherwise, `areaOC` variable is added instead. In the end, the area values are average to number of data points added. This makes the score independent from the sequence length.

Algorithm 6.2 Calculate ABCScore.

Input: *curve, splitVector, index, modelCurve*
Output: *areaUC, areaOC*
   Initialize area under and over model's curve:
1: *areaUC, areaOC* = 0
2: *ucPoint, ocPoint* = 0
   Get the selected Sub-Curve:
3: *subCurve* = *getSubCurve(curve, splitVector, index)*
   Find the shortest iteration:
4: *shortestItr* = *shortestItr(subCurve, modelCurve)*
   Accumulate area under and over model's curve:
5: **for** i = 1 to *shortestItr* **do**
6:    **if** (*subCurve(i)* $\geq$ *modelCurve(i)*) **then**
7:       *areaOC*+ = *subCurve(i)* − *modelCurve(i)*
8:       *ocPoint*+ = 1
9:    **else**
10:      *areaUC*+ = *modelCurve(i)* − *subCurve(i)*
11:      *ucPoint*+ = 1
12:   **end if**
13: **end for**
   Normalize the area with total number of points:
14: *areaUC* = *areaUC/ucPoint*
15: *areaOC* = *areaOverCurve/ocPoint*
16: **return** *areaUC, areaOC*

Finally, the element feature vector $S_{i\lambda}$, which consists of `areaUC` and `areaOC`, is computed. This iterative process is performed for all HMM ($\lambda_1, \ldots, \lambda_6$) that generates a feature vector F from the testing program i denoted by $F_i = \{S_{i\lambda_1 1}, S_{i\lambda_1 2}, S_{i\lambda_2 1}, S_{i\lambda_2 2}, \ldots, S_{i\lambda_6 1}, S_{i\lambda_6 2}\}$.

6.3.4 Malware Detection

The last step is to classify unknown programs into either clean or malware using the feature vector, i.e. 12 features from each program. The study we conducted has chosen the four following well-known binary classifiers used in related work [3, 21, 22]: OneR (One Rule) [38], J48 (C4.5 Decision Tree) [39], RF (Random Forest) [39], and SVM [40]. OneR and SVM work based on finding an optimal linear threshold to separate between two classes of programs, whereas J48 and RF build a tree of decision rules for classification. Only one classifier is needed in this method, and others are used for a benchmark. The details about the training and testing classifiers are as follows.

6.3.4.1 Training Detection Classifier

Let O^{F_j} denotes the training API sequences from malware family F_j, whereas B denotes a set of API sequence from benign software. The detection classifier X_{F_j} for malware family F_j is trained by:

$$\{O^{F_j}, B\} \rightarrow X_{F_j} \quad j \in \{1, \dots, 6\}. \tag{6.6}$$

The training data varies in balance of classes and average length of API calls. Since the number of available malware is different in each family, the proportions of malware per benign used to train the binary classifier are not the same. Also, as the training samples consist of various application types (e.g. console, wizard, web page, and win32 application with or without GUI), the sequences of executing instructions vary in length depending on group of software.

6.3.4.2 Detect Malware

During this step, the trained classifiers are used to classify unknown programs into either malware or clean software. Each program i has its features F_i extracted using the described Sub-Curve extraction method. Afterward, the trained classifier X is used to determine whether the observed API call sequence belongs to malware or clean software.

The set of classifiers $X = \{X_{F_1}, \dots, X_{F_6}\}$ are used to test each malware family separately. For example, the classifier X_{F_1} is used to classify unknown which consists of malware samples from F_1 and clean software B. During the evaluation of the proposed method, this study did not include samples from other malware families in the wild. In other words, the testing samples were members of either benign or one out of six selected malware families that were not used in training.

6.4 Evaluation

This section describes the experimental environment and the various conducted steps. The intent here is to benchmark the efficiency of Sub-Curve HMM against well-known and relevant methods.

6.4.1 Datasets

Various API call-based datasets have been used by the methods summarized in Section 6.2, such as VX Heavens [41], Malicia [42], Malheur [32], and APIMDS [6] datasets. These unfortunately are no longer published or outdated. This research therefore collected the most recent malware binary samples from Virusshare.com [43], one of the largest malicious repositories in the world. However, with over 30 million samples, our study cannot process all the data as Virusshare.com only provided malware binary files without meta-data descriptions. What is needed is to manually query each malware meta-data (i.e. file type and malware family) from the separated web service. Therefore, only malware samples submitted to Virusshare's database in 12 months period (i.e. April 2017–March 2018) will be used as Virrushare.com limited the number of query results.

Based on malware behavior that considered as data exfiltration threats reported by Symantec Corporation [16] and Check Point Research [17], the following six malware families were selected for this experiment:

- *Keylogger*: This variant steals user information directly by captures keystrokes and may save locally or send out via email [44].
- *Zeus*: It is also known as Zbot. It steals banking information via logging keystroke or form on a browser and creates a botnet from compromised machines [45].
- *Ransom*: The old variant that became popular again in the recent year. It is well known as a malware captures victim's data and asks them paying money to unlock their own files [46].
- *Ramnit*: This group considered a removable drive Trojan that steals banking credentials, FTP passwords, session cookies, and personal data [47].
- *Hivecoin*: Since cryptocurrency has become popular recently, Hivecoin is a new tool to harvest digital money using victims' machines. It is a web-based malware that uses website visitors' computer to mine the cryptocurrency. In addition, they also try to steal a coin from victims [48].
- *Lokibot*: The Trojan that steals various sensitive information, including keystroke, FTP, ssh, and email credentials. It could turn into Ransom when users try to remove it [49].

Since there was no precise measurement to associate a label with a suspicious sample, labeling cannot be done by looking at the family name given by a particular antivirus engine. As a given binary may be detected and classified differently by a number of antivirus software, a binary that was labeled as a particular malware family by less than three disparate AV engines was discarded. The reason was to avoid false negative from malware family assignment. The meta-data provided by Virusshare's database [43] is used in samples selection.

Table 6.3 Malware dataset.

Family	No. of malware	AVG API INS	Malware/benign
Hivecoin	115	4819	0.55
Ramnit	121	12,680	0.58
Lokibot	110	24,805	0.52
Ransom	192	27,082	0.91
Zeus	127	34,936	0.60
Keylogger	93	76,101	0.44

Table 6.3 shows the malware dataset used in the experiments. The number of files used varies depending on the actual data collected. A few numbers of samples were dismissed in the experiment because they were not working on the testing environment. For example, the malware did not find the library required to execute its own code, or the malware detected the sandbox setup and refused to work. If the length of instruction series was shorter than 100, then this was also discarded. The length of API sequence was different between group sets. The average number of API INS was presented under *Average API INS* column.

Table 6.3 *column Malware/benign* depicts the ratio of malware vs. benign population. Although there were 42 original benign instances (see Table 6.4), the number of benign instances in the classification stage was 210. This is because malware and benign software were processed differently under the proposed method. First, no benign software was used in the HMM training during the training phase. Secondly, fivefold cross-validation was used to ensure the result

Table 6.4 Benign dataset.

alg	calc	certUtil	charmap
cipher	cleanmgr	cliconfg	ctfmon
cmdl32	dpicaling	driverquery	dvdplay
eventcreate	edit	eventvwr	grpconv
ipconfig	magnify	mrt	mspaint
narrator	netstat	notepad	nslookup
osk	regedit	sndvol	snippingtool
sort	soundrecorder	stikynot	syskey
taskmgr	taskchd	verifier	wf
where	winhlp32	wmimgmt	write
wscript	systempropertiescomputername		

was accurate throughout the dataset. Hence, each group of data was separated into five partitions. Across five iterations, four folds were used for training and one fold for testing. A new fold was chosen every round until all group set has been used for testing. As a result, the number of original benign was multiplied by five folds, which resulted in 210 instances. For this reason, Malware/Benign ratio varied from 0.44 to 0.91 with respect to the number of malicious specimen. Apart from that, the undersampling method [50] was used to normalize the Malware/Benign portion with the non-HMM method (i.e. Information Gain) to maintain the same class balance ratio as the HMM-based methods.

For the dataset of benign software, 42 pre-installed programs in Microsoft Windows 7 32-bit edition were chosen. This benign dataset is mostly identical to the one in [3], which is the reference baseline for the experiments. Names of the benign software are listed in Table 6.4.

6.4.2 Experimental Settings

The machine used in the experiments was CPU Intel Xeon E5-1650@3.2 GHz, 32 GB of RAM, and 500 GB of storage space. The operating system was Linux Ubuntu 16.04 LTS 64-bit edition. API sequence behavior was extracted by using Cuckoo Automate Malware Analysis sandbox 2.0.1 [31], since it was a trampoline-based module for API hooking. Cuckoo was chosen as the preferred sandbox as it was found to be faster and more secure than other open-source sandboxes [30]. The web-based analysis framework was also suitable for large-scale malware binaries. Furthermore, since it was under active development, so it was a better option for analyzing a newer malicious code compared to Sandboxie [51] or CWSandbox [52]. Since our study focused on Windows-based malware, the honeypot machine was configured with Microsoft Windows 7 32-bit edition and running on Virtualbox 5.1.34r121010.

Tools for processing API sequence data were MATLAB R2017b and Weka 3.8 [53]. Initial HMM training parameters such as transition matrix A and observation probability matrix B were random with $\sum_j a_{ij} = 1$ and $\sum_k b_i(o_k) = 1$. However, since the length of training set was long, these random parameters did not affect the output model.

6.4.3 Malware Classification Methods

Since the dataset used in this work was new, Sub-Curve HMM will be thus compared with the commonly used algorithms (i.e. IG by Yang and Pedersen [54], an existing HMM-based method by Damodaran et al. [3]) to evaluate its performance. Additionally, as described in Section 6.3.3, Sub-Curve HMM has two subcomponents (i.e. **Step 4**: *Sub-Curve replacement* and **Step 5**: *Compute* *the feature score*) which will need to be evaluated. To isolate the results from each subcomponent, three sets of malware classification systems were implemented based on Sub-Curve HMM that either partly included a subcomponent or included all components. The details of the classification systems used for benchmarking are as follows:

- **IG** (Information Gain) [54] uses frequencies of total number of each API INS observed and selects discriminating features by choosing the topmost features that give discriminated information. For example, the total number of a particular API INS can distinguish malicious from benign programs. In this chapter, the six top discriminating API INS were used as features. The structural entropy-based method is one of the effective solutions because malware family shares common functions and behaviors.
- **STD-HMM** (Standard HMM) [3] is chosen because it has shown good accuracy in malware detection, and Sub-Curve HMM is built based on the same HMM method. The feature vector of program i comes from a LLPO score, which is computed using the α-pass algorithm.
- **SC-HMM** (Sub-curve HMM) has a subcomponent method, called SC (Sub-Curve), which applied a *sub-curve replacement* to modify the log-likelihood curve if Sub-Curve is presented (see Section 6.3.3 Step 4). However, AUCScore in Step 5 is not used here. Hence, a vector of feature scores comes from LLPO score $\delta(C^r)$ of the selected Sub-Curve C^r directly.
- **ABC-HMM** (Area Between Curves HMM) has a second subcomponent, called ABC-HMM method, which does not apply *sub-curve replacement* step. Instead, the original curve C is compared with model's curve (C^λ) to generate *ABCScore* by using AUC method described in Section 6.3.3 Step 5.
- **SABC-HMM** (Sub-Curve and Area Between Curves HMM) is the complete Sub-Curve HMM method, which includes all subcomponents from *SC-HMM* and *ABC-HMM* methods as described in Section 6.3.

Additionally, the SABC-HMM method has been compared with well-known real-world antivirus engines. The aim is not to directly compare the Sub-Curve HMM's system with the complete antivirus software solutions but to give a reference of how the presented method performs compared to the real-world antivirus scanner. A detailed comparisons are discussed in Section 6.5.4.

6.4.4 Metrics

To evaluate the efficiency of the Sub-Curve HMM method in detecting malware, three different metrics were chosen based on the coverage of both positive and negative prediction results. These metrics are *accuracy*, *precision*, and *recall*. Specifically, the classifying information consists of two classes: malware (positive) and benign software (negative). Metrics used to benchmark the proposed method with existing baselines are *accuracy (ACC), precision (PR)*, and *recall (RC)*.

Let *TP* and *FP* denote true/false positive, which are number of correct or incorrect predictions of the malware (i.e. positive). Also, let *TN* and *FN* denote true/false negative, which refer to the number of correct and incorrect classifications of the legitimate software. Metrics used in the evaluation are described as follows:

Accuracy (ACC) shows overall performance of malware classification method. It covers correct prediction of both malware and benign software in combination. *ACC* defined as:

$$ACC = \frac{(TP + TN)}{(TP + TN + FN + FP)}. \tag{6.7}$$

Precision (PR) focuses on the number of malware that is not detected by the detection system. *PR* is a proportion between the number of malware detected (*TP*) compared to total number of malicious programs in the testing dataset (*TP + FP*). *PR* can be calculated by:

$$PR = \frac{TP}{(TP + FP)}. \tag{6.8}$$

Recall: In order to highlight the rate of false detection on benign software, Recall (*RC*) is used by including a proportion of correctly classified malware (*TP*) compared to all malware prediction (*TP + FN*). *RC* is defined as:

$$RC = \frac{TP}{(TP + FN)}. \tag{6.9}$$

Although the higher ACC indicates a better efficiency of a given detection system, PR and RC can be used in conjunction to further analyze how a given system performs in detecting malware and benign software. For instance, the system is considered inefficient even if is it has detected all malicious programs (i.e. PR = 1.0), but it has also included false alarming (FP) that detected a clean program to be malignant. Additionally, the experiments compared the aforementioned metrics on different lengths of API sequences to evaluate robustness in detecting malicious behaviors from the long API sequences.

6.5 Experimental Results

This section summarizes the experimental results of every component of the Sub-Curve HMM method as well as comparing them with baseline methods. Section 6.5.1 discusses the results from SC-HMM method, and the outcomes from ABC-HMM are presented in Section 6.5.2. Finally, outputs from the complete Sub-Curve HMM implementation SABC-HMM) is analyzed in Section 6.5.3.

6.5.1 Results for SC-HMM Method

Table 6.5 shows the detection accuracy results for six malware variants. The column Tech. depicts the implementation of different methods, whereas the column CLF indicates classifier used. Malware Family (INS Length) column presents a family name of malware sorted by average length of API call INS, ascending from left to right. Rows are grouped by implementation methods, namely IG, STD-HMM, SC-HMM, ABC-HMM, and SABC-HMM. Each row consists of results based on the different classifiers, namely OneR, J48, RF,

Table 6.5 A comparison of malware detection accuracy (%) of proposed method[a].

Tech	CLF	Malware family (INS length)						
		Hivecoin (4819)	Ramnit (12,680)	Lokibot (24,805)	Ransom (27,082)	Zeus (34,936)	Keylogger (76,101)	AVG
IG	OneR	78.46	92.42	67.19	70.00	67.16	71.67	74.25
	J48	86.15	92.42	79.68	77.50	80.60	70.00	81.10
	RF	92.31	92.42	87.50	76.25	79.10	73.33	83.12
	SVM	80.00	92.42	80.00	53.75	64.18	70.00	71.88
STD-HMM	OneR	**100.00**	96.98	87.81	83.58	88.13	80.20	89.23
	J48	**100.00**	96.68	86.56	79.10	86.94	82.84	88.10
	RF	**100.00**	98.49	91.25	85.57	87.83	83.83	90.89
	SVM	**100.00**	88.52	84.06	52.24	62.31	69.31	74.20
SC-HMM[a]	OneR	**100.00**	97.89	85.94	85.07	82.49	84.49	89.07
	J48	**100.00**	**99.40**	94.38	94.28	92.58	87.79	94.86
	RF	**100.00**	99.09	93.13	93.78	94.07	92.74	95.41
	SVM	**100.00**	97.58	84.38	78.61	64.69	79.21	83.60
ABC-HMM[a]	OneR	**100.00**	98.79	84.69	81.84	86.05	69.31	86.86
	J48	99.69	98.49	93.44	92.78	93.77	90.10	94.68
	RF	**100.00**	98.79	**96.25**	94.78	95.25	92.08	96.18
	SVM	**100.00**	97.58	85.31	79.35	63.20	79.54	83.71
SABC-HMM[a]	OneR	**100.00**	98.49	83.75	82.09	83.38	82.84	88.07
	J48	99.69	96.98	92.25	92.29	94.07	88.45	93.83
	RF	99.69	99.09	95.63	**95.77**	**96.44**	**94.72**	**96.86**
	SVM	**100.00**	97.58	86.25	79.85	74.78	85.15	86.25

The highest value (which is the average result for each malware type) in each column is highlighted in **bold**.
a) Proposed method refers to SC-HMM, ABC-HMM ad SABC-HMM.

and SVM. The column AVG shows detection accuracy (%) weighted by total number of malware in the particular family compared to the total number of the experimenting dataset.

Overall, the SC-HMM method outperforms the STD-HMM method in all cases. Furthermore, it had a larger improvement over the IG compared to the HMM baseline. As shown in Table 6.5: column Hivecoin and Ramnit, the HMM-based methods performed very well compared to the other methods (i.e. ranging from column Lokibot to Keylogger, where the accuracy decreased over the increasing API INS length). Specifically, SC-HMM and STD-HMM detected 100% of Hivecoin malware and nearly all of Ramnit variants (around 98–99%). The high accuracy was consistent with existing work [6] when API INS was short. The experiment observed no negative results from SC-HMM implementation over the baseline STD-HMM method, where Algorithm 6.1 was implemented.

On the other hand, the SC-HMM method detected malware at a higher rate (approximately 92–94%) even if the sequence length increased from 24k INS (Lokibot family) up to around 76k INS (Keylogger variant) when using RF classifier (see Figure 6.7a). Meanwhile, the baseline IG performed worse when the number of INS was rising. For instance, the accuracy went down from around 87% to 73% that was around 6–20% lower than SC-HMM method. Also, the HMM baseline was affected when the API INS series was longer. For instance, its accuracy went down from just over 91% to less than 84%. Hence, gaps between the baseline methods and the proposed method were widened when API sequences getting longer.

Since the finding Sub-Curve method helped to separate the whole sequence of program behaviors into smaller subsequences of behavior, some of the activities that did not attract the testing HMM were discarded (i.e. Sub-Curves with lower log-likelihood values). Therefore, Algorithm 6.1 showed an improvement over the baseline HMM. However, as malware and benign software shared common API code to perform basic functionalities, these overlapped activities were inevitably included in the training data. Hence, the inaccurate predictions partly came from the limitation of impurities in the training data itself. Additionally, as the current method determined Sub-Curve based on graphical data (visualized character of curves), optimizing the best thresholds for separating Sub-Curve (i.e. lowTHOLD and upTHOLD in Algorithm 6.1) for any length of API INS needed to be addressed further in the future work.

6.5.2 Results for ABC-HMM Method

ABC-HMM implemented the new feature extraction method using area between log-likelihood curves of the testing sample and the model (denoted ABCScore, as described in Algorithm 6.2). This implementation did not apply finding Sub-Curve method, instead, the whole API sequence data had been used to calculate ABCScore.

Figure 6.7a,b illustrates that ABC-HMM had also performed better than STD-HMM with RF and J48 classifiers. The improvement is closed to the SC-HMM method. The line graph of ABC-HMM laid just above SC-HMM method excepted for the group of the longest API sequence (76k INS), which the accuracy dropped to just under SC-HMM at around 92%.

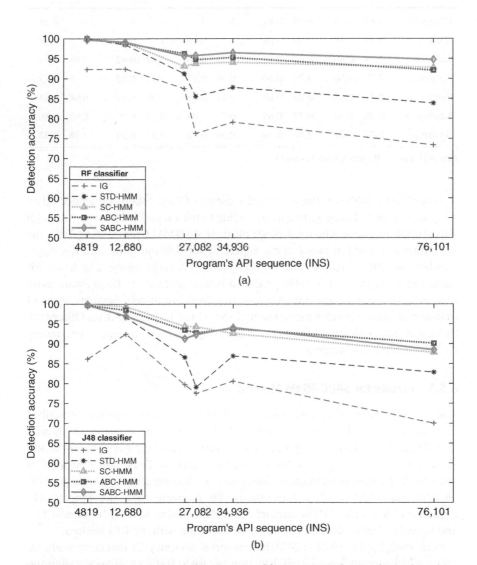

Figure 6.7 Comparison the detection accuracy of feature extraction methods when the API Calls sequence is growing from 4819 to 76,101 INS based-on classifiers: (a) RF (Random Forest) and (b) J48 (C4.5 Decision Tree).

Table 6.6 Comparison of precision and recall of malware detection methods.

Family	Feature extraction methods									
	IG		STD-HMM		SC-HMM		ABC-HMM		SABC-HMM	
	PR	RC	PR	RC	PR	RC	PR	RC	PR	RC
Hivecoin	0.85	0.96	0.99	0.97	1	1	1	1	1	0.99
Ramnit	0.85	0.96	0.98	0.98	1	0.98	1	0.97	1	0.98
Lokibot	0.79	0.86	0.92	0.82	0.93	0.86	0.97	0.92	0.98	0.89
Ransom	0.79	0.68	0.78	0.80	0.96	0.91	0.97	0.92	0.98	0.93
Zeus	0.74	0.68	0.87	0.80	0.94	0.90	0.98	0.89	0.98	0.93
Keylogger	0.56	0.50	0.77	0.68	0.92	0.84	0.95	0.79	0.96	0.86
Average	**0.77**	**0.77**	**0.88**	**0.84**	**0.96**	**0.92**	**0.98**	**0.92**	**0.98**	**0.93**

Results based on Random Forest classifier.

According to Table 6.6, the increased accuracy of ABC-HMM was traded off by a higher number of false alarming, according to the PR and RC metric. Although ABC-HMM produced a better average PR than SC-HMM (from 0.96 to 0.98), the RC values worsened in many cases. Especially for Ramnit, Zeus, and Keylogger families, the PR decreased to 0.97, 0.89, and 0.79, respectively. The lower PR value indicated that ABC-HMM predicted benign software to be malware more than SC-HMM (i.e. having a higher false negative). Intuitively, from an aspect of malware detection development, the tool should not be too sensitive. Otherwise, this could affect efficiency of the system in raising alarms to the user in preventing the data exfiltration incident.

6.5.3 Results for SABC-HMM Method

The last implementation combined both feature extraction methods described in Section 6.3.1: Algorithms 6.1 and 6.2 altogether. The experiment showed that SABC-HMM further improved the detection accuracy over SC-HMM and ABC-HMM. Specifically, in Table 6.5 column Ransom, Zeus, and Keylogger, it showed the highest percentage of detection overall comparing methods (95.77%, 96.44%, and 94.72%). Most importantly, for malware with the longest API sequence (76k), SABC-HMM outperformed the baseline STD-HMM almost 11% and up to 21% better than IG method when working with the RF classifier.

Even though, the SABC-HMM had dropped accuracy in detecting malware group which already have a high detection rate up to 100%, i.e. Hivecoin, Ramnit, and Lokibot, the changes were less than 1%. We suspected the limitation of

ABCScore method that caused false alarm on the benign software to decrease performance on this group of malicious programs. As shown in Table 6.5 column Hivecoin and Ramnit, SC-HMM detected 99–100% of malignant, whereas ABC-HMM had dropped the accuracy a little to around 98%. Lokibot was the only exception where ABC-HMM gave the best result.

Figure 6.8a,b indicate that OneR and SVM classifiers performed much worse compared to RF and J48 classifiers, as shown in Figure 6.7a,b, regardless of baseline method in the conducted experiment. Since the proposed Sub-Curve HMM solution worked based on existing binary classifiers, we conducted experiments on four aforementioned classification tools to find the best compatible classifier with the proposing method.

The outcome indicated that there were subclusters of malware features data in one family. Hence, the classifiers with a single detection threshold, including linear (OneR) and nonlinear (SVM), could not compete with the classifiers based on set of decision rules (i.e. RF and J48). Intuitively, the overlapping characteristics between different malware families or benign software are out of control. Also, one instance of program might perform several tasks that are not common in the group.

6.5.4 Comparison with Other Antivirus Scanners

This section compares the detection rates of SABC-HMM and other antivirus engines. For the facts that the methods used by various commercial antivirus scanners are not available, and the antivirus software is a complete commercialized product and not a research prototype. Several of antivirus scanners use a static signature (i.e. YARA [56]) to train the detection engines as well as other runtime heuristic analysis. Hence, this is not a fair comparison but serves as a reference. In fact, the proposed method could be incorporated in an antivirus engine to improve its heuristic analysis.

The following 10 well-known consumer antivirus scanners were used here to compare with the Sub-Curve HMM method: AVG [57], Avira [58], Baidu [59], BitDefender [60], ESET-NOD32 [61], Kaspersky [62], McAfee [63], Microsoft Windows Defender [64], Symantec [65], and TrendMicro [66]. All selected antivirus engines have been randomly assigned label as AV1 to AV10 for anonymously reference. The detection results were queried from the VirusTotal database [55], where the most up-to-date virus signatures were used by antivirus engines (i.e. January 2020).

Figure 6.9 illustrates the distributions of detection accuracy over six malware families. The box plot [67] shows detection accuracy between quartile 1 and quartile 3. The horizontal line inside the box represents median, whereas the dotted lines and the plus sign show maximum/minimum values and outliers respectively.

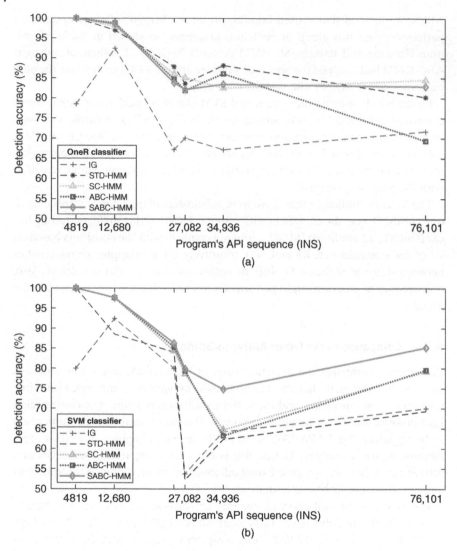

Figure 6.8 Comparison the detection accuracy of feature extraction methods when the API calls sequence is growing from 4819 to 76,101 INS based on classifiers: (a) OneR (One Rule) and (b) SVM (Support Vector Machine).

Generally, SABC-HMM performed consistently good for all malware families (between 95% and 99%), whereas all antivirus scanners showed at least one malware family with the detection accuracy lower than 90%. Besides, differences between median value of the accuracy of SABC-HMM and other antivirus software, especially AV1–AV8, are negligible. Some products, e.g. AV9 and AV10, perform poorly in detecting malware from the dataset used in this chapter.

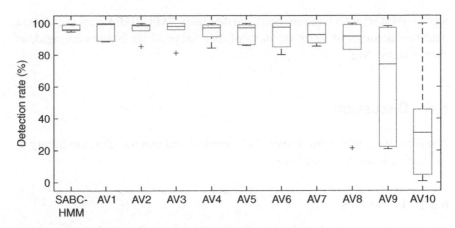

Figure 6.9 Distribution of detection accuracy over six malware families of SABC-HMM and antivirus engines.

Table 6.7 Keyloggers detection rates (%) of Sub-Curve HMM, IG, and 10 antivirus scanners.

Method	Keylogger	Best	Average
SABC-HMM	**94.7**	99.7	**96.9**
STD-HMM	83.8	**100**	90.9
IG	73.3	92.4	83.1
AV1	88.5	**100**	96.5
AV2	85.4	**100**	96.5
AV3	81.3	**100**	96.2
AV4	84.4	**100**	94.8
AV5	86.5	**100**	93.8
AV6	80.2	**100**	92.9
AV7	87.5	**100**	92.3
AV8	83.3	**100**	80.9
AV9	64.6	98.4	66.1
AV10	26.0	**100**	35.7

The highest result of each row is highlighted in **Bold**.

Table 6.7 highlights the effectiveness of SABC-HMM, specifically in detecting Keylogger family which generated the longest API calls sequence out of the six families. Our method detects up to 94.7% compared to 88.5% by the best antivirus scanner (i.e. AV1). Regarding the best case, most antivirus scanners obtain at least 100% detection accuracy on one malware family, whereas the best case of

SABC-HMM is 99.7% (see row Best). Furthermore, SABC-HMM gives the highest detection accuracy of 96.9% vs. 96.5% of AV1 out of all six families averaged, as shown in row Avg.

6.6 Discussion

The limitations of the Sub-Curve HMM method and computation complexity of its overheads are discussed here.

6.6.1 Limitations

Although the empirical study shows promising results that could lead to interesting directions for future work, we realize aspects that need further study as follows:

- *No-op invasion*: Although this method could detect fractions of suspicious activity from the long API sequence of legitimate activities, no-op API inserted between series malignant commands could still degrade the detection system (i.e. Mimicry attack [68]).
- *The use of static threshold*: In Algorithm 6.1, the threshold (i.e. window, lowTHOLD, and upTHOLD) are fixed values set up by manually observed characters of log-likelihood curve. These thresholds should be dynamically chosen according to the trend of sub-curve to accurately determine the sub-curve across datasets. We aim to improve in future study.
- *The HMM training data*: Although the Sub-Curve HMM works based on assumption that HMM is able to match suspicious series of API commands, we currently use the model that trained by the whole sequence of malware behavior. The training data could still contain activities that overlapped between malware and benign software/malware from a different family. Hence, the preprocess of the training API sequence is needed to eliminate unrelated/overlapped calls sequence.
- *Size of the testing dataset*: Although we conducted experiment on similar number of malware sample is our reference method [3], this number is still far from real-world scale. Since we have limited resources to label and test a large volume of recent malicious samples (i.e. with the sandbox connected to the Internet), only six families were tested. In future, we plan to employ the solution [69] to automatically label a large volume of the most recent sample.
- *Dependence of API version*: It is undeniable that a set of API instructions varies on the platform (e.g. operating system or runtime); hence, the changing parameters will impact the prediction result [70]. However, from aspect of the

end user, the heuristic monitoring system is still useful to immediately issue the alarm. On the other hand, a static or hybrid method might use more complex sources of information (e.g. binary, network traffic, etc.) to deeply analyze and create a more specific signature of the threat.

6.6.2 Performance Overheads

When extracting feature from API calls, the Sub-Curve HMM method has additional overhead to the HMM α-pass algorithm. The baseline has time complexity $\mathcal{O}(M^2T)$, where M is the number of unique API commands and T is the length of the API sequence. The additional Sub-Curve extraction (Algorithm 6.1) passes through likelihood curve T/W times, where W is the fixed window size. Also, the feature generation method (Algorithm 6.2) requires T passes through the API sequence. Therefore, the total performance overhead is $(T/W) + T$, whereas the worst-case complexity remains $\mathcal{O}(M^2T)$. In practice, the baseline HMM method and our proposed method can benefit from parallel execution on a multicore CPU system as these methods consist of several matrix multiplication operations. However, we did not have the parallel computing toolbox license for MATLAB; hence, we could not show the speed improvement on the multicore system in this thesis.

On the other hand, time complexity of classifier is minor compared to API feature extraction. RF classifier, which gives the best detection accuracy, has computational complexity of $\mathcal{O}(fn\log(n))$, where f is the number of features and n is total number of the testing sample.

6.7 Summary

This chapter described a feature extraction method based on HMM that makes use of API call sequences. The main element of the Sub-Curve HMM method is subcontained behavior extraction. This allows small pieces of malicious activities contained in a long sequence of observation to be detected.

The limitations of the detection efficiency of HMM and information gain methods were presented, especially when long API call sequences were examined. Compared to existing methods, Sub-Curve HMM outperforms baseline methods across datasets with various average API sequence lengths. This result confirms the ability to match interesting behavior from subsequences of the whole activities observed. Unlike the previous work that focuses on using all information gathered from the specimen, this work requires only parts of activities in detection. Hence, Sub-Curve HMM can be applied in a real-time context where it is not possible to gather all information from suspicious processes. In addition, if this method can be used to monitor only a set of processes accessing sensitive information to prevent data exfiltration incidents. Despite the promising outcomes of Sub-Curve HMM, the feature extracting HMMs are sensitive to the training API sequences with indiscriminate features. As a result, the prediction accuracy is limited by the false alarming rate.

The upcoming chapter will be focusing on detecting the actual sensitive data being accessed by the program, instead of monitoring for the malicious behavior of the running process. Such a method directly checks the physical memory. Hence, the use of sensitive data can be tracked regardless of the program being classified as malicious or benign.

References

1 Faheem Ullah, Matthew Edwards, Rajiv Ramdhany, Ruzanna Chitchyan, M. Ali Babar, and Awais Rashid. Data exfiltration: a review of external attack vectors and countermeasures. *Elsevier Journal of Network and Computer Applications*, 101:18–54, 2018.

2 Dan Conifer. Defence contractor's computer system hacked, files stolen, cyber security report reveals. https://www.abc.net.au/news/2017-10-10/defence-contractors-files-stolen-in-hacking:-security-report/9032290, October 2017.

3 Anusha Damodaran, Fabio Di Troia, Corrado Aaron Visaggio, Thomas H. Austin, and Mark Stamp. A comparison of static, dynamic, and hybrid analysis for malware detection. *Springer Journal of Computer Virology and Hacking Techniques*, 13(1):1–12, 2017.

4 Chinmayee Annachhatre, Thomas H. Austin, and Mark Stamp. Hidden Markov models for malware classification. *Springer Journal of Computer Virology and Hacking Techniques*, 11(2):59–73, 2015.

5 Gerardo Canfora, Francesco Mercaldo, and Corrado Aaron Visaggio. An HMM and structural entropy based detector for android malware: an empirical study. *Elsevier Journal on Computers & Security*, 61:1–18, 2016.

6 Youngjoon Ki, Eunjin Kim, and Huy Kang Kim. A novel approach to detect malware based on API call sequence analysis. *SAGE International Journal of Distributed Sensor Networks*, 11(6):659101, 2015.

7 Sultan Alneyadi, Elankayer Sithirasenan, and Vallipuram Muthukkumarasamy. A survey on data leakage prevention systems. *Journal of Network and Computer Applications*, 62: 137–152, 2016. http://dx.doi.org/10.1016/j.jnca.2016.01.008.

8 Swathi Melkundi and Chaitali Chandankhede. A robust technique for relational database watermarking and verification. In *Proceedings of the International Conference on Communication, Information & Computing Technology*, pages 1–7, Mumbai, India, 2015.

9 Pratik C. Patel and Upasna Singh. Detection of data theft using fuzzy inference system. In *Proceedings of the 3rd IEEE International Advance Computing Conference*, pages 702–707, Ghaziabad, India, 2013.

10 Kevin Richards, Floris van den Dool, and Joshua Kennedy-White. Cost of cyber crime study: insights on the security investments that make a difference. Technical report, Accenture, 2017.

11 Saurabh Verma and Abhishek Singh. Data theft prevention & endpoint protection from unauthorized USB devices-implementation. In *Proceedings of the 4th IEEE International Conference on Advanced Computing*, pages 1–4, Chennai, India, 2012.

12 Damian Poddebniak, Christian Dresen, Jens Müller, Fabian Ising, Sebastian Schinzel, Simon Friedberger, Juraj Somorovsky, and Jörg Schwenk. Efail: breaking S/MIME and OpenPGP email encryption using exfiltration channels. In *Proceedings of the 27th USENIX Security Symposium*, pages 549–566, Baltimore, MD, USA, 2018.

13 Gary Cantrell and David D. Dampier. Experiments in hiding data inside the file structure of common office documents: a stegonography application. In *Proceedings of the ACM International Symposium on Information and Communication Technologies*, pages 146–151, Las Vegas, NV, USA, 2004.

14 Wei Huang, Yao Dong, Ana Milanova, and Julian Dolby. Scalable and precise taint analysis for android. In *Proceedings of the 2015 International Symposium on Software Testing and Analysis*, pages 106–117, Baltimore, MD, USA, 2015.

15 Songyang Wu, Pan Wang, Xun Li, and Yong Zhang. Effective detection of android malware based on the usage of data flow APIs and machine learning. *Elsevier Journal on Information and Software Technology*, 75:17–25, 2016.

16 Symantec Corporation. Symantec internet security threat report 2017. Technical report, Symantec Corp. https://www.symantec.com/content/dam/symantec/docs/reports/istr-22-2017-en.pdf, 2017.

17 Check Point Research. H2 2017 Global Threat Intelligence Trends Report. Technical report, Check Point Technologies Ltd. https://research.checkpoint.com/h2-2017-global-threat-intelligence-trends-report, 2018.

18 Wing Wong and Mark Stamp. Hunting for metamorphic engines. *Journal in Computer Virology*, 2(3):211–229, 2006.

19 Edward Raff, Richard Zak, Russell Cox, Jared Sylvester, Paul Yacci, Rebecca Ward, Anna Tracy, Mark McLean, and Charles Nicholas. An investigation of byte n-gram features for malware classification. *Elsevier Journal of Computer Virology and Hacking Techniques*, 14(1):1–20, 2018.

20 Fengguo Wei, Sankardas Roy, Xinming Ou, et al. Amandroid: a precise and general inter-component data flow analysis framework for security vetting of android apps. In *Proceedings of the ACM SIGSAC Conference on Computer and Communications Security (CCS)*, pages 1329–1341, Scottsdale, AZ, 2014.

21 Yujie Fan, Yanfang Ye, and Lifei Chen. Malicious sequential pattern mining for automatic malware detection. *Elsevier Journal of Expert Systems with Applications*, 52:16–25, 2016.

22 Bojan Kolosnjaji, Apostolis Zarras, George Webster, and Claudia Eckert. Deep learning for classification of malware system call sequences. In *Proceedings of the Australasian Joint Conference on Artificial Intelligence*, pages 137–149, Hobart, Australia, 2016. Springer.

23 Shahid Alam, Zhengyang Qu, Ryan Riley, Yan Chen, and Vaibhav Rastogi. DroidNative: semantic-based detection of android native code malware. *arXiv preprint arXiv:1602.04693*, 2016.

24 Andrew Henderson, Lok Kwong Yan, Xunchao Hu, Aravind Prakash, Heng Yin, and Stephen McCamant. DECAF: a platform-neutral whole-system dynamic binary analysis platform. *IEEE Transactions on Software Engineering*, 43(2):164–184, 2017.

25 Shamsul Huda, Jemal Abawajy, Mali Abdollahian, Rafiqul Islam, and John Yearwood. A fast malware feature selection approach using a hybrid of multi-linear and stepwise binary logistic regression. *Concurrency and Computation: Practice and Experience*, 29(23):e3912, 2017.

26 Itzik Kotler and Amit Klein. The adventures of AV and the leaky sandbox. https://www.safebreach.com/resources/in-plain-sight-the-perfect-exfiltration-research-report/, 2017.

27 Lorenzo Martignoni, Mihai Christodorescu, and Somesh Jha. OmniUnpack: fast, generic, and safe unpacking of malware. In *Proceedings of the 23rd Annual Computer Security Applications Conference*, pages 431–441, Miami Beach, FL, USA, 2007.

28 Amin Kharraz, Sajjad Arshad, Collin Mulliner, William K. Robertson, and Engin Kirda. UNVEIL: a large-scale, automated approach to detecting ransomware. In *Proceedings of the 25th USENIX Security Symposium*, pages 757–772, Austin, TX, USA, 2016.

29 Abir Awad, Sara Kadry, Guraraj Maddodi, Saul Gill, and Brian Lee. Data leakage detection using system call provenance. In *Proceedings of the 2016 International Conference on Intelligent Networking and Collaborative Systems*, pages 486–491, Ostrawva, Czech Republic, 2016.

30 Yong Qiao, Yuexiang Yang, Jie He, Chuan Tang, and Zhixue Liu. CBM: free, automatic malware analysis framework using api call sequences. In *Proceedings of the 7th Springer International Conference on Intelligent Systems and Knowledge Engineering*, pages 225–236, Beijing, China, 2014.

31 Digit Oktavianto and Iqbal Muhardianto. *Cuckoo Malware Analysis*. Packt Publishing Ltd., 2013.

32 Konrad Rieck, Philipp Trinius, Carsten Willems, and Thorsten Holz. Automatic analysis of malware behavior using machine learning. *Journal of Computer Security*, 19(4):639–668, 2011.

33 Aziz Mohaisen, Omar Alrawi, and Manar Mohaisen. AMAL: high-fidelity, behavior-based automated malware analysis and classification. *Elsevier Journal on Computers & Security*, 52:251–266, 2015.

34 Gernot A. Fink. *Markov Models for Pattern Recognition: From Theory to Applications*. Springer, 2nd edition, 2014.

35 Antonio Torralba, Kevin P. Murphy, William T. Freeman, and Mark A. Rubin. Context-based vision system for place and object recognition. In *Proceedings of the IEEE International Conference on Computer Vision*, pages 1–8, Nice, France, 2003.

36 Lawrence R. Rabiner and Biing-Hwang Juang. *Fundamentals of Speech Recognition*, volume 14. Prentice-Hall, Inc., Upper Saddle River, NJ, USA, 1993. ISBN 0-13-015157-2.

37 Leonard E. Baum and Ted Petrie. Statistical inference for probabilistic functions of finite state Markov chains. *The Annals of Mathematical Statistics*, 37(6):1554–1563, 1966.

38 Robert C. Holte. Very simple classification rules perform well on most commonly used datasets. *Springer Journal of Machine Learning*, 11(1):63–90, 1993.

39 Leo Breiman. Random forests. *Springer Journal of Machine Learning*, 45(1):5–32, 2001.

40 S. Sathiya Keerthi, Shirish Krishnaj Shevade, Chiranjib Bhattacharyya, and Karuturi Radha Krishna Murthy. Improvements to platt's SMO algorithm for SVM classifier design. *Neural Computation*, 13(3):637–649, 2001.

41 VX Heavens. Virus collection. http://vxheaven.org/vl.php, 2008.

42 Antonio Nappa, M. Zubair Rafique, and Juan Caballero. The MALICIA dataset: identification and analysis of drive-by download operations. *Springer International Journal of Information Security*, 14(1):15–33, 2015.

43 J.-Michael Roberts. https://VirusShare.com, 2018.

44 S Shetty. Introduction to spyware keyloggers. Technical report, Symantec Security Response, 2010. https://www.symantec.com/connect/articles/introduction-spyware-keyloggers.

45 Nicolas Falliere and Eric Chien. Zeus: King of the bots. Technical report, Symantec Security Response, 2009. https://www.symantec.com/content/en/us/enterprise/media/security_response/whitepapers/zeus_king_of_bots.pdf.

46 Kevin Savage, Peter Coogan, and Hon Lau. The evolution of ransomware. Technical report, Symantec Corp., Mountain View, CA, USA, 2015. https://www.symantec.com/content/en/us/enterprise/media/security_response/whitepapers/the-evolution-of-ransomware.pdf.

47 Trend Micro. RAMNIT - threat encyclopedia. https://www.trendmicro.com/vinfo/us/threat-encyclopedia/malware/ramnit, 2014.

48 Tim Hux and Norris Brazier. Malware mines, steals cryptocurrencies from victims. Technical report, McAfee Labs, 2017. https://securingtomorrow.mcafee.com/mcafee-labs/malware-mines-steals-cryptocurrencies-from-victims/.

49 Alexandra Golovina. LokiBot: if not stealing, then extorting. Technical report, Kaspersky, 2017. https://www.kaspersky.com/blog/lokibot-trojan/20030/.

50 Yunan Zhang, Qingjia Huang, Xinjian Ma, Zeming Yang, and Jianguo Jiang. Using multi-features and ensemble learning method for imbalanced malware classification. In *Proceedings of the IEEE Trustcom/BigDataSE/ISPA Conferences*, pages 965–973, Tianjin, China, 2016.

51 R. Tzur. Sandboxie trust no program: getting started. https://community.sophos.com/sandboxie/, 2012.

52 Carsten Willems, Thorsten Holz, and Felix Freiling. CWSandbox: towards automated dynamic binary analysis. *IEEE Security & Privacy*, 5(2):32–39, 2007.

53 Ian H. Witten, Eibe Frank, Mark A. Hall, and Christopher J. Pal. *Data Mining: Practical Machine Learning Tools and Techniques*. Morgan Kaufmann, 2016. http://dx.doi.org/10.1016/C2009-0-19715-5.

54 Yiming Yang and Jan O. Pedersen. A comparative study on feature selection in text categorization. In *Proceedings of the 14th International Conference on Machine Learning*, volume 97, pages 412–420, San Francisco, CA, USA, 1997.

55 Virus Total. VirusTotal-Free online virus, malware and URL scanner. https://www.virustotal.com/en, 2018.

56 Virus Total. VirusTotal/YARA: the pattern matching swiss knife. https://github.com/virustotal/yara#whos-using-yara, 2020.

57 Avast Software s.r.o. AVG 2020 Free Antivirus. https://www.avg.com/, 2020.

58 Avira Operations GmbH & Co. KG. Avira Antivirus. https://antivirus.avira.com/, 2020.

59 Baidu. Baidu Antivirus. http://antivirus.baidu.com/, 2016.

60 Bitdefender Australia. Bitdefender Australia - Cybersecurity Solutions for Business and Personal Use. https://www.bitdefender.com.au/, 2020.

61 ESET North America. Antivirus and Internet Security Don't Get Hacked. Get ESET. https://www.eset.com/, 2020.

62 Kaspersky Lab Australia. Computer Security Products for Home Users. https://www.kaspersky.com.au, 2020.

63 McAfee, LLC. McAfee Total Protection. https://www.mcafee.com/, 2020.

64 Microsoft. Windows 10 Security, Windows Defender Antivirus, Firewall and Windows Hello. https://www.microsoft.com/en-au/windows/comprehensive-security, 2020.

65 Broadcom Inc. Symantec - Global Leader In Next Generation Cyber Security. https://www.symantec.com/, 2020.

66 Trend Micro Inc. Antivirus Plus Security Software Trend Micro. https://www
.trendmicro.com/en_au/forHome/products/antivirus-plus.html, 2020.

67 Robert Dawson. How significant is a boxplot outlier? *Journal of Statistics
Education*, 19(2), 2011. https://doi.org/10.1080/10691898.2011.11889610.

68 David Wagner and Paolo Soto. Mimicry attacks on host-based intrusion detection systems. In *Proceedings of the 9th ACM Conference on Computer and
Communications Security (CCS)*, pages 255–264, 2002.

69 Marcos Sebastián, Richard Rivera, Platon Kotzias, and Juan Caballero.
AVCLASS: a tool for massive malware labeling. In *Proceeding of the Springer
International Symposium on Research in Attacks, Intrusions, and Defenses*,
pages 230–253, Paris, France, 2016.

70 Davide Canali, Andrea Lanzi, Davide Balzarotti, Christopher Kruegel, Mihai
Christodorescu, and Engin Kirda. A quantitative study of accuracy in system
call-based malware detection. In *Proceedings of the ACM International Symposium on Software Testing and Analysis*, pages 122–132, 2012.

7

Memory-Based Data Exfiltration Detection Methods

Monitoring a system's running processes to detect if there is a tendency of program's behaviors toward data exfiltration is a crucial measure to prevent ongoing data breaches, especially by malware. However, a sophisticated attacker or insider threat could simply evade the behavior monitoring system by using a benign program to export or transfer sensitive data. Hence, it is advantageous to know whether a program is possessing a sensitive document regardless of being classified as malicious or benign by the malware scanner. Intuitively, this knowledge can be analyzed either by a security specialist or an automated software to detect the abnormal behavior of an employee or to simply identify an advanced data exfiltration malware that could not be detected using existing methods.

Instead of scanning for malicious programs, this chapter describes Fast-lookup Bag-of-Words (so-called FBoW) as an effective method for the data exfiltration problem based on monitoring for the presence of a sensitive document in the physical memory. Section 7.1 motivates the problem, and existing solutions and their limitations are discussed in Section 7.2. Section 7.3 formally defines the problem and also describes the terms used in this chapter. Section 7.4 provides details of the FBoW method followed by the experimental evaluation in Section 7.5. A summary of this chapter is given in Section 7.6.

7.1 Motivation

Existing data leakage prevention (DLP) methods attempt to prevent data exfiltration by limiting access to a host machine/network [1]. The host-based prevention method includes, but is not limited to, access control, encryption [2], and scanning the data-in-use or data-at-rest. The network-based method includes firewall, network traffic monitoring for the data in-transit transit, anomaly detection, and log-based detection. However, sensitive data can be exfiltrated through various

Data Exfiltration Threats and Prevention Techniques: Machine Learning and Memory-Based Data Security, First Edition. Zahir Tari, Nasrin Sohrabi, Yasaman Samadi, and Jakapan Suaboot.

means or applications, and this, therefore, is not properly captured by existing DLP methods. For instance, a malicious insider can simply use an outbound email or upload it to personal cloud storage. An automated malicious program could evade the detection system by using encryption or steganography methods to hide the exfiltrated data while being exported. Additionally, some recent research works have shown that sensitive data can be transmitted with side channels using either noise over the electric power line [3] or acoustic signals for the data transmission [4].

To monitor data exfiltration on various channels, this chapter focuses on analyzing the runtime data of the random access memory (RAM). Intuitively, RAM is the single place that all the data needs to be loaded into before any application can process the data, e.g. encrypting, duplicating, or transmitting out of the system. Even if an insider threat attempts to steal sensitive information by reading from the screen and typing on an instant messaging(IM) application, that information exists as fragments of data accessed by the IM client process in the memory. The threat actor does not need to use any special application or communication channel for the mentioned exfiltration. Even though the appearance of sensitive data in the physical memory does not necessarily mean data leakage, as mentioned, the data stealing could be done by using benign software as well. Therefore, the monitoring for sensitive data in the main memory helps to shortlist processes that could cause the data exfiltration, for instance, malicious or benign software that could be hiding the nefarious purposes in accessing the sensitive data. The list of processes involve with the sensitive information, therefore, will be very useful for the anomaly detection system to determine the suspicious behaviors of the user or programs.

The type of sensitive data varies from fixed-format content (e.g. credit card number, tax file number, etc.) to free-form text (e.g. emails, articles, or internal documents). This work focuses on the latter since the textual content covers a wider range of sensitive data compared to individual fixed-format data. For example, sensitive data can be stored in unformatted text, which can be presented in different formats, e.g. web-page, mobile application, or PDF format.

The memory-based textual sensitive data detection poses new challenges to the existing pattern-matching methods. First, the database of sensitive data contains many documents. The single-pattern-matching methods were designed to detect only one pattern at a time (e.g. Knuth–Morris–Pratt [5], Boyer and Moore [6]). Alternatively, a hash value can be used to match each text document. However, this has weaknesses against document spanning or small alterations as it causes changes in the hash value. Furthermore, applying a single-pattern-matching algorithm repeatedly for multiple pattern could lead to runtime inefficiency. On the other hand, the multiple-pattern-matching methods (e.g. Aho–Corasick [7], Commentz-Walter [8]) are capable of matching all the patterns simultaneously.

However, these methods were designed to be used with patterns rather than corpora of text documents. As a result, they are not memory efficient when patterns are replaced with text corpora. Hence, memory and runtime scalability are the main issues. Second, the text content extracted from memory contains noise. This could be caused by decoding the nontextual elements in the memory to extra characters or re-ordering the content as per memory paging [9]. This issue raises a serious practical impediment to using the exact matching algorithms mentioned earlier. Obviously, approximate matching is more robust in this context; however, approximate matching methods are either runtime inefficient (e.g. Smith–Waterman [10]) or unable to accurately identify free-form text (e.g. using regular expression [11]).

This chapter provides details of FBoW as the mentioned issues in matching the RAM's textual sensitive data, i.e. scalability and robustness. FBoW's effectiveness can be summarized as follows: (i) an effective pattern-matching algorithm for multiple long text corpus that is memory and runtime efficient; (ii) a customizable approximate search algorithm that allows a user to fine-tune a trade-off between scalability (i.e. memory footprint and processing time) and the detection accuracy; and (iii) a series of experimental evaluations that benchmark single and multiple-pattern-matching algorithms (e.g. inference of regular expressions [RegEx] [11], Smith Waterman [10], and Aho–Corasick [7]) for both exact and inexact solutions in the context of matching sensitive data in three different formats: only keywords, whole text files, and sensitive data in the physical RAM.

7.2 Existing Methods

This section provides a summary of existing methods, consisting of tools used to acquire physical memory and various pattern-matching methods.

7.2.1 Physical Memory Acquisition Tool

To allow a user program to access content in the physical memory, the software requires privileged instructions, i.e. running in the kernel mode [12]. For instance, Linux needs the memory acquiring software to be loaded as a kernel module. Similarly, Windows allows device drivers to execute privileged commands that are needed to dump a memory image. On the other hand, Mac OS does not allow user software to directly access the main memory. In this case, the main memory can be accessed by exploiting FireWire interface [13]. The trick works by pretending to be a device that requires the direct memory access (DMA) for fast data transfer. Once the DMA is granted by the operating system, the software can read or write the lower 4 GB of the main memory and bypass the operating system. Various memory imaging tools are available for the three major operating systems:

- *Linux OS*: For Linux, the memory imaging tools include Linux Memory Extractor (LiME) [14], Linux Memory Grabber [15], Imap and pmem [16], and the GNU dd command.
- *Microsoft Windows OS*: For Microsoft Windows there is the WindowsSCOPE software suite [17], Belkasoft Live RAM Caputer [18], Helix 3 Pro [19], and Mdd [20].
- *Mac OS*: For Mac OS, options are Goldfish [21], Mac Memory Reader [22], and OSXPMem [23].

On the other hand, most of the virtualization software (e.g. VMWare, KVM, or Microsoft Hyper-V, etc.) allows its guest OS's memory to be extracted at the hypervisor level; hence, no special software is needed to install in the guest OS. Since a vast majority of the commercial servers are running on the cloud as virtual machines (VM), capturing the memory image can be done at the hypervisor level without affecting the running VMs. Apart from the aforementioned methods, the physical memory content could be acquired via several different other methods [12]. This includes, for example, emulation [24], debuggers [25], crash dumps [26, 27], and rootkits [28].

7.2.2 Pattern-Matching Method

Pattern matching is crucial in text search, and it aims to find all occurrences of a given string in a text. Let us denote by p a pattern, which is in the form of $p = [0, \dots, m-1]$, where m is the length of p. The text can be defined as $t = [0, \dots, n-1]$, where the length is equal to n. The pattern-matching problem aims to efficiently compare a pattern with the available text. From the perspective of searching in a corpus of a sensitive database, the pattern-matching methods are categorized into two types: (i) single-pattern matching and (ii) multipattern matching. If D_s denotes a corpus of sensitive documents containing N number of files, the single-pattern-matching method requires to run N times on the extracted string content M_p, whereas the multipattern-matching method needs to run only once to compare M_p with all N sensitive documents. Details of some common algorithms in each category are as follows.

7.2.2.1 Single-Pattern-Matching Method

Brute force or the naïve algorithm checks all positions in the text between 0 and $n - m$ to find whether a pattern is in the text or not. The pattern is aligned with the text that starts from left to right. If there is a mismatch, the brute force algorithm shifts the pattern by one position. Therefore, the time complexity for the search is $O(m \times n)$ and the number of comparisons is $2n$ [29].

The Knuth–Morris–Pratt (KMP) method [5] aims to improve the length of shifts and remember some characters that matched the pattern by generating the prefix table. The table is used to determine how many characters can be shifted when a mismatch occurs. The value in the prefix table indicates the length of the longest prefix that matches the suffix in the same subpattern. The prefix table requires $O(m)$ space and time complexity, whereas the searching time is reduced to $O(m + n)$ with $2n - 1$ comparisons in the worst-case scenario.

In contrast to the KMP method, the Boyer Moore method [6] performs comparisons from right to left. To skip as many characters as possible, Boyer Moor algorithm needs to build a *bad match table*, which consists of good suffix shift and bad character shift. The table is used to determine how many characters to shift when a mismatch occurs. The preprocessing time and space complexity are in order of $O(m + \sigma)$, where σ is the size of the alphabet set. Even though the worst-case search time complexity remains equal to $O(m \times n)$, the best complexity is $O(n/m)$. This makes the Boyer Moore method one of the most efficient string-matching methods used in text editors [29]. This group of string-matching methods (e.g. Brute force, KMP, Boyer Moore, etc.) requires the pattern and the search text to be exactly matched; hence, they are not resilient to a noise being added into the searching text. On top of that, carrying multiple searches could degrade the overall performance.

On the other hand, the Smith–Waterman [10] method carries out an inexact search that can search, for example, the longest common subsequences between two DNA strands. It works by building a two-dimensional matrix, where each cell of the matrix corresponds to a pairing of characters from the pattern and text. The matching processes are divided into filling the matrix with the similarity score and the backtracking search for an optimal alignment. The backtracking phase allows a short mismatched in the sequence to occur (i.e. specified by gap penalties). Although the time and space complexity of the Smith–Waterman method are in the order of $O(m \times n)$, this method is more resilient to regions with low similarity (i.e. memory extraction noise). This makes the Smith–Waterman method suitable for contexts where the sensitive information is visualized and paraphrased by a malignant user, such as reading the sensitive document and writing the sensitive information into email or note applications.

7.2.2.2 Multiple Patterns Matching Method

One of the most widely used multipattern-matching methods is the Aho–Corasick [7] method. This extends the KMP [5] method to support the matching of multiple patterns simultaneously. The corresponding algorithm builds a trie structure that is a finite state machine containing all the patterns that are needed to be matched. The runtime complexity of Aho–Corasick is $O(n)$ over N documents. Similarly, the Commentz-Walter algorithm [8] was designed based on Boyer Moore method [6] to perform larger jumps when a mismatch occurs. The Commentz-Walter method combines reversed patterns into a trie structure. Hence, the Commentz-Walter method claims to be the fastest average multipattern-matching algorithm. However, since Aho–Corasick algorithm is optimal in the worst case, it is slightly faster than Commentz-Walter with a large number of keywords [30].

Alternatively, the search patterns can be replaced by a sequence of characters (also called regular expression or RegEx). Each character of the RegEx method represents either a regular character or meta-character. For example, the RegEx 'A.', 'A' refers to letter "A," whereas '.' is a meta-character represents any letter except a newline. The regular expression is translated by the *RegEx processor* to the deterministic finite automaton (DFA) [31]. The finite automaton can represent an infinite set of patterns, and hence the RegEx method not only defines multiple variations of patterns but also as efficient as (if not better than) other multipattern string searching algorithms. As a result, RegEx has been widely used to detect known patterns, for instance, antiviruses and malware scanners [32] or intrusion detection systems [33]. However, the application of the RegEx method is limited by the conversion from patterns to RegEx. One of the solutions is to use AI to automatically infer the RegEx method from examples of patterns [11]. However, this method is limited to patterns with common format or definitions, e.g. credit card, hospital patient or driving license number, etc. When considering a corpus of text documents as sensitive data, the space of monitoring keywords will be too large for regular expressions to comprehend all the relevant information into a single search.

7.3 Concepts

This section explains the concepts of the FBoW method and provides examples for the illustration of memory extraction noises. Formal problem definitions are given, and all the used notations are depicted in Table 7.1. These will be useful for the various parts of Section 7.4.

7.3.1 Notation

Figure 7.1 illustrates the overall concepts of the FBoW method. In general, there are two inputs and one output. *Input #1* consists of the corpora of sensitive and nonsensitive documents. On the other hand, *Input #2* is a memory snapshot, which can be acquired by operating system's API or other memory acquisition

Table 7.1 Frequently used notations.

Notation	Description
D_s	A corpus of N sensitive documents to monitor (also referred to as a sensitive database)
D_r	Samples of regular or nonsensitive documents from the same organization
M_p	An extracted string content from memory address space of the running process p
t	A term of one word or n words separated by white space (e.g. when n-gram is applied)
$f_{t,d}$	The frequency or number of times that a term t appears in the document d
tf_d	A term-frequency pair $(t, f_{t,d})$ in the document d
t_d	The term frequency invert document frequency (tf-idf) value of term t
t^d	The term t that appears in document d
BoW_d	Bag-of-words consists of one or more pairs of term frequency $tf_d = (t, f_{t,d})$, where the particular term t appears in document d for f number of times
BoW_{seq}	A sequence of Bag-of-Words (BoW) from D_s, which are grouped by the frequency of occurrence and sort alphabetically (see Section 7.4.1.4)
BoW_{mem}	A sequence of BoW from M_p, which are grouped and sorted using the same method as BoW_{seq} from D_s
$Dict_s$	A set of terms that are unique from a corpus of sensitive documents, where all terms $t \in D_s$
$FBoW$	The Fast lookup BoW, a data structure which represents the database that is used to query the similarity between M_p and the individual sensitive document $d \in D_s$. $FBoW$ contains the summarized sensitive database D_s in such a way that allows the quick lookup
α	A threshold for selecting terms based on a comparison between terms that appear in D_s (see Section 7.4.1.3)
β	A threshold for selecting terms based on a comparison between terms that appear in D_s and others, which are in either D_s or D_r (see Section 7.4.1.3)

tools (see Section 7.2.1). Overall, the FBoW method involves five different steps: (i) establish the FBoW detection model, (ii) extract the memory snapshot from the host machine being monitored, (iii) process unstructured (i.e. binary) data to the textual representation, (iv) convert the text data from the memory into the Bag-of-Words (BoW) by using the dictionary of sensitive keywords from the first step, and (v) detect the sensitive data from the extracted memory information. These steps produce the matching likelihood between the text content extracted from the memory snapshot to a sensitive document in the corpus of sensitive text files as an *Output*. All details of each step are provided in Section 7.4.

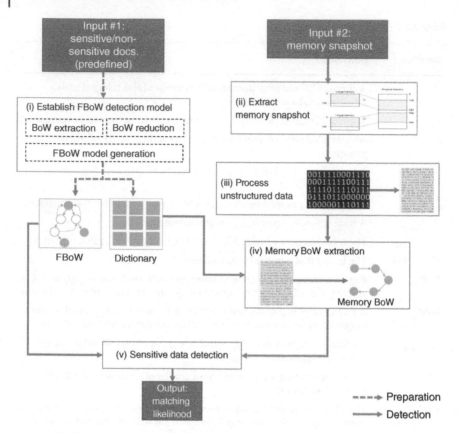

Figure 7.1 The Fast lookup BoW conceptual diagram.

7.3.2 Memory Data

Figure 7.2 illustrates how text data is extracted from the memory snapshot of a given process, which loaded several text files into its memory space (top-left). The arrows link text from Lines 5–7 of the memory image to the original text paragraph. Parts of the text from the original paragraphs in documents A, B, and C (top-right and bottom left-right) are highlighted in gray. This is an example of noise from data being stored in the memory and managed by the operating system, of which, the text order in the original document cannot be guaranteed [9].

Apart from that, the noise from the memory extraction process could also originated from the string and other variables contained in the executable image, function names or XML code (see Figure 7.3). The build in string could be parts of the graphic user interface, file names and locations, user agreement, and so on. This type of string could be matched with parts of the sensitive document and result in the false positive. On the other hand, the machine code, empty space, array, or

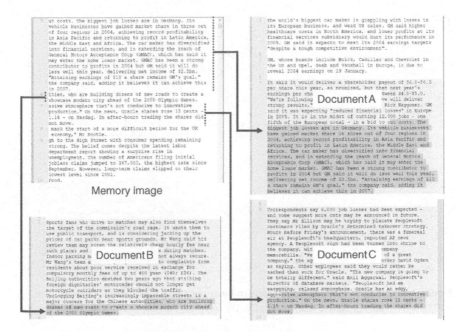

Figure 7.2 Example of text data extracted from the memory image compared to original text from Documents A, B, and C (highlighted in gray).

Figure 7.3 Example of noise from: string and other variables contained in the executable image (a); and function names and XML code as parts of the executable image (b).

(a)   (b)

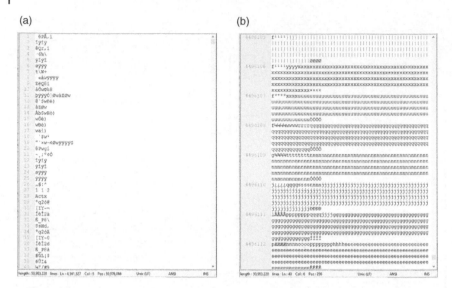

Figure 7.4 Example of noise from: program binary header (a); and other random patterns from empty space, array, stack, etc. (b).

stack, as shown in Figure 7.4, have a lower chance of matching with the sensitive document. This memory data with the noises (i.e. as in Figure 7.2) is referred to as M_p. It will form the search terms, which are used to match with the sensitive document in the matching process.

Formally, the memory data M_p can be described as a block of string content extracted from a computer's main memory for each process p. The raw memory image M_p is decoded using e encoding standard, such as 8/16/32-bit Unicode Transformation Format (UTF-8/16/32). Intuitively, the data owner knows the encoding type of the sensitive files, hence the appropriate type can be selected in advance. The data that cannot be decoded as a printable character are discarded. On the contrary, some data might be decoded into character regardless of what was interpreted by the process that had access to the memory. Hence, the string content extracted from the memory image should contain noise from data that has accidentally been decoded by e.

7.3.3 Sensitive Documents

Let D_s be a collection of sensitive documents, which contains N sensitive text documents $D_s = \{D_1, \dots, D_N\}$. This research assumes that a corpus of sensitive documents that have been already identified either manually (by the data owner) or using an automated process (such as document redaction/sanitization algorithms [34]).

7.3.4 Sensitive Data Matching

Given a sensitive dataset of documents $D_s = \{D_i | i \in 1, \ldots, N\}$ and a string content M_p extracted from the memory snapshot of a process p, the sensitive data matching is defined as $(\exists M_p \in D_i \wedge \exists t_i \subseteq T_i \wedge t_p \subseteq T_p : t_i \approx t_p)$. That is string content M_p and a sensitive document D_i sharing common string content. Let T_i and T_p be all characters in D_i and M_p, respectively. With the matching threshold τ, $M_p \approx D_i \Longleftrightarrow t_i \approx t_p$ with differences $e : e \le \tau$.

In the context of this work, the string content T_i and T_p are replaced with BoW_i and BoW_p. Hence, the problem definition is to find $(\exists M_p \in D_i : BoW_i \approx BoW_p)$, where $e : e \le \tau$.

7.4 Fast Lookup Bag-of-Words (FBoW)

Figure 7.5 provides an overview of the FBoW method. The sensitive database D_s and samples of nonsensitive documents D_r are required to generate the detection model for detecting sensitive data. The FBoW method is divided into three main steps: (i) detection model generation, (ii) memory data extraction, and (iii) sensitive data detection. Details are as follows.

7.4.1 Detection Model Generation

The detection model of the FBoW method consists of two data structures $Dict_s$ and $FBoW$. The first data structure is a dictionary that contains BoWs that are

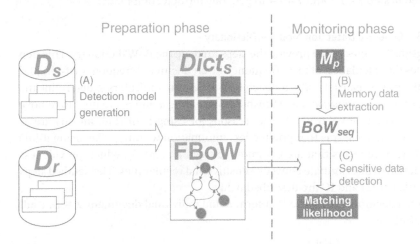

Figure 7.5 The Fast lookup BoW method.

present in all sensitive files in the database. The second data structure, *FBoW*, is a collection of BoW sequences extracted from sensitive files that are compacted into a DFA, using a trie-based data structure. Details of the detection model generation in Algorithm 7.1 are as follows.

7.4.1.1 Extract Bag-of-Words from Nonsensitive Dataset

Samples of regular documents D_r (i.e. nonsensitive) are required, in addition to a corpus of sensitive documents D_s. The intuition is that documents from both D_r and D_s are expected to be discovered in the memory of workstations in that particular corporation. Hence, the common terms that appear in both sensitive and nonsensitive documents would be less informative to detect the sensitive data and can be removed from the detection model later in step 7.4.1.3, to reduce the size of the detection model while maintaining the detection efficiency.

Algorithm 7.1 Lines 1–4 show the steps to extract BoWs from D_r. String from each document D_j is split into terms. BoW_j consists of unique term-frequency pairs for D_j. The extracted BoW is kept in D_r.

7.4.1.2 Extract Bag-of-Words from Sensitive Dataset

Similar to the previous step, BoW_i is extracted from string content of document D_i in the sensitive dataset D_s. Additionally, the hash map *DictOl* is instantiated. It contains pairs of *unique term* used by all documents and the *cluster* number of each term. The cluster c, defined as $c = \sum_{d \in D_s} |t^d|$, where $c \in \mathbb{Z}^+$ denotes the number of documents in D_s sharing common term t, and $|t^d| = 1$ when the term t appears in document $d \in D_s$ (see Algorithm 7.1 Lines 5–9). This map of BoW-Cluster is required in step 7.4.1.3 and 7.4.1.4 to generate the detection model.

7.4.1.3 Generate Detection Model – Dictionary

Algorithm 7.1 Lines 10–19 provide the steps to create the BoW dictionary. This step includes the calculation of term frequency invert document frequency (tf-idf) [35] and information gain (IG) [36] for each BoW. These are indicators to determine the level of BoW's *informativeness*. Thresholds, including α and β, are used to remove less informative BoWs from D_s. The reasons for using both tf-idf and IG are as follows: (i) reduce terms that provide less information within D_s (i.e. using tf-idf) and (ii) remove terms that are common between D_s and D_r, which provide less information to discriminate between sensitive and regular files. The detailed steps to calculate tf-idf and IG are described below.

Given a document database D, a term t, and individual document $d \in D$, tf-idf t_d is defined as:

$$t_d = f_{t,d} \times \log\left(\frac{|D|}{f_{t,D}}\right),$$

Algorithm 7.1 Detection model generation.

---

input : D_s, D_r, α and β
output: $Dict_s$ and $FBoW$

```
/* D_s and D_r are sensitive and nonsensitive dataset. α
   and β are BoW reduction thresholds. Dict_s and FBoW are
   components of the detection model.                       */

   /* A.1 extract Bow from D_r                               */
```
1 **foreach** $D_j \in D_r$:
2 $\quad$ $BoW_j \leftarrow$ extract BoW D_j;
3 $\quad$ $D_r \leftarrow$ associate BoW_j with D_j;
4 **end**
```
   /* A.2 extract BoW from D_s                               */
```
5 **foreach** $D_i \in D_s$:
6 $\quad$ $BoW_i \leftarrow$ extract BoW D_i;
7 $\quad$ $DictOl \leftarrow$ add BoW_i;
8 $\quad$ $D_s \leftarrow$ associate BoW_i with D_i;
9 **end**
```
   /* A.3 generate detection model - dictionary              */
   /* A.3.1 calculate tf-idf                                 */
```
10 **foreach** $D_i \in D_s$:
11 $\quad$ $BoW_i \leftarrow$ get BoW D_i;
12 $\quad$ **foreach** $tf \in BoW_i$:
13 $\quad\quad$ $t_d \leftarrow$ calTFIDF $(tf, DictOl)$;
14 $\quad\quad$ $D_i \leftarrow$ associate BoW_i with t_d;
15 $\quad$ **end**
16 **end**
```
   /* A.3.2 calculate IG                                     */
```
17 calculateIG (D_s);
18 $\alpha', \beta' \leftarrow$ boundTH (D_s, α, β)
```
   /* A.3.3 reduce BoW from dictionary)                      */
```
19 selectBoW $(Dict_s, D_s, \alpha', \beta')$;
```
   /* A.4 generate detection model - automaton               */
   /* A.4.1 sort BoW sequences                               */
```
20 sortBoWSequence $(D_s, DictOl)$
```
   /* A.4.2 build document links                             */
```
21 **foreach** $D_i \in D_s$:
22 $\quad$ $FBoW \leftarrow$ addDoc (D_i)
23 **end**

Algorithm 7.1 (Continued)

```
/* A.4.3 build failure links                                    */
24 for D_i ∈ D_s do
25 |   createFLink(D_i, FBoW)
26 end
27 return Dict_s, FBoW
```

---

where $f_{t,d}$ and $f_{t,D}$ represent the number of times that the term t appears in the individual document d, and among the database D, respectively. $|D|$ represents the total number of files in the database [37].

On the other hand, IG [36] is applied to help reduce the common terms between sensitive and nonsensitive documents. The calculation of IG from corpora of sensitive (D_s) and nonsensitive files (D_r) are as follows.

Let $H(D)$ be the entropy of the database D when partitioned by a feature a, where $D \subset (D_s \cup D_r)$. The output of function $H(D)$ (so-called Shannon entropy [38]) is a value between [0,1]. When the entropy is equal to 0, this means that a is not useful to classify the document $d \in D$ into a category of sensitive or nonsensitive. Conversely, the entropy of 1 means that a is a good feature to classify sensitive documents.

The well-known Shannon entropy is defined as follows:

$$H(D) = - \sum_{d \in \{D_s, D_r\}} P(d)\log_2 P(d),$$

where $P(d)$ denotes probability of a document $d \in D$ being sensitive $(d \in D_s)$ or nonsensitive document $(d \in D_r)$.

Although there can be several features in a document dataset, the Shannon's function only defines the entropy of the dataset when it is split using a single feature. Each feature has different capabilities to discriminate between sensitive and nonsensitive information. By definition, IG indicates the reduction of entropy when the document dataset D is partitioned using the feature a. Therefore, the IG function is used to measure the level of information gained from different features. The function $IG(D, a)$ is defined as

$$IG(D, a) = H(D_a) - \sum_{v \in V} \frac{|D_v|}{|D|} H(D_v),$$

where V denotes all the remaining features after excluding a. $|D_v|$ represents the total number of documents with the feature v. $|D|$ denotes the total number of documents.

To establish features V for each document, tf-idf (t_d) is used as a feature v instead of the term frequency tf_d. That is because the number of features could be close to the size of the data, in case all tf_d are unique. For instance, documents share common terms t but different frequencies ($f_{t,d}$). On the other hand, t_d can be grouped into intervals, despite being a real number. Hence, several term-frequency pairs can be attributed as having the same feature, if they share the same t_d or interval of t_d.

Since value of features is not bounded ($t_d, IG(D, a) \in \mathbb{R}^+$), the BoW selection thresholds can be varied according to the distribution of t_d and $IG(D, a)$ values. To limit this variation and bound the BoW selection thresholds, normalization is required. This limits the thresholds to absolute values between [0,1]. In Algorithm 7.1 Line 18, the bounded thresholds are converted to α' and β'. The output will be the actual tf-idf or IG score of BoW, which varies depending on the distribution of these scores in the database D_s.

Algorithm 7.2 describes the normalization of the bounded threshold with respect to tf-idf or IG scores to the individual tf-idf or IG score. The inputs are the feature vector FV and the threshold Γ (α or β), whereas the output is the value of an individual feature at the index i (i.e. $F[i]$). The FV is first sorted in Line 1. Afterward, the index i is computed by the bounded threshold Γ. Finally, the individual value of the input feature vector is returned to be used as the selection threshold, i.e. tf-idf or IG.

Algorithm 7.2 Features-threshold normalization.

---

input : FV, Γ
output: $FV[i]$
```
/* (A.3.2)  FV is a vector of features; Γ is bounded
      threshold. FV[i] is value at index i of sorted FV      */
```
1 sort (FV) ;   /* sort ascending */
2 $i \leftarrow \Gamma \times$ size (FV);
3 **return** $FV[i]$;

In Line 19 of Algorithm 7.1, the function `selectBoW()` removes BoW that has tf-idf or IG score lower than the α' and β' thresholds in the BoW sequence. The output of `selectBoW()` is kept in $Dict_s$, which is a hash map data structure that allows constant time lookup of a term. Formally,

$$Dict_s = \{\{t^1, stat_t^1\}, \{t^2, stat_t^2\}, \dots, \{t^n, stat_t^n\}\},$$

where the term t is a key and $stat_t = \{f_t, t_d, c\}$ is the associated value. $stat_t$ consists of the frequency f_t, tf-idf t_d, and the cluster number c, i.e. the number of times that term t is found across the database D_s.

7.4.1.4 Generate Detection Model – Automaton

In this step, the FBoW automaton is built. First, the BoW sequence of each document is grouped by the cluster number and sorted alphabetically (see Algorithm 7.1 Line 20). For instance, let tf_i be a term-frequency pair in D_i, which has a cluster number $c \in K$. tf_i will be added to cluster c. Within this cluster, BoWs are sorted by term t alphabetically. After every term-frequency pair is grouped, a BoW sequence of D_i is rearranged by clusters. The largest cluster will be added to the front, followed by the smaller cluster. An example of grouping and sorting by the cluster number is illustrated in Figure 7.6.

Each document $D_i \in D_s$ with the sorted BoW sequences is added into a trie-based automaton [39], which is called *FBoW* (refer to Lines 21–23 of Algorithm 7.1). Since BoW sequences begin with the largest cluster, this gives a chance for the more common term-frequency pair to share the same node in a BoW trie and helps reduce the size of the FBoW.

The formal definition of the *FBoW* automaton is as follows: $FBoW = (V, E, F)$, where $V = dp, id[]$ is the node that consists of dp and $id[]$. Here, dp is the remaining depth to reach the deepest leaf node, and $id[]$ is the list of the document ID(s) along the path. The remaining depth can be used to estimate the similarity in the

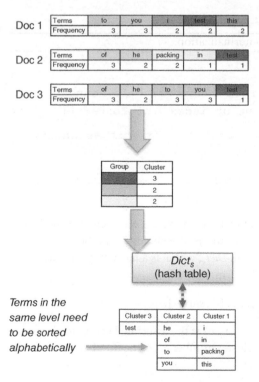

Figure 7.6 Example of grouping and sorting of the term-frequency pairs.

matching process. $E = [\{t, f_t\}, V]$ is list of link(s) to the children nodes V with the term-frequency $\{t, f_t\}$ as a search key. Lastly, F is the failure link that points to the longest possible suffix of BoW sequences in the *FBoW*. The failure link serves the same function as the one in Aho–Corasick string matching [7].

The final step of creating the *FBoW* data structure is to build the failure link for every node. The BoW sequence is broken down into BoW prefix sequences, and the longest suffix BoW sequence in *FBoW* is linked together with the last node of the BoW prefix. The failure link allows extra BoW to be added before the matched sequences. Details of the failure link generation are shown in Algorithm 7.3.

Algorithm 7.3 Failure link generation.

input : D and *FBoW*

output: *FBoW*

```
/* (A.4.3) Find the longest suffix in FBoW for each
   prefix of BoW_seq from D and create the failure link    */
```
1 $BoW_{seq} \leftarrow \text{getBoW}(D)$;
2 **foreach** $bow_{px} \in BoW_{seq}$ **do**
3 | $last \leftarrow \text{getLastNode}(bow_{px}, FBoW)$;
4 | **if** $\text{length}(bow_{px}) = 1$ **then**
5 | | $last.f\,Link = FBoW.root$;   /* first node */
6 | **else**
   | | /* link to the longest suffix node or root   */
7 | | $longest \leftarrow \text{getLongestSuffix}(bow_{px}, FBoW)$;
8 | | $last.f\,Link = longest$
9 | **endif**
10 **end**
11 **return** *FBoW*

The detection model represents static signatures of sensitive files. Hence, $Dict_s$ and *FBoW* can be processed in advance from the given sensitive dataset D_s and the nonsensitive dataset D_r. The BoW reduction thresholds α and β can be adjusted to limit the memory footprint of the detection model. The effects related to the variations of these parameters are discussed in Section 7.5.

7.4.2 Memory Data Extraction

7.4.2.1 Prerequisite

Physical memory acquisition is a prerequisite for the FBoW method. This process can be done using several methods at different software layers (i.e. user, kernel, hypervisor, rootkit or hardware) [12]. The choice depends on the operating system, platform (i.e. physical or virtual machine), and the security policy of the targeted organization. A comprehensive list of memory acquisition tools for different operating systems is discussed in Section 7.2.1. Since this work focuses on the real-time memory monitoring algorithm, the details about content extraction from the memory are not included in this chapter. It is assumed that the snapshot of the memory image has been acquired and preextracted in advance using existing memory acquisition tools [12]. Further details of the tool used in this work are discussed in Section 7.5.1.

7.4.2.2 BoW Sequence Extraction

Algorithm 7.4 provides details of the sensitive document detection on data extracted from physical RAM. The memory image M_p is manually captured from the running Windows machine by acquiring memory allocated to the process p by the operating system. M_p is matched with the sensitive database D_s, which was transformed into *FBoW* and *Dict$_s$* as described in Section 7.4.1. The output of the algorithm is the likelihood x of matching with the closest BoW sequence in *FBoW*, where $x \in \mathbb{R} | 0 \leq x \leq 1$.

First, the binary image M_p is decoded into a printable string. The function decodeStr() in Line 1 of Algorithm 7.4 decodes the memory image M_p using UTF-8/16/32 encoding standard. It is assumed that the data owner will know in advance the encoding type of their sensitive files. In Line 2 of Algorithm 7.4, BoW_{mem} is extracted from M_p by selecting all terms $t \in Dict_s$. The elements in BoW_{mem} are grouped by cluster and sorted alphabetically following the same steps in Section 7.4.1.4 to generate the BoW sequences.

7.4.3 Sensitive Data Detection

In Lines 3–15 of Algorithm 7.4, each *bow* selected from the BoW_{mem} of the memory M_p is searched into the FboW trie data structure containing the summary of the sensitive documents. From the root node, *current* checks if that node contains the particular *bow*. If the *current* node does not contain the *bow*, the next node to be checked will be the node in the failure link (i.e. *current.fLink*). For the current path that has no prefix or suffix BoW sequence, it indicates a mismatch. Hence, the failure link will be the root node. If the leaf node is reached, then the match has been found. As a result, the function returns the likelihood of 1.0.

When the search traversal reaches the end of BoW_{mem} by has not hit any leaf node, then the match is not found. In this case, the estimated likelihood is computed instead. Since each node contains the min remaining hop to travel to reach the closest leaf node, the estimated likelihood is computed with the fraction of the

---

Algorithm 7.4 Memory-based sensitive data detection.

input : $Dict_s$, $FBoW$ and M_p
output: Matching likelihood
```
/* Dict_s, FBoW are a detection model (i.e. dictionary and
   automaton), and M_p is a memory image                    */

/* (B) memory data extraction                               */
```
1   $M_p \leftarrow$ decodeStr (M_p);
2   $BoW_{mem} \leftarrow$ extract BoW from M_p with $Dict_s$;
```
/* (C) sensitive data detection                             */
```
3   $bow \leftarrow$ nextBoW (BoW_{mem});
4   $current \leftarrow FBoW.root$;
5   **while** $bow \neq \emptyset$
6     $child \leftarrow$ getChild $(current, bow)$;
7   **if** $child = \emptyset$ **then**
8 | $current \leftarrow current.f\,Link$;   /* Follow the failure link */
9   **else if** isLeaf $(child)$ **then**
10 | **return** 1.0 ;   /* Matched */
11   **endif**
12    $current \leftarrow child$;   /* Continue */
13    $bow \leftarrow$ nextBoW (BoW_{mem})
14 **end**
```
/* End of BoW_mem return the estimate matching             */
```
15 **return** currentDepth $(current)$ / closestLeafDepth $(current)$

---

current depth and the min remaining depth (i.e. using function currentDepth and closestLeafDepth).

The estimation matching in Algorithm 7.4 is designed to cope with the noise from memory content extraction. For instance, if M_p contains parts of the sensitive data then the matching likelihood will not be 0 but should be a value that reflects any partial matching of sensitive data. This may be interpreted as the initial stage of an exfiltration process, or an intentional way to circumvent memory-based detection by loading pieces of sensitive data at a time. Either way, depending on the likelihood, alarms can be raised to isolate the process p and look into its runtime behavior more closely.

7.5 Evaluation

This section benchmarks the performance and scalability of the FBoW method against the state-of-the-art methods in matching sensitive data from the memory image. It first describes the experimental settings followed by a number of experimental evaluations.

7.5.1 Experimental Settings

The machine used in the experiments was CPU Intel Xeon E5-1650@3.2 GHz, 32 GB of RAM, and 500 GB SSD storage space. The operating system was Microsoft Windows 10 Enterprise 1809. The state-of-the-art and the FBoW method were implemented in Java and tested on Java Virtual Machine version 10.0.2 amd64 edition.

Memory acquisition problems are simplified here by using preextracted data from the memory snapshot of a VM running Microsoft Windows 7 on Virtualbox [40] virtualization software. When a VM was started, the user executed software that loaded the testing text documents into its memory space (i.e. sensitive and nonsensitive documents). By using `VBoxManage` command of VirtualBox, the memory snapshot was taken while the VM was running. The `VBoxManage` command dumped the memory snapshot into an ELF64 image file, and the file was processed using the Volatility [41] software. The raw memory image of the particular process (i.e. the process that opened text files) was extracted using Volatility plug-ins. The string contents were extracted using *strings* decoder on Ubuntu 16.04 LTS [42] (e.g. `$strings < memory.dmp -e S > plaintext_8bit.txt`). The exacted contents were stored in text files, which were used in the series of experiments detailed in this section.

7.5.2 Benchmarked Methods

To evaluate the FBoW method, this is compared with the following three state-of-the-art methods that are widely used for pattern-matching problems.

Aho–Corasick method [7] is a multipattern matching method, which produces exact matching and is widely used in many real-world applications, including searching for the virus signatures in the executable code [33]. Aho–Corasick collects all sensitive documents in a single DFA. This enables Aho–Corasick to match multipattern simultaneously in linear time complexity. Thus, it is one of the promising candidate methods for monitoring the sensitive files in RAM, especially from the aspect of runtime efficiency.

Smith–Waterman method [10] is an approximate matching method. Unlike Aho–Corasick, the Smith–Waterman method uses a penalty system that allows mismatch to occur in the matching. This makes this method more robust to noisy input. Intuitively, the string content extracted from the RAM could contain lots of noise, as illustrated in Figure 7.2. Hence, the Smith–Waterman was included in the benchmark.

RegEx method is the regular expression (RegEx) based approach by Bartoli et al. [11]. RegEx is a sequence of characters used by *RegEx processor* to create the DFA [31], which processes string input in linear time complexity. RegEx is considered an approximate matching method. It is more lightweight compared to Aho–Corasick, as the DFA does not contain all information of the search content. Hence, RegEx is potentially the most efficient method as far as the memory footprint is concerned.

7.5.3 Datasets

We used nine different datasets to benchmark FBoW with the state-of-the-art methods. These datasets can be divided into three groups according to the format and goals of the dataset. Groups (i) and (ii) were used to determine the suitability of the algorithms in different formats of sensitive files. The dataset group (iii) was used to benchmark the algorithms in detecting text documents from the memory image. Details of the total number of records, the number of matched/unmatched items, and the character size are depicted in Table 7.2. Format and objectives of datasets in each group are described as follows:

(i) *The fixed format sensitive keywords*: The datasets #1–#6 are annotated strings datasets from [43], which were originally designed for text extraction research, e.g. [11]. The task of the benchmarked search algorithms was to look for information with a known format or uniformly presented (e.g. extracting author names from latex bib file, IP addresses from the network logs, content from HTML source code, etc.).

Table 7.2 Characteristics of a dataset.

#	DS name	Total doc. (file)	Matched (item)	Unmatched (item)	Matched (char)	Unmatched (char)
1	IPGOD	100,000	1,000,000	1,000,000	10,000,000	161,879,029
2	Bibtex author	200	589	789	789	8996
3	Bibtex title	200	200	400	13,137	40,780
4	Congress bill	600	3085	3685	38,960	16,471,840
5	Web heading	49,026	1083	48,761	206,580	4,363,373
6	Web content	49,026	1083	50,109	193,261	4,375,692
7	News	1000	500	500	979,501	1,599,042
8	Product review	150,000	75,000	75,000	34,209,763	34,196,698
9	Memory dump	80,102	9517	70,585	972,316	4,097,844

(ii) *The whole text documents*: The datasets #7–#8 relate to the news articles dataset [44] and the 150,000 product reviews dataset [45], respectively. The task of the experiment was to differentiate between each text document. The news in [44] was categorized into 10 topics: business, entertainment, food, graphics, historical, medical, politics, space, sport, and technology. The dataset from [45] contains a raw of 150,000 reviews of products sold on Amazon.com.

(iii) *The memory dump*: The dataset #9 is a memory dump. cppAES [46] is used and this was designed for testing anti-ransomware tools. It was implemented using C++. The program searched and read the sensitive text documents from the specified location of the honeypot machine. By using a unique AES key, the program encrypted contents and the decrypting key using a hard-coded public RSA key. This program represented the process that loaded sensitive documents into its memory address space. The memory image of the implemented software was captured and extracted to printable characters using UTF-8 standard. There were 9517 sensitive items and 70,585 nonsensitive items (i.e. contents from news articles) loaded into the memory. Indeed, the decoded data consisted of a mixture of contents from sensitive documents, nonsensitive documents, and noise from memory data extraction. The task was to identify any part of the sensitive documents in the memory dump.

The labeling of the testing data for keywords (i.e. the datasets #1–#6) and for text documents (e.g. the datasets #7–#9) was different. In the keywords datasets, texts were annotated as *matched* or *unmatched*, where the *matched* part was used as *sensitive* and the *unmatched* counterpart was used as *nonsensitive*. On the other hand, files in text datasets were randomly given a label as either *sensitive* or *nonsensitive*. Intuitively, as the nature of sensitive text documents is unstructured and random, most organizations identify sensitive documents by using human expertise [34]. Despite using random labeling, the comparison results were intuitive because both the state-of-the-art and the FBoW method were tested using the same set of labels.

7.5.4 Implementation

Four versions of the multiple sensitive document detection programs were fully implemented. All programs performed the same tasks, classifying sensitive files in datasets #1–#8 and detecting sensitive documents in dataset #9. The difference was the pattern-matching method used in each program. This was done as follows:

- The FBoW method was implemented using Java (Oracle JDK 11) to experimentally measure efficiency and scalability. The standard Java Map Data structure (e.g. `HashMap`, `TreeMap`, etc.) is used to implement the collection of BoW.

- The Smith–Waterman method was implemented in Java from scratch based on the description given in [10]. The core implementation included the scoring matrix for two strings and the backtracking method to estimate the similarity between two strings.
- The inference of a regular expression was publicly available at [47]. The default parameter settings is used to generate a regular expression using genetic algorithms. The output regular expressions is recorded to query for the sensitive document detection program.
- The Aho–Corasick library from [48] was used to implement the testing of the sensitive document detection program. The Aho–Corasick library is set to ignore overlaps (i.e. two documents that share the common sentences) as well as to ignore the letter's case.

Java Object Layout (JOL) [49] was used to measure the size of a data structure. It was used for all implementations except for the inference of a regular expression. That was because the step of generating the regular expression required much more memory to run compared to the step of using the regular expression to match with the input string. On top of that, inferring a regular expression required a much larger memory compared to other methods. Hence, in Table 7.3, the maximum memory used to search for a regular expression was considered instead of the actual memory for matching strings using RegEx.

7.5.5 Experimental Results

This section benchmarks the FBoW method against the state-of-the-art methods based on specific metrics (i.e. runtime, memory footprint, and accuracy) using the datasets #1–#9 detailed in the previous section. The results were discussed separately for each group of datasets (i.e. fixed format, whole text, and the memory dump datasets).

7.5.5.1 Runtime

The column *runtime* in Tables 7.3 and 7.4 is divided into two. The *Offline* column depicts the processing time that can be prepared offline, namely the time for [11] to generalize the regular expression from examples, time to build trie for Aho–Corasick, and time to generate the detection model for FBoW. However, there was no offline preparation time for the Smith–Waterman method because the comparison matrix needs to be made in real time. The column *Avg./d* depicts the average runtime per document. As various datasets were different in the number of documents, the average processing time divided by the total number of documents was used (see Table 7.2, column *Total Doc.*).

Table 7.3 Benchmark the state-of-the-art and the FBoW method on the fixed format keywords datasets.

DS name	Matched	Un-matched	Method	Acc.	Runtime (μs) Offline	Avg./d	DS size (bytes)
IPGOD	5000	5000	Aho–Corasick	1.000	52,000	114.00	6,050,864
			Smith–Waterman	1.000	0	3586.00	14,494,872
			RegEx	1.000	4.39 h	62.00	6,293,504[b]
			FBoW	1.000	44,667	155.33	2,589,280
Bibtex author	589	789	Aho–Corasick	1.000	27,000	150.00	2,099,192
			Smith–Waterman	0.995	0	810.00	6,475,296
			RegEx	0.885	0.93 h	59.26	10.91 GB[b]
			FBoW	0.840	21,000	70.00	451,064
Bibtex title	200	400	Aho–Corasick	1.000	30,000	100.00	341,184
			Smith–Waterman	0.990	0	850.00	8,024,104
			RegEx[a]	—	—	—	—
			FBoW	0.720	32,667	95.00	762,824
Congress bill	3085	3685	Aho–Corasick	1.000	31,000	448.33	5,244,928
			Smith–Waterman	0.990	0	2,096,637.00	1.45 GB
			RegEx[a]	—	—	—	—
			FBoW	0.825	2,288,333	8.89	401,448
Web heading	1083	48,761	Aho–Corasick	1.000	131,000	3.67	17,623,000
			Smith–Waterman	0.999	0	55.17	352,734,472
			RegEx[a]	—	—	—	—
			FBoW	0.610	1,199,333	0.66	2,753,944
Web content	1083	50,109	Aho–Corasick	1.000	116,000	4.16	14,646,496
			Smith–Waterman	0.999	0	2340.00	47,848,304
			RegEx[a]	—	—	—	—
			FBoW	0.330	1,220,666	14.46	2,595,704

a) The result was not available due to timeout or out-of-memory.
b) The memory used to infer the regular expression (i.e. preparation phase) is used instead of the data structure size because the size of RegEx is very small and negligible.

Table 7.4 Benchmark the state-of-the-art and the FBoW method on the whole text datasets.

DS name	Matched	Un-matched	Method	Acc.	Runtime (μs) Offline	Avg./d	DS size (bytes)
News articles	500	500	Aho–Corasick	1.000	5,030,000	420.33	202,810,392
			FBoW	0.992	889,000	281.00	6,512,104
Product review	25,000	25,000	Aho–Corasick	1.000	9,302,667	17.07	2,247,307,592
			FBoW	0.980	53,888,666	54.58	5,614,968

(a) *Fixed format sensitive datasets*: The result in Table 7.3 shows that the regular expression-based method was the fastest in terms of matching time per document. It took only around 62 and 59 μs per document for the dataset IPGOD and Bibtex author, respectively. The runtime of FBoW was similar in general to the Aho–Corasick method. FBoW outperformed Aho–Corasick for most of the datasets, except for the IPGOD and web content datasets where it was just over 41 and 10 μs per document slower than Aho–Corasick. On the other hand, Smith–Waterman was the worst in terms of performance. For the Congress bill dataset, Smith–Waterman took significantly longer than other methods, up to roughly 2000 ms compared to FBoW that finished in less than 10 μs.

(b) *Whole text datasets*: Since FBoW was intentionally designed to be used with a text document, the results from this group of datasets provided a better indication of the efficiency of the FBoW method. As can be seen in Table 7.4, FBoW outperformed Aho–Corasick for the news articles dataset, where the content to be compared had several paragraphs of news content. FBoW ran faster during the preprocessing step, e.g. in summarizing sensitive news into the dictionary of sensitive keywords, compared to Aho–Corasick's preprocessing step of building its searching trie (i.e. 281 vs. 420 μs). Since FBoW processes streams of input based on *words* instead of *characters* as used by the Aho–Corasick method, the number of rounds to add each node into the trie has been reduced. Hence, Aho–Corasick took much more time to process long news articles. Conversely, the product reviews dataset contained much shorter strings content compared to the news article. As a result, FBoW took a much longer time to process each document because of the overhead time to extract the BoWs. On top of that, the product reviews had more diverse terms used to describe products and users' opinions (as opposed to news articles that used more common terms). When combined with the dataset size (i.e. 150 k), FBoW was much slower in terms of offline processing time. However, the time was a trade-off with the memory space, which will be discussed in the next section.

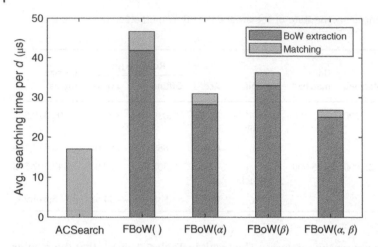

Figure 7.7 Average runtime comparison between Aho–Corasick and FBoW.

Figure 7.7 compares variations of FBoW to Aho–Corasick by focusing on the same dataset. Since the Aho–Corasick method had no preprocessing step, the runtime part consisted of a single step, i.e. the matching step. On the other hand, FBoW had two steps, i.e. BoW extraction and matching. It is clear that the FBoW method spent more time to preprocess the input into BoW than to match with information in the sensitive database. Variations of the α and β thresholds helped to reduce the preprocessing time. Indeed, the threshold filtered out less significant keywords, and as a result, less BoW to be extracted and faster searching time per document. Once can notice that the average comparison time from FBoW variations was slower than Aho–Corasick, i.e. 10–30 μs per document.

Figure 7.8 compares the average document searching time and detection accuracy of FBoW method when varying the thresholds α and β. Once can notice that α threshold reduced the searching time continuously, whereas the variations of β threshold resulted in fluctuations of the searching speed. By varying α threshold, the average searching time gradually reduced from 54 to 40 μs. On the other hand, β threshold variations observed fluctuation in the searching speed between around 43 and 46 μs. The document searching time was the fastest when $\alpha = 0.8$ and slowest when $\alpha = 0.2$. The fluctuating behavior of the average searching time for β and α is not straightforward. That is because the reduction thresholds (i.e. β and α) remove some terms from the FBoW model based on *the level of informativeness* but not the term's frequency. Hence, the number of terms deleted from the FBoW model results in fluctuation when adjusting the thresholds, as shown in Figure 7.8. Moreover, the fluctuation can also depend on the distribution of terms across multiple documents and the total number of documents in a corpus of sensitive data.

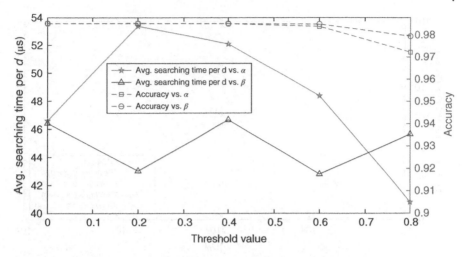

Figure 7.8 The average searching time per *d* vs. accuracy on variation of thresholds.

Regarding the results for the Smith–Waterman and RegEx methods depicted in Table 7.4, experiments show that both methods failed to complete/run. Indeed, the Smith–Waterman method required a larger memory space than what our machine had, whereas the RegEx based method spent more than 24 hours and still could not find the best regular expression solution that represented all documents. This was not a surprise since the whole text datasets consist of several documents, and hence no specific regular expression can be generalized from the data.

7.5.5.2 Memory Footprint

The column *DS size* of Tables 7.3 and 7.4 shows the sizes of data structures that stored sensitive information to be maintained in the memory in order to search for the memory strings. The results indicate that in most cases FBoW outperformed the state-of-the-art methods. For example, as shown in Table 7.4, FBoW used 31 times less memory compared to Aho–Corasick for the news articles datasets, Also, FBoW performed 400 times better than Aho–Corasick method for the product review dataset. On the other hand, when the IPGOD dataset was used (see Table 7.3), the size of data structure used in FBoW was more than two times smaller compared to Aho–Corasick method. For the Bibtex title dataset, however, FBoW generated approximately two times larger data structure compared to Aho–Corasick. The *n*-gram method [50] was needed to be applied for the Bibtex title dataset to extract BoW. This was because the Bibtex titles were not easy to be differentiated from other parts of the Bibtex code.

Figure 7.9 compares variations of FBoW and Aho–Corasick based on the size of the data structure and the number of documents to be added to the sensitive

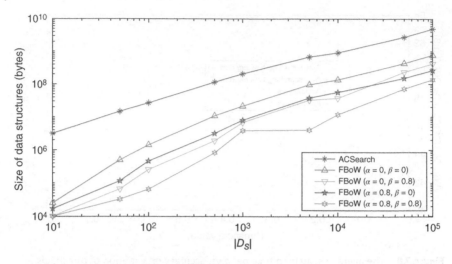

Figure 7.9 The data structure size comparison.

database. Overall, the trend of the growing data structure size per the number of documents in the database was similar for all the methods, and all variations of FBoW needed less memory than the Aho–Corasick method. FBoW, without memory reduction, i.e. $FBoW(\alpha = 0, \beta = 0)$, required a larger memory compared to other methods, whereas the aggressive memory reduction, i.e. $FBoW(\alpha = 0.8, \beta = 0.8)$, required the least memory. Note that the threshold values higher than 0.8 removed most of the data from the detection model and resulted in a dramatic reduction of the accuracy. Hence, the highest α and β threshold values were limited to 0.8.

Figure 7.10 shows a reduction of the data structure size and accuracy when the thresholds α or β were varied. One can notice that α reduced the size of the data structure much faster than β. When α was increased from 0.0 to 0.6, the detection accuracy was roughly the same. However, the size of the data structure decreased nearly by half from over 700 MB down to just under 400 MB. When α was set to 0.8, it limited the data structure size to roughly 250 MB, whereas the detection accuracy slightly decreased by less than 2% from 98.5% to 97.1%. The threshold β affected the size and accuracy similarly, and it reduced less the data size however offered a better detection accuracy.

In this experiment, the Smith–Waterman and RegEx methods were not compared with the FBoW and Aho–Corasick methods for the following reasons. The regular expression method was not included because it failed to infer a regular expression that matches our sensitive data, particularly for the text documents. On top of that, the memory requirement for the RegEx's process of inference was relatively large compared to other methods (see Table 7.3). The Smith–Waterman

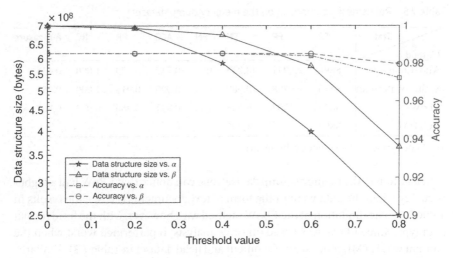

Figure 7.10 The data structure size vs. accuracy on the variation of threshold values.

method is not included in this comparison as the method was unable to scale enough (failed to complete execution) to generate the testing results for all the datasets. Several experiments have failed due to out-of-memory errors. Therefore, the Smith–Waterman method performed the worst with regard to memory footprint.

7.5.5.3 Accuracy

To evaluate the detection accuracy, the memory dump dataset that contained noises from the extraction process was used to examine the robustness of the various methods. Table 7.5 illustrates a confusion matrix as well as other statistical measurements for the Aho–Corasick, Smith–Waterman, and FBoW methods. The correct solution (i.e. *ACTUAL*) was obtained by manually counting the memory dump file for the detected sensitive items. Overall, FBoW was the most accurate method with an accuracy of 99.1%. Although the Aho–Corasick method detected all of the sensitive items, it did have a higher number of false alarms (i.e. false positive). As a result, the Aho–Corasick method achieved only 71.3% accuracy, and this confirmed the lack of robustness of the exact search method on the memory dump dataset compared to the approximate search method. The FBoW and Smith–Waterman methods were very similar with regard to accuracy. However, as explained in the previous section, Smith–Waterman did not have good performance results: it took up to **one day and six hours** to complete the experiment, compared to the other methods that completed in fractions of a second.

Table 7.5 Robustness comparison on the memory dump dataset.

Stat Method	TP	FP	TN	FN	ACC	PR	RC	F-measure
Aho–Corasick	8894	22,971	48,237	0	0.713	0.279	1.000	0.436
Smith–Waterman	8615	798	70,689	0	0.990	0.915	1.000	0.955
FBoW	8672	303	70,745	382	0.991	0.966	0.957	0.962
ACTUAL[a]	8894		71,208					

a) Manual search from memory dump file.

In addition to the memory dump dataset, one can notice that FBoW had a higher accuracy when the data were in the form of text documents (i.e. see the results in Table 7.4). The limitation of the FBoW method was, however, with the fixed format data type. Since FBoW was based on BoW analysis, it performed worst when the content was HTML code (see web content and head dataset in Table 7.3). Similarly, FBoW did not perform well with the bibtex author names because names, which consisted of initials and surnames, were short and hard to differentiate from the nonmatching parts using BoW.

Figures 7.11 and 7.12 show the detection accuracy for the Aho–Corasick method and compared with the different variations of FBoW with α and β thresholds. For the news articles, FBoW with no threshold behaved similarly to Aho–Corasick, whereas the FBoW method with thresholds, i.e. $FBoW(\alpha = 0.8, \ \beta = 0.8)$, was getting better accuracy when more documents were added into the sensitive

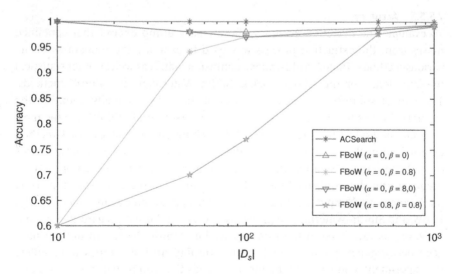

Figure 7.11 The accuracy on news articles dataset.

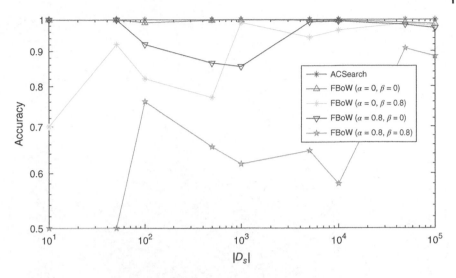

Figure 7.12 The accuracy dataset product reviews dataset.

database. With 1000 documents, the accuracy of $FBoW(\alpha = 0.8, \beta = 0.8)$ was very close to 100%. Similarly, FBoW with thresholds performed better on the product review dataset (see Figure 7.12) when more documents were added to the sensitive database. However, the reduction of data using α and β thresholds affected the accuracy when the number of documents grew up to 10,000 items. This was because the FBoW data structure had reduced too much information that was needed to differentiate between sensitive and nonsensitive documents. Moreover, one can notice that the observed nonmonotonic behaviors and trends of the matching accuracy for the product reviews dataset. The news articles dataset has only 10 subjects, and articles from the same subject usually share common words. On the other hand, the product reviews dataset has more variations in the customers' writing style. For instance, text lengths often differ from one review to another. Also, reviewers use many different terms to describe various products. Therefore, the size of the FBoW model could not be reduced as much as needed with the news articles dataset because the product review dataset has more diverse terms and styles than the news article dataset.

7.5.6 Sensitivity Analysis of FBoW

This section evaluates the sensitivity of the FBoW method to variations of FBoW's parameters and the effects on runtime, memory, and accuracy. The variations of α and β thresholds allowed FBoW to reduce the size of the data structure used to store information about sensitive documents (e.g. sensitive database). FBoW was

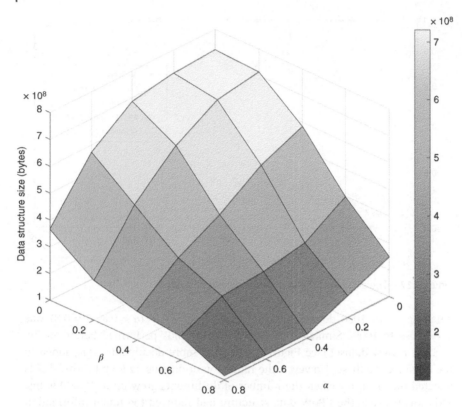

Figure 7.13 The data structure size on variation of α and β threshold.

designed to work in realtime. Hence, the design focused on scalability and performance when a large number of documents were added to the sensitive database. Therefore, the reduction of the memory footprint was the key factor to indicate the scalability of the FBoW method.

Figure 7.13 depicts the reduction of the data structure size from around 700 MB down to around 200 MB by varying the thresholds α and β. One can notice that both thresholds gradually reduced the size of the data structure, and the combination of both thresholds further decreased the data size, where the smallest size was around 200 MB when $\alpha = 0.8$ and $\beta = 0.8$.

Similarly, the average search time per document can be reduced by adjusting the thresholds α and β. When using both thresholds in combination, they produced the fastest processing time at around 32 μs down from around 44 μs without applying the reduction thresholds (see Figure 7.14).

Figure 7.15 illustrates the effects on the detection accuracy when the thresholds were used to filter out less significant BoWs. In overall, the accuracy dropped from

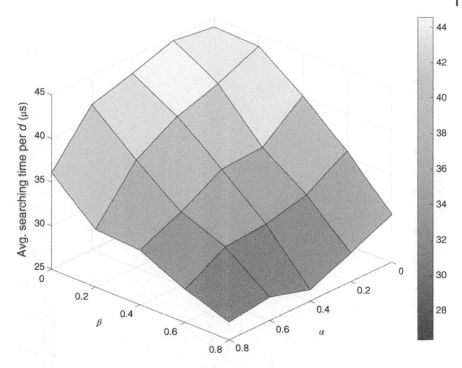

Figure 7.14 The average searching time per *d* on variation of α and β threshold.

close to 100% to around 97%. The β threshold affected the detection accuracy less than the α threshold. It is clear that the use of β threshold from $\beta = 0.0$ to $\beta = 0.6$ slightly reduced the accuracy, whereas the α threshold reduced accuracy faster from $\alpha = 0.2$ to $\alpha = 0.8$.

7.5.6.1 Features Comparison

Table 7.6 compares pattern matching features of the FBoW method to existing state-of-the-art string searching methods: Smith–Waterman [10], Aho–Corasick [7], and inference of RegEx [11]. The following describes the features for comparison.

- The *exact* and *inexact* features indicate the resilience of a given method to noise when searching using text extracted from the memory. In particular, the monitoring of data in the memory (M_p) could contain partial, and not the complete content of the sensitive documents. Additionally, since M_p is decoded from the raw binary (i.e. memory image), it is likely that some of the binary data cannot be converted to printable characters. Hence, this "faulty" decoding is considered as noise, which could reside between chunks of the sensitive data

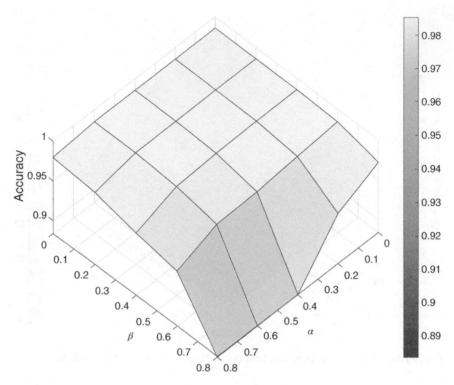

Figure 7.15 The accuracy on variation of α and β threshold.

Table 7.6 Features comparison between state-of-the-art and the FBoW method.

Method / Feature	Matching	Multi-document	Context sensitive	Uniform format	Scalability	Application
Aho–Corasick [7]	Exact	Multiple	Yes	No	No	Multiple patterns matching
RegEx [11]	Inexact	Multiple[a]	No	Yes	Yes	Various fix-format pattern matching
Smith–Waterman [10]	Inexact	Single	Yes	No	No	DNA sequence alignment or plagiarism detection
FBoW	Inexact	Multiple	Yes	No	Yes	RAM-based textual document matching

a) Match terms across multiple documents which share the same pattern only.

content (e.g. Figure 7.2). The exact solution (e.g. Aho–Corasick [7]) is the only method that needs all the information to be exactly matched.

- The *multiple document* feature refers to the ability to match M_p with multiple sensitive documents in the dataset D_s. The multiple documents matching is crucial when the sensitive data is a corpus of documents rather than a set of keywords. The Smith–Waterman method [10] allows only a single document to be checked at the same time, whereas the Aho–Corasick [7] and FBoW methods can examine all the sensitive documents D_s at once. The regular expression (e.g. [11]) can be used to check multiple documents at the same time. However, keywords in sensitive documents need to share common patterns to allow the regular expression to be inferred; and hence the use case is limited compared to the other methods.
- The *context sensitive* methods preserve different behavior of words depending on the situations/contexts in a given sentence. Except for the regular expression-based method [11], all the other methods (e.g. [7, 10]), including the FBoW method, do preserve the contexts of words.
- The *uniform format* feature is only required by the inference of RegEx method [11].
- Using the *scalability* feature shows that the FBoW method is the most scalable one, followed by the Aho–Corasick [7] method. Specifically, FBoW required a significantly smaller memory footprint to run the similarity matching compared to the Aho–Corasick and Smith–Waterman methods. On the other hand, the least scalable method was the Smith–Waterman [10] method, and this is due to the memory limitation when the size of sensitive documents grew. Note that when sensitive data are uniform, the regular expression [11] can be precisely inferred from a given example, and therefore it could be the most scalable method. Unfortunately, the regular expression method is not applicable in the context of text documents, as this fails to efficiently generate regular expressions (see Table 7.3–7.5).
- The *targeted application* feature depicts the targeted application a method that was originally designed for or mostly used. Since the detection of data exfiltration on memory was a novel security and privacy method, there was no direct competitor for the FBoW method. Hence, the state-of-the-art methods, which were designed for various other applications, were used for benchmarking against the FBoW method.

7.6 Summary

FBoW has improved the traditional data exfiltration methods as a memory-based sensitive data detection method. This chapter has also explained the limitations of state-of-the-art methods in monitoring the existence of sensitive content in the physical memory (e.g. memory footprint, runtime, accuracy, and robustness). The FBoW method matches multiple sensitive text documents simultaneously using the automation of BoW. It allows the administrator to fine-tune the performance and security trade-off by using filtering thresholds, enabling to alternate/balance between performance and security levels. Experimental results showed that the FBoW method outperforms the state-of-the-art methods with regard to memory requirements and robustness to noise, with negligible reductions in runtime and accuracy. Hence, the FBoW method is a multipattern matching method, which is scalable and efficient to monitor a corpus of sensitive text documents in the physical memory.

Even though the FBoW method has shown a promising ability to efficiently detect the program that possesses sensitive information, the sophisticated or state-sponsored hacktivist could still evade the detection system by accessing multiple minuscule pieces of the sensitive data at a time. This will minimize the chance of being detected by the FBoW method as the fraction of sensitive data could be too small to be detected. Still, they could keep collecting pieces of sensitive information for over a prolonged period of time and combine them back together later after all the data are transferred out of the system. Chapter 8s will address one of the most challenging data exfiltration attacks, the temporal or the time-delay data-stealing method.

References

1 Asaf Shabtai, Yuval Elovici, and Lior Rokach. *A Survey of Data Leakage Detection and Prevention Solutions.* Springer Science & Business Media, 2012.

2 Saurabh Verma and Abhishek Singh. Data theft prevention & endpoint protection from unauthorized usb devices-implementation. In *Proceedings of the 4th IEEE International Conference on Advanced Computing (ICoAC)*, pages 1–4, 2012.

3 Zhihui Shao, Mohammad A. Islam, and Shaolei Ren. Your noise, my signal: exploiting switching noise for stealthy data exfiltration from desktop computers. *Proceedings of the ACM on Measurement and Analysis of Computing Systems*, 4(1):1–39, 2020.

4 Mordechai Guri, Yosef Solewicz, Andrey Daidakulov, and Yuval Elovici. Acoustic data exfiltration from speakerless air-gapped computers via covert hard-drive noise ('diskfiltration'). In *Proceedings of the Springer European Symposium on Research in Computer Security*, pages 98–115, 2017.

5 Donald E. Knuth, James H. Morris, Jr., and Vaughan R. Pratt. Fast pattern matching in strings. *SIAM Journal on Computing*, 6(2):323–350, 1977.

6 Robert S. Boyer and J. Strother Moore. A fast string searching algorithm. *Communications of the ACM (CACM)*, 20(10):762–772, 1977.

7 Alfred V. Aho and Margaret J. Corasick. Efficient string matching: an aid to bibliographic search. *Communications of the ACM (CACM)*, 18(6):333–340, 1975.

8 Beate Commentz-Walter. A string matching algorithm fast on the average. In *Springer International Colloquium on Automata, Languages, and Programming*, pages 118–132, 1979.

9 Abraham Silberschatz, Peter B. Galvin, and Greg Gagne. *Operating System Concepts*. John Wiley & Sons, 2006.

10 William R. Pearson. Searching protein sequence libraries: comparison of the sensitivity and selectivity of the Smith–Waterman and fasta algorithms. *Elsevier Journal of Genomics*, 11(3):635–650, 1991.

11 Alberto Bartoli, Andrea De Lorenzo, Eric Medvet, and Fabiano Tarlao. Inference of regular expressions for text extraction from examples. *IEEE Transactions on Knowledge and Data Engineering (TKDE)*, 28(5):1217–1230, 2016.

12 Tobias Latzo, Ralph Palutke, and Felix Freiling. A universal taxonomy and survey of forensic memory acquisition techniques. *Elsevier Journal of Digital Investigation*, 28:56–69, 2019.

13 Carsten Maartmann-Moe. Inception is a physical memory manipulation and hacking tool exploiting PCI-based DMA. https://github.com/carmaa/inception, 2020.

14 Joe Sylve. LiME-Linux memory extractor. https://github.com/504ensicslabs/lime, 2012.

15 Hal Pomeranz. Script for automating Linux memory capture. https://github.com/halpomeranz/lmg/, 2020.

16 Michael Cohen. Scanning memory with Yara. *Elsevier Journal of Digital Investigation*, 20:34–43, 2017.

17 WindowsSCOPE Group. WindowsSCOPE Windows memory forensics tools. http://www.windowsscope.com/, 2020.

18 Belkasoft. Belkasoft RAM Capturer: Volatile Memory Acquisition Tool. https://belkasoft.com/ram-capturer, 2020.

19 e-fense Carpe Datum. e-fense:: Cyber Security & Computer Forensics Software. http://www.e-fense.com/helix3pro.php, 2020.

20 ManTech International Corporation. Memory DD. https://sourceforge.net/projects/mdd/, 2020.

21 Digital Forensics Investigation Research Laboratory. Goldfish. http://digitalfire.ucd.ie/?page_id=430/, 2020.

22 Cyber Marshel. Mac Memory Reader. http://cybermarshal.atc-nycorp.com/index.php/cyber-marshal-utilities/mac-memory-reader, 2011.

23 Johannes Stuettgen. OSXPMem - Mac OS X Physical Memory acquisition tool. https://code.google.com/archive/p/pmem/wikis/OSXPmem.wiki, 2020.

24 Kevin P. Lawton. Bochs: a portable PC emulator for Unix/X. *Linux Journal*, 1996(29es):7, 1996.

25 Microsoft Corporation. Debugging Tools for Windows (WinDbg, KD, CDB, NTSD). https://docs.microsoft.com/en-us/windows-hardware/drivers/debugger/, 2020.

26 Vivek Goyal, Eric W. Biederman, and Hariprasad Nellitheertha. Kdump, A Kexec-based Kernel crash dumping mechanism. In *Proceedings of the Linux Symposium*. Citeseer, 2005.

27 He Sun, Kun Sun, Yuewu Wang, Jiwu Jing, and Sushil Jajodia. TrustDump: reliable memory acquisition on smartphones. In M. Kuty?owski and J. Vaidya, editors, *European Symposium on Research in Computer Security*, pages 202–218. Springer, 2014.

28 Dmytro Oleksiuk. SmmBackdoor. https://github.com/Cr4sh/SmmBackdoor, 2020.

29 Christian Charras and Thierry Lecroq. *Handbook of Exact String Matching Algorithms*. Citeseer, 2004.

30 Akinul Islam Jony. Analysis of multiple string pattern matching algorithms. *International Journal of Advanced Computer Science and Information Technology (IJACSIT)*, 3(4):344–353, 2014.

31 Michael O. Rabin and Dana Scott. Finite automata and their decision problems. *IBM Journal of Research and Development*, 3(2):114–125, 1959.

32 Cisco Systems Inc. Clam AntiVirus User Manual. https://www.clamav.net/documents/clam-antivirus-user-manual, 2020.

33 Viorel Negru. *Heterogeneous Pattern Matching for Intrusion Detection Systems and Digital Forensics*. PhD thesis, West University of Timisoara, 2012.

34 David Sánchez and Montserrat Batet. Toward sensitive document release with privacy guarantees. *Elsevier Journal of Engineering Applications of Artificial Intelligence*, 59:23–34, 2017.

35 Karen Sparck Jones. A statistical interpretation of term specificity and its application in retrieval. *Journal of Documentation*, 28:11–21, 1972.

36 Yiming Yang and Jan O. Pedersen. A comparative study on feature selection in text categorization. In *Proceedings of the 14th International Conference on Machine Learning*, volume 97, pages 412–420, San Francisco, CA, USA, 1997.

37 Gerard Salton and Christopher Buckley. Term-weighting approaches in automatic text retrieval. *Elsevier Journal of Information Processing & Management*, 24(5):513–523, 1988.

38 Jianhua Lin. Divergence measures based on the shannon entropy. *IEEE Transactions on Information Theory*, 37(1):145–151, 1991.

39 Rene De La Briandais. File searching using variable length keys. In *Papers presented at the Western Joint Computer Conference*, pages 295–298, 1959.

40 Oracle Corporation. Oracle VirtualBox. https://www.virtualbox.org/manual/ch08.html, 2017.

41 Aaron Walters. Volatility Wiki. https://github.com/volatilityfoundation/volatility/wiki, 2020.

42 Free Software Foundation Inc. strings - print the strings of printable characters in files. http://manpages.ubuntu.com/manpages/bionic/man1/arm-none-eabi-strings.1.html, 2020.

43 Machine Learning Lab. Annotated Strings for Learning Text Extractors. https://machinelearning.inginf.units.it/data-and-tools/annotated-strings-for-learning-text-extractors, 2020.

44 Jensen Baxter. (10)Dataset Text Document Classification. https://www.kaggle.com/jensenbaxter/10dataset-text-document-classification, 2020.

45 Yury Kashnitsky. Hierarchical text classification. https://www.kaggle.com/kashnitsky/hierarchical-text-classification, 2020.

46 Connor Zufelt. GitHub - cjzufelt/cppAES: C++ Cryptography Program Designed for Testing Anti-Ransomware Tools. https://github.com/cjzufelt/cppAES, 2019.

47 Machine Learning Lab. SearchAndReplaceGenerator. https://github.com/MaLeLabTs/SearchAndReplaceGenerator, 2020.

48 Robert Bor. Aho-Corasick. https://github.com/robert-bor/aho-corasick, 2020.

49 OpenJDK. Java Object Layout. https://openjdk.java.net/projects/code-tools/jol/, 2020.

50 Daniel S. Soper and Ofir Turel. An *n*-gram analysis of *Communications* 2000–2010. *Communications of the ACM (CACM)*, 55(5):81–87, 2012.

8

Temporal-Based Data Exfiltration Detection Methods

This chapter discusses a more advanced data exfiltration problem, called *temporal data exfiltration*, which is commonly known as *time-delay data exfiltration*. Together with the description of temporal attacks, details of a novel memory-based temporal data exfiltration countermeasure will also be provided in this chapter. Specifically, Section 8.1 provides the specific motivations for this research, and an overview of existing solutions and their limitations is given in Section 8.2. Section 8.3 provides formal definitions of the problem to be addressed (i.e. *temporal data exfiltration*) as well as the corresponding concepts. Section 8.4 describes in detail the Temporary Memory Bag-of-Words (TMBoW) method (for the detection of time-delay data extrafiltration), followed by an experimental evaluation in Section 8.5. Concluding remarks are given in Section 8.6.

8.1 Motivation

The detection of sensitive data leakage is a challenging issue and one that must be addressed effectively, especially if the sensitive data is the internal information of a company. In this context, authorized employees may be required to use sensitive data for a broad range of diverse business activities; hence, it is not a matter of just storing the data in a safe place. Hence, determining whether the data leaving the organization is legitimate or malicious is not a straightforward process. This chapter addresses the data exfiltration issue when an attacker uses several exfiltration channels to export sensitive data. For instance, malicious insiders could simply attach subtle information as a file or include it as a message in an outbound email, upload it to a personal cloud drive, or transfer it to insecure external storage. Or, data extrusion can be done automatically using malware. For instance, by using a *traditional covert channel*, a malicious program could exploit a benign web server process to export sensitive information using the normal HTTP header, i.e. If-Modified-Since or ETag [1]. However, a sophisticated or state-sponsored

Data Exfiltration Threats and Prevention Techniques: Machine Learning and Memory-Based Data Security, First Edition. Zahir Tari, Nasrin Sohrabi, Yasaman Samadi, and Jakapan Suaboot.
© 2023 John Wiley & Sons, Inc. Published 2023 by John Wiley & Sons, Inc.

adversary could still evade this memory-based detection method by applying the temporal or time-delay data exfiltration method. Specifically, an intruder could delay the data-stealing activity by exfiltrating tiny pieces of information over a long period instead of transferring several files at once. This causes the data exfiltration detection systems to return a false-negative detection result. This is simply because the detected data fragment is too small for the detection threshold. The fragment could be an overlapping region between sensitive and nonsensitive files, which is common. Or, it could be the nefarious data extrusion that utilizes the time-delay exfiltration channel.

The aim of the solution discussed in this chapter is to address the temporal data exfiltration issue, which is one of the hardest problems facing data leakage detection. Specifically, the focus is still on monitoring the sensitive data from the memory to prevent the multichannel data extrusion as mentioned earlier. This chapter emphasizes, however, on the monitoring of the collective activities of processes, whereby fractions of sensitive information are extracted over a period of time. The data to be protected are in the format of text-based sensitive files. Generally, the format of the sensitive information varies from a fixed-format text or keywords (e.g. email address, credit card number, healthcare identifier, and so on) to free-form text, such as patient records, instant message conversations, articles, or internal documents. While the sensitivity of the former is apparent, the latter covers a broader range of sensitive data compared to the fixed-format text or keywords. For instance, the data owner could save sensitive data in unformatted text, which can be presented later in different formats such as a web page, mobile app, or PDF depending on the applications. Therefore, the focus here is on the monitoring of the sensitive text documents instead of just the fixed-format keywords.

The mitigation of temporal data exfiltration raises however new challenges. First is the scalability issue of the monitoring algorithm. The size of sensitive data, particularly of text files, can be much larger compared to the size of sensitive keywords. Hence, a straightforward comparison between the text-based sensitive data and the memory content cannot scale when the number of sensitive files in the database is large. Second, there is the challenge of detecting the temporal attack pattern itself. In particular, the detection model needs to deal with confusion between several temporal data leakage attacks and accidental matching of the sensitive text to the random content in the RAM. Third, the detection model needs to deal with noise from multi-time-step memory data extraction. Ultimately, very few of the previous studies have investigated the temporal data exfiltration issue. One plausible data breach prevention suggested by Google [2] is to limit the rate at which data can be read. This thwarts the adversary's attempt to exfiltrate a large volume of sensitive data. However, the attacker could still exfiltrate the sensitive data by using the temporal data exfiltration at a transfer rate lower than the limit. The simple algorithm, such as hashing [3] of the sensitive file, does scale well for detecting several sensitive documents. Nevertheless, the hash-based method is prone to noises from a slight change from original data. Therefore, the temporal data exfiltration problem remains unsolved over years since being raised by Giani et al. [4]. Despite having great potential and being practical solution for the problem of threat actors, not much research specifically addressing this type of timing attack has been conducted thus far.

This chapter describes the TMBoW method for detecting the sophisticated temporal data exfiltration for the free-form sensitive text document. By representing the sensitive text with Bag-of-Words (BoW) and transforming the BoW to SDR (sparse distributed representation) Boolean vector, the size of sensitive data can be reduced dramatically. Hence, the TMBoW method allows more files to be added to the database of sensitive data. Furthermore, various SDR operations [5] enable the temporary memory functionality. Specifically, TMBoW is capable of memorizing words that appear in the sensitive files and continues to update the temporary memory over time to detect the temporal data exfiltration. The key aspects of TMBoW discussed in this chapter are: (i) the leakage detection of sensitive data in the memory using time-delay channel, (ii) the scalability issue of the pattern-matching algorithm for the text-based sensitive data, and (iii) the noise issue when extracting string from the memory snapshot over multiple time steps.

8.2 Existing Methods

8.2.1 Fingerprinting

The fingerprinting method is intended to efficiently create a fingerprint or signature that represents the actual sensitive content. Two major limitations of using content signature to detect data exfiltration are the alteration of the content (e.g. rephrasing or modification) and the overlap of sensitive and nonsensitive documents. Shapira et al. [6] described a solution to the problem by using a sorted k-skip-n-grams method. Their method requires the company to provide samples of sensitive and nonsensitive documents to be kept in the fingerprint database. These data help to remove the overlapping parts. The k-skip-n-grams method reduces the effects of small rephrasing and modification. In contrast, Zhuang et al. [7] solve the data leakage problem from a private to a public cloud storage using a hashing-based method. They proposed the BFSMinHash algorithm that creates hashes from multiple data chunks of sensitive content. With the Bloom filter method, only random chunks of data will be compared using the Jaccard similarity. This allows BFSMin to roughly monitor sensitive documents being exposed to the public cloud.

8.2.2 Token or Tagging

This method is intended to monitor the meta-data of the file before it is being exported by the cloud service, e.g. moved or copied to the public service. The idea of tagging is similar to that of fingerprinting; however, this requires tags/tokens to be stored as a meta-data of sensitive documents instead of creating the signature from the file's content. Zhang et al. [8] propose extension to the MapReduce framework to allow a programmer to tag and track sensitive files being transferred over the private or public cloud services. The tagged sensitive data is checked by the cloud scheduler/worker before the map-reduce process begins. In contrast, Li et al. [9] present a data leakage prevention method that enables companies to monitor the unstructured data being transferred over a network. Their method integrates key-word filtering and data signature verification to allow the network traffic monitor server to detect a data leakage. First, the keyword is used to filter the suspicious traffic. Then, the public–private key pairs are used as a data label to verify the sensitivity level of the data being transferred over the network.

8.2.3 Machine Learning (ML)

Machine learning (ML) advances offer a wide range of automated information processing. The data leakage prevention solution exploits different ML methods to classify entities and find an anomaly, such as documents, network traffic, and structured query language (SQL) query. Alneyadi et al. [10] analyze the content of sensitive documents using term-frequency-invert document frequency (tf-idf) statistical attribute. This enables small changes/rephrasing to be dismissed. Then, the tf-idf attributes are processed with the singular value decomposition (SVD) method to reduce data dimension and allow noise to be eliminated. This allows the data lost prevention (DLP) solution to deal with known, partially known, and unknown data. In contrast, Li et al. [11] focus on preventing the known malicious threats to exfiltrate the sensitive information by monitoring the domain name system (DNS) log. Since a great deal of malware uses domain generation algorithms (DGAs) to evade detection systems by exporting sensitive data to many servers (i.e. domains), a deep neural network is used to predict a DGA attack. Similarly, Powell [12] used regular network traffic to build a one-class model that can be used to detect the abnormal data transfer by remote attackers over time. ML can also be used to heuristically detect an SQL injection attack. For instance, Li et al. [13] propose a deep-forest-based method to detect complex SQL injection attacks. This can be integrated into the database server to prevent data breaches. Song et al. [14] deal with issues in memory forensics. Although the memory forensic is a very effective tool for recovering evidence from the compromised machine, it is still vulnerable to DKOM attacks. The attack prevents the memory detective from rebuilding kernel objects from the memory image. To do so, attackers manipulate the header of the kernel object data structure to avoid reconstruction of the kernel objects using signature. The authors in [14] proposed a deep neural network-based method that is capable of learning characteristics of the kernel object and helps to efficiently rebuild the usable information of the memory snapshot.

It is clear that there is no single solution that can address data breaches. For instance, an insider or a bribed individual can still steal data using a combination of different channels (e.g. printer, email, USB drive, and instance message) [15]. To the best of our knowledge, none of the current solutions monitor sensitive data in the RAM, and only a few works (e.g. [4, 12]) have paid attention to the temporal or time-delay data exfiltration. Therefore, the solution described in this chapter is a novel means of preventing temporal data exfiltration. However, rather than relying on a single monitoring system, having more protection for different components of the system should be considered.

8.3 Definitions

This section establishes the definitions of terms and problem statements. The frequently used terminologies are listed in Table 8.1.

8.3.1 Sensitive Data

A *sensitive data document* is defined as one that includes confidential (or secret) and/or private information. The degree of data sensitivity depends on the data owner's justification. This can be determined either manually by specialists or automatically using a classification software, Sánchez and Batet [16]. Sensitive data also differs in terms of content, and this depends on businesses activities of the data owners and/or business sectors. For instance, sensitive data could be the meeting minutes, articles, resource planning strategy, source code, patient records, and so on. Types of sensitive data also include fixed-format keywords such as email address and customer's credit card number. However, as discussed previously in Section 8.1, this chapter focuses only on the free-form text.

This work assumes that sensitive documents have already been identified and collected in a database of sensitive documents (so-called sensitive database). Formally, the sensitive database D_s consists of total N document $d_i \in D_s | 1 \geq i \geq N$. Each document d consists of terms t that occur f_t times in d. BoW_d denotes a set of term-frequency pairs (t, f_t), which is called a *Bag-of-Words* of the document d.

8.3.2 Memory Content

A memory content $M_{p,t}$ refers to the string decoded from a RAM snapshot of the running process p at the time step t. If the memory content of the process p

Table 8.1 Terminology.

Notation	Description
Π	Global maximum transfer rate of sensitive data from a controlled storage into memory space of a process
D_s	A corpus of N sensitive documents to monitor
M_t	An extracted string content from memory address space of the running process p at time t
$Dict_w$	A set of terms t from a corpus of sensitive documents, where all terms $t \in D_s$
$Dict_{BoW}$	A set of term-frequency pairs (t, f_t) from a corpus of sensitive documents, where all terms $(t, f_t) \in D_s$
SDR_x	The sparse distributed representation (SDR) vector represents BoWs in $Dict_{BoW}$ of string x
$\lvert SDR \rvert, n$	Size of the SDR vector in bit. $\lvert SDR \rvert$ and n are used interchangeably throughout the chapter
$\lVert SDR \rVert_1, w$	Number of bit ON in SDR vector. $\lVert SDR \rVert_1$ and w are used interchangeably throughout the chapter
$SDRList[]$	Array of SDR vector of files in sensitive database grouped by $\lVert SDR \rVert_1$
τ_t	Minimum time to memorize BoW_t discovered in memory at time t
Γ	Global similarity detection threshold
Θ_w	Similarity threshold for inhibition Rx, where $w = \lVert R_x \rVert_1, \Theta_w = \Gamma \times w$
$\lVert D \rVert_{min}$	Size of smallest file in the sensitive database D_s
ψ	Maximum period of time the monitoring program waits until the memory content M of process p is rechecked

contains any term associated with the sensitive data, the monitoring system will be activated. Hence, the memory content in the next step $t + 1$ and so on will be acquired to track the temporal data exfiltration. For instance, $M_{p,t}$ and $M_{p,t+1}$ are the memory content of the process p acquired at the different time step.

A string content is decoded using Unicode Transformation Format (UTF-8/16/32) standard. The data that cannot be decoded as a printable character is discarded. The reasoning is that the original format of the sensitive data is known to the data owner. Hence, the decoding format can be set in advance. Note that, some binary data might be accidentally decoded to characters regardless of how it was interpreted by the process that has access to the memory.

8.3.3 Noise from Multi-time-Step Memory Data Extraction

The illustrations in Figures 8.1 and 8.2 show noises from memory data extraction and multiple time steps monitoring. In this example, the program has loaded

(a)   (b)

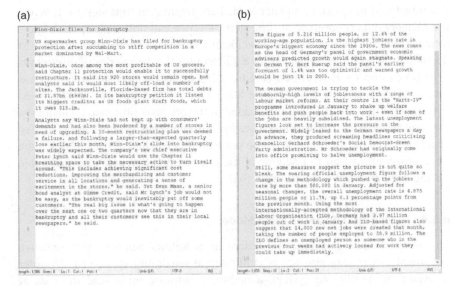

Figure 8.1 Example of original text document A lines 1–7 (a) and text document B lines 5–9 (b).

(a)   (b)

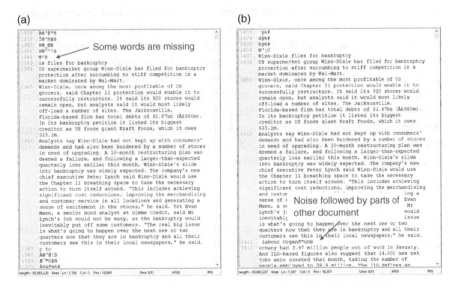

Figure 8.2 Decoded text from a memory snapshot shows two discoveries of the text document A at time step $t + 1$: the first is almost complete with some words missing (a); and the second is complete followed by noise and parts of line 9 from text document B which involved at time step t (b).

document B at time step t and later loaded document A at time step $t + 1$. When the memory data is observed at time step $t + 1$, one can notice that parts of documents A and B were combined. Specifically, Figure 8.1 shows the original text documents A and B, whereas Figure 8.2 illustrates the discoveries of documents A at time t and $t + 1$. At time t (Figure 8.2a), an incomplete document A was found, whereas at time $t + 1$ (Figure 8.2a) a complete document A was mixed with parts of document B that was loaded in the previous time step t. Obviously, the organization of the memory (i.e. by the operating system) leads to two observations of the document A at the same time step, whereas the multiple time steps observations lead to fractions of the document B that still was observable during more than one time step after that.

8.3.4 Temporal Data Exfiltration Model

The temporal data exfiltration is described as follows. Suppose that sensitive document d_i with the size $|d_i|$ is exfiltrated at maximum speed of r. In order to evade the monitoring system, a malicious software must read the data at speed,

$$r < \Pi,$$

where Π is the limit amount of data transferred per day that a user process allows. It is assumed here that all sensitive files have been stored in the restricted storage, and all processes' access to the special storage are logged and examined by the security team. The Π threshold can be set according to reasonable normal usage of authorized individuals who work with the sensitive data. Hence, the setting is arbitrary and determined by the company, depending on normal usage of that particular sensitive document by the data owner or user.

Moreover, sophisticated malware could be reading multiple parts of several sensitive documents, say d_1, d_2, ..., d_n, at a safe speed in order to evade the detection system. In this case, the total data size s to be exported will be

$$s = \sum_{i=1}^{n} |d_i|,$$

hence, a malicious program needs a minimum time τ to complete the data transfer, which is equal to

$$\tau = \frac{s}{r}.$$

Although the malware could still transfer data at a slower speed over a longer period of time $x \gg \tau$, this will give the security team more opportunity to discover an abnormal activity and minimize the total data loss. Therefore, it is assumed that attackers will need to steal the sensitive data as fast as possible before being logged by the monitoring system. In other words, this work focuses on detecting the temporal data exfiltration that occurs during the period τ of time, where a malware reads s bytes of sensitive data of a total n files at r bytes per day.

8.4 Temporary Memory Bag-of-Words (TMBoW)

This section provides details of the TMBoW method for the detection of time-delay data exfiltration. First, a system overview is presented, and the steps involved in the preparation of the sensitive database are discussed. Finally, the steps of the TMBoW's countermeasure are explained in detail.

8.4.1 System State Diagram

Figure 8.3 provides an overview of the TMBoW method. The system begins with the state (a), i.e. the *monitoring state*. In this state, if a process loads data from the controlled storage more than Π byte per second, the system will start logging that activity so that it will end up in state (b). Since the transfer rate Π is based on the normal usage of sensitive files in the database, accessing a larger volume of data will be considered suspicious. This log can be monitored by the security administrator or other anomaly detection systems.

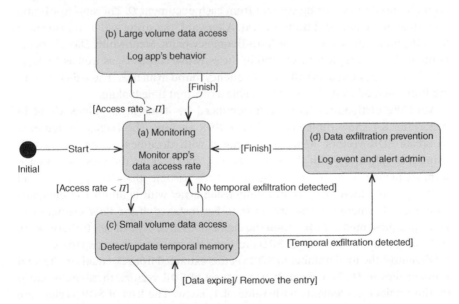

Figure 8.3 State diagram of the temporal data exfiltration detection system.

The smaller volume of data access will trigger the monitoring system into state (c). In this state, the memory data of a particular process is monitored. If the content extracted from the RAM contains terms associated with a sensitive document, these terms will be remembered. In this case, if the data read by that process in the past is combined with any of the sensitive documents, then an alarm will be triggered in state (d). This will alert system administrator to manually investigate for any data breach.

8.4.2 Preparation of Sensitive Database

The preprocessing of the sensitive database is a prerequisite step for the TMBoW method. In general, this process transforms all important documents that need to be monitored to two dictionaries and a set of SDR vectors [5]. These data structures are required during the monitoring phase. Specifically, the two dictionaries are used to extract SDR from the memory content, which later will be compared with a set of SDRs of the sensitive database. More details are provided in Section 8.4.3.

Initially, the sensitive files must be tagged either automatically or manually [16], depending on context of the company. After that, sensitive documents are stored in a database, referred to as D_s.

Algorithm 8.1 explains how to prepare the data structures from the sensitive database D_s. This algorithm extracts two dictionaries (i.e. $Dict_w$ and $Dict_{BoW}$) and a set of SDR vectors that is stored in $SDRList[]$. In lines 1–9, the process begins with the input of raw string content from each document D. The stop words and punctuation are removed from the text. Afterward, the string will be transformed to BoW_d that represents a set of term-frequency pairs. Meanwhile, $Dict_w$ is being populated with unique terms found in the sensitive corpus D_s as well as $Dict_{BoW}$, which are being built using all term-frequency found in all files. These dictionaries are implemented using hash set to enable a constant time lookup.

After the dictionaries have been populated by items in D_s, Lines 10–14 in Algorithm 8.1 show the construction of SDR vectors. The $Dict_{BoW}$ is required to create SDR vectors. SDR_d is associated with document d, and it is built using a simple array with the size of $Dict_{BoW}$ by checking the presence of each term-frequency in BoW_d with $Dict_{BoW}$. Let's assume that $|Dict_{BoW}| = n$ and $\|SDR_d\|_1 = w_d$, then SDR_d is an n-dimension array with w number of elements containing 1, where the rest are set to 0. For instance, if the BoW element i in $Dict_{BoW}$ is presented in BoW_d, then the element ith in SDR_d will be 1 (otherwise 0). Indeed, only a few elements of SRD are 1 and the rest are 0 (hence sparse).

Obviously, the total number of SDR vectors extracted from D_s equals to the total number files in D_s. To efficiently access a set of SDR vectors, these are grouped by the number of elements with value of 1, i.e. w. The lists of SDR vectors are stored in the $SDRList$ array. For instance, $SDRList[w]$ points to list of SDRs where $\|SDR\|_1 = w$ is satisfied.

Algorithm 8.1 Preprocess sensitive database.

---

input : Database of sensitive document
output: $SDRList[]$, $Dict_w$, $Dict_{BoW}$

1 **foreach** $D \in D_s$ **do**
2   Remove stop words and punctuations from D.
3      $BoW_d \leftarrow$ extract bag-of-word from D.
4   **foreach** $Word \in BoW_d$ **do**
5         $Dict_w \leftarrow$ add $Word$.
6   **end**
7      $Dict_{BoW} \leftarrow$ add BoW_d.
8      $D \leftarrow$ store BoW_d.
9 **end**
10 **foreach** $BoW_d \in D_s$ **do**
11      $SDR_d \leftarrow$ generate from BoW_d and $Dict_{BoW}$.
12      $w_d \leftarrow \|SDR_d\|_1$.
13      $SDRList[w_d] \leftarrow$ add SDR_d.
14 **end**
15 **return** $SDRList[]$, $Dict_w$, $Dict_{BoW}$

8.4.3 Sensitive Data Leakage Discovery

This section explains in detail the various processes used to monitor sensitive files in order to detect any temporal data exfiltration. Algorithm 8.2 shows details of these processes. Initially, three data structures from Algorithm 8.1 (i.e. $SDRList[]$, $Dict_w$, and $Dict_{BoW}$) and one content from memory M_t obtained at time t are required as inputs. The monitoring processes are comprised of five major steps.

Step 1: **Preprocess the memory content.** First, stop words and punctuation are removed from the string M_t. After that, $Dict_w$ is used to select only those terms present in the sensitive database D_s. These terms are collected as BoW_t. Obviously, BoW_t contains terms in D_s, but the frequencies might be different from the original files in D_s.

Step 2: **Estimate the monitoring lifetime.** During this step, the minimum time required to memorize the discovered terms from M_t is estimated. If parts of document D_i are found, then the minimum time required to exfiltrate the whole D_i will be $\tau_i = \frac{|D_i|}{R}$, where $R < \Pi$ (see Section 8.3.4). In contrast, if parts of more than one document were discovered, the minimum time will be computed using the combined size of all files that related to the discovery.

Lines 4–6 of Algorithm 8.2 estimate τ_t by generating SDR_t from BoW_t and $Dict_{BoW}$. Then, they calculate the inhibition vector (i.e. R_t) of SDR_t with $SDRList[]$.

Algorithm 8.2 Detect the temporal data exfiltration.

input: M_t, $SDRList[]$, $Dict_w$, $Dict_{BoW}$

1 **while** *true* **do**

/* Step 1: preprocess memory content   */

2   Remove stop words and punctuations from M_t.

3     $BoW_t \leftarrow$ extract M_t using $Dict_w$.

/* Step 2: estimate monitoring life time   */

4     $SDR_t \leftarrow$ generate from BoW_t and $Dict_{BoW}$.

5     $R_t \leftarrow$ calculate inhibition vector of SDR_t with $SDRList[]$.

6     $\tau_t \leftarrow$ minimum timeout of BoW_t from R_t.

7     $BoW_t \leftarrow$ store τ_t.

8     $BoWList[] \leftarrow$ add BoW_t.

9   **foreach** $\tau \in BoWList[]$ **do**

10   **if** $\tau \leq 0$ **then**

11         $BoWList[] \leftarrow$ remove BoW_τ.

12   **else**

13         $\tau \leftarrow$ deduct by ψ.

14   **end**

15   **end**

/* Step 3: combine temporal data   */

16     $BoW_{mem} \leftarrow$ merge $BoWList[]$.

17     $SDR_{mem} \leftarrow$ generate from BoW_{mem} and $Dict_{BoW}$.

/* Step 4: detect temporal exfiltration   */

18     $R_{mem} \leftarrow$ calculate inhibition vector of SDR_{mem} with $SDRList[]$.

19   **foreach** *elem* $\in R_{mem}$ **do**

20   **if** *elem* $= 1$ **then**

21   Log document *elem* is detected.

22   **end**

23   **end**

/* Step 5: sleep and refresh memory content   */

24   Sleep ψ seconds.

25   Refresh M_t.

26 **end**

The R_t vector estimates the total number of matches BoW between BoW_t and documents in $SDRList[]$.

Algorithm 8.3 Calculate inhibition R_x vector.

---

input : $SDRList[], SDR_x$

output: R_x

1   $w \leftarrow \|SDR_x\|_1$.

2   $\Theta_w \leftarrow \Gamma \times w$.

3   $\beta_w \leftarrow \frac{w}{\Gamma}$.

4   $R_x \leftarrow SDR_x \cdot SDR_i$ where
     $SDR_i \in SDRList[] \land \|SRD_i\|_1 \leq \beta_w \land \|SRD_i\|_1 \geq \Theta_w$.
     /* Inhibition R_t with Θ_w */

5   **foreach** $i \in R_x$ **do**

6   **if** $i/w \geq \Theta_w$ **then**

7         $i \leftarrow 1$.

8   **else**

9         $i \leftarrow 0$.

10   **end**

11 **end**

12 **return** R_x

Algorithm 8.3 shows the steps for calculating the inhibition R_x vector. First, $SDRList[]$ and SDR_x are taken as inputs. The Θ_w are calculated using the global similarity detection threshold Γ:

$$\Theta_w = \lceil \Gamma \times w \rceil,$$

where $w = \|R\|_1$. The R_x vector is a dot product between SDR_x and $SDR_i \in SDRList[]$:

$$R_x = SDR_x \cdot SDRList[],$$

where $\|SRD_i\|_1 \leq w \land \|SRD_i\|_1 \geq \Theta_w$. For instance, if $w = 10$ and the $\Gamma = 0.5$, then the Θ_w is 5. Thus, if the document i and strings from memory x both have 10 BoWs in total, the string x will be considered as matching the document i if and only if the total number of matching BoWs is equal to or greater than 5 (i.e. $x \simeq i \iff R_x[i] \geq \Theta_w$, where $R_x[i] = SDR_x \cdot SDR_i$). The matching result is kept as an element of R_x. Lines 4–9 iterate each element of R_x and change the value to 1 or 0 to indicate a *match* or *no match* using the Θ_w threshold. The matching estimation is known as the *inhibition*.

In Lines 7–8 of Algorithm 8.2, the estimated τ_t is associated with BoW_t. Then, $BoWList[]$ is used to temporarily memorize the input string M_t. In Lines 9–15, the estimated time τ of each input string in the temporary list is updated (i.e. reduced by ψ). The outdated string will be removed from the list when $\tau \leq 0$.

Step 3: **Combine the temporal data.** All BoWs from strings in the *BoWList* are presumably parts of the sensitive data being exfiltrated. In this step, all the suspect data are merged. In Line 16 of Algorithm 8.2, temporary *BoWList*[] are merged into BoW_{mem}. At this stage, frequencies of the same term are combined. Therefore, BoW_{mem} has all unique terms in all elements of *BoWList*[]. In other words, the total number of occurrences of individual terms over τ second are combined into one term-frequency (i.e. BoW).

Step 4: **Detect temporal exfiltration.** The detection of similarity between BoW_{mem} and all sensitive documents in the database can be done using the process discussed in *Step 2*. First, BoW_{mem} is converted to SDR_{mem} using $Dict_{BoW}$, where SDR_{mem} indicates the term-frequency pair that exists in the sensitive database. Then, the inhibition vector R_{mem} can be formulated from the SDR_{mem} and $SDRList$[]. Although BoW_{mem} could have BoWs from more than one document merged into one list, the matching process checks only for a match and disregards a mismatch.

From Lines 19 to 23 of Algorithm 8.2, each element of R_{mem} that indicates a match with a sensitive document will be logged and reported to the security team.

Step 5: **Sleep and refresh the memory content.** The monitoring will pause for ψ seconds and data from the memory M_t is refreshed. Let $\|D\|_{min}$ denotes the size of the smallest sensitive file:

$$\|D\|_{min} = \min(|D_i|),$$

where $D_i \in D_s$. Since the described model is based on BoW, a minimum of Θ bytes of data is needed in order to detect a sensitive file (i.e. $\Theta \approx \Gamma \times \|D\|_{min}$). At the maximum transfer rate R, the waiting period is calculated as:

$$\psi = \frac{\Gamma \times \|D\|_{min}}{R}.$$

In other words, the monitoring system needs to recheck the memory content at least every ψ seconds so as to detect Θ bytes of a sensitive file being exfiltrated at the speed R. The faster refreshing time $\psi' \ll \psi$ is not necessary, as too little information will be obtained and the model will not detect very small fractions of sensitive files. In contrast, if too much time is taken to re-read the memory $\psi'' \gg \psi$, it might be too late to detect small sensitive files being exported from the database.

8.5 Experimental Results

This section presents preliminary implementation results and discusses the robustness of the TMBoW method in detecting false alarms.

8.5.1 Experimental Setup

The machine used for the experiments was CPU Intel Xeon E5-1650@3.2 GHz, 32 GB of RAM, and 500 GB solid state drive (SSD) storage space. The operating system was Microsoft Windows 10 Enterprise 1809. The TMBoW method was implemented in Java and tested on Java Virtual Machine version 10.0.2 AMD64 edition.

The memory acquisition problems are simplified here by using pre-extracted data from the memory snapshot of a virtual machine (VM). The VM instance was installed with the Microsoft Windows 7 operating system, and the hypervisor software was Virtualbox version 6.0.24 [17]. The memory content of the demo data exfiltration malware software was repeatedly acquired at five-minute intervals. All the acquisition commands placed in a MS-DoS batch file. Specifically, batch instructions invoked the VBoxManage function of VirtualBox to gather a memory image of the VM. The batched commands dumped the memory snapshot into an ELF64 image file, and the file was processed using Volatility [18] to help extract data from the raw image file. The raw memory image of the particular process (i.e. the process that opened text files) was extracted using Volatility plug-ins. The string contents were extracted using the *strings* decoder on Ubuntu 16.04 long term support (LTS) [19] (e.g. `$strings < memory.dmp -e S > plaintext_8bit.txt`). The extracted contents were stored in text files, which were used in the series of experiments detailed in this section.

The dataset used for the experimental evaluation comprised news articles obtained from [20] and categorized into 10 topics: business, entertainment, food, graphics, historical, medical, politics, space, sport, and technology. Ten documents are randomly chosen from this dataset.

8.5.2 Implementation

TMBoW as well as the naïve method were implemented using Java programming language version 11. Both programs were tested using the same input files containing string extracted from memory snapshots. A demonstration of the data exfiltration was conducted by using a program implemented in C++. The testing dataset was populated by memory snapshots captured when the program was running. The implementation details are as follows:

- *TMBoW program*: This takes a decoded string from the memory snapshot as an input and then splits the input into smaller data blocks, each of which has a size equal to half of the smallest sensitive document in the database. In the worst-case scenario, half of the smallest sensitive document should be detected. By using a sliding window method, two blocks are included in a single monitoring window, and the window slides one block at a time until the end of the memory image is reached. SDR vector is generated for each sliding window. The output is a set of monitoring results for each individual sliding window, in particular, the matching result between SDR vectors from the memory and the one in the sensitive database. The database of stop words to be excluded from the sensitive database is derived from [21].

- *Naïve program*: This is a straightforward method used to read the input file as a string line by line. Each line is compared with every line from all the sensitive documents in the database using Java String `compareTo` API [22]. Obviously, this is not a very efficient method, especially when there is a large number of sensitive files; however, the result is supposed to be accurate or close to perfect. In rare cases, if the noise from the memory extraction process occurs in between the original text and the newline character, then the string comparison-based method will not be able to detect that line in the sensitive document as it is not exactly matched.

- *Temporal data exfiltration program*: Since real-world sophisticated temporal data exfiltration malware could not be found, a demo program is implemented based on the publicly available ransomware testing tool cppAES [23]. The original version of cppAES was designed for testing anti-ransomware tool, which was implemented using C++. The program searches for and reads sensitive text documents from the specified location of the honeypot machine. By using a unique AES key, the program encrypts contents and the decryption key using a hard-coded public Rivest–Shamir–Adlema (RSA) key. Hence, the file can be decrypted only by the one who owns the private key. In reality, the attacker can use a similar program to silently exfiltrates the sensitive data without damaging the original file. In the experiments, cppAES is modified so that it periodically read one sensitive file into the memory and performed the encryption task. After that, the software sleeps for five minutes before it resumes reading the next targeted file.

8.5.3 Attack Scenario

Figure 8.4 depicts the attack scenario where the demo ransomware was acquiring sensitive files from the honeypot, and the timeline showing when the memory dataset was captured. The demon ransomware was programmed to read the file F1–F10 within one hour. In the host machine outside the VM, the batched VBoxManage command was taking a memory snapshot every five minutes. In

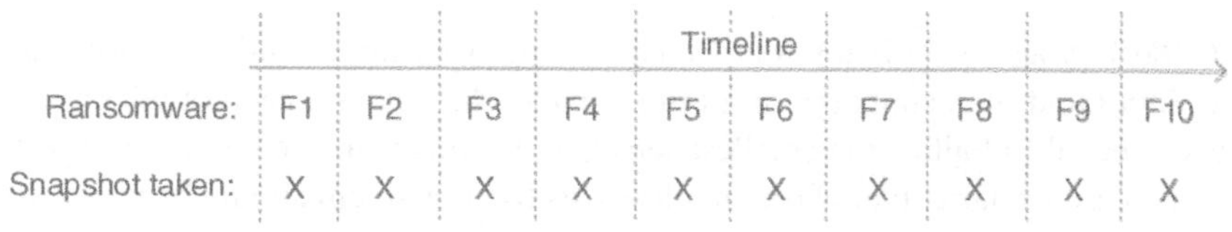

					Timeline					
Ransomware:	F1	F2	F3	F4	F5	F6	F7	F8	F9	F10
Snapshot taken:	X	X	X	X	X	X	X	X	X	X

Figure 8.4 Attack timeline of the temporal-based ransomware.

total, 10 snapshots were taken during 50 minutes. As shown in the timeline, the snapshot is captured every five minutes. Indeed, this was not long after the demo malware performed each data exfiltration.

The ransomware is purposely programmed to acquire sensitive files at fixed intervals in order to simplify the determination of the detection accuracy. This is because data from the previous time step could remain in the memory and be seen again several time intervals later. Hence, the variation in the memory snapshot acquisition intervals was a control variable. This prevented confusion when the data are analyzed, particularly when comparing evidence found in random access memory (RAM) with the actual activities of the demo ransomware.

8.5.4 Results

This section discusses the experimental results from perspectives of scalability and robustness.

8.5.4.1 Detection Results
Figure 8.5 shows IDs of documents found in the memory snapshots from time steps 1 to 10. The marks indicate that at least one element of the particular document was detected. In other words, the marks in Figure 8.5 do not indicate the full

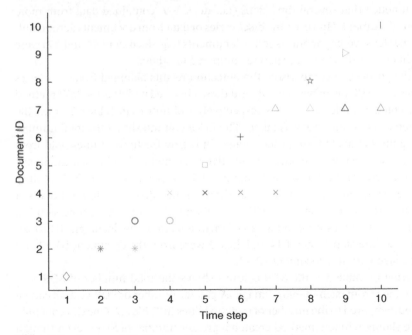

Figure 8.5 Document ID discovered from multiple time steps.

Table 8.2 Detection result using naïve method.

TS	LINE	MATCH	MATCHED ID	A:B
1	4,581,652	7	1 1 1 1 1 1 1	7:0
2	4,658,064	11	2 2 2 2 2 2 2 2 2 2 2	11:0
3	4,646,362	14	2 2 2 3 3 3 3 3 3 3 3 3 3 3	3:11
4	4,629,881	12	4 4 4 4 4 4 4 3 3 3 3 3	7:5
5	4,625,855	8	4 5 5 5 5 5 5 5	1:7
6	4,563,398	10	4 6 6 6 6 6 6 6 6 6	1:9
7	4,569,620	10	4 7 7 7 7 7 7 7 7 7	1:9
8	4,565,385	13	8 8 8 8 8 8 8 8 8 7 7 7 7	9:4
9	4,563,521	11	9 9 9 9 9 9 9 7 7 7 7	8:4
10	4,562,389	11	10 10 10 10 10 10 10 7 7 7 7	7:4

discovery of the particular document. In regard to document ID, one can notice that some documents that were loaded into the memory remained in the memory for several time steps after that, whereas some documents disappeared immediately after the document was unloaded by the program. In terms of the time step, one can notice that several time steps (i.e. steps 3–9) contained data from more than one document. However, the discoveries of data from documents across multiple time steps were random, as some documents (e.g. document #4 and #7) were found in the RAM for a longer period compared to others.

For the purpose of comparison, the detection results obtained from String's compareTo API (i.e. naïve method) and those obtained with the TMBoW method are presented in Tables 8.2 and 8.3, respectively. Column *TS* in Table 8.2 shows the time step when a snapshot was taken. The *LINE* column shows the total number of string lines extracted from each image. Only tiny fractions of lines read from the memory image were related to sensitive documents. Specifically, the image files contained around 4.5–4.6 million lines of decoded string, but only 7–14 lines belonged to the sensitive documents, as shown in the *MATCH* column. Details of the match are given in the *MATCHED ID* column. For instance, at time step 1, a total of seven matches were found, all of them related to the document ID #1. In contrast, at time step 3, out of 14 matches, 3 were from the document ID #2 and 11 associated with the document ID #3.

Referring to Table 8.3, the *SDR* column shows the total number of SDR vectors obtained from each memory image. A greater number of SDR vectors can be observed compared to the number of matched lines in Table 8.2. One can conclude that the sliding window method created a greater number of SDRs, even though the strings without terms in the sensitive database (i.e. $Dict_w$) were discarded. Also,

Table 8.3 Detection result using TMBoW method.

TS	SDR	MATCH	MATCHED ID	A:B
1	6	3	1.1.1.	3:0
2	44	4	.......2........2.........2.........2......	4:0
3	72	7	.......2........2...........3.........3.........3.........3.........3..	2:5
4	73	7	....4........4........4........4...............3.........3.........3...	4:3
5	71	5	...4.....................5..........5.........5.........5............	1:4
6	71	5	...4....................................6......6.......6........6..	1:4
7	74	5	...4......................7.........7.........7.........7............	1:4
8	74	6	....8........8........8........8............7.........7............	4:2
9	73	6	.9.9........9.........9.......................7.........7............	4:2
10	74	6	......10.........10.........10.........10............7.........7............	4:2

a) *Note*: "." denotes UNMATCH.

the naïve method reads the text file line by line, whereas the TMBoW method splits the input string into the fixed-size block. If the block contained at least one term from $Dict_w$, the SDR vector of that block was created. As a result, a greater number of SDR vectors can be observed in Table 8.3 compared to the number of matched lines in Table 8.2. Indeed, the column *MATCH* of Tables 8.2 and 8.3 have different units, in particular with regard to the *matched lines* vs. the *matched blocks* of input. The SDR vector that had a match with the sensitive database less than the detection threshold ($\theta_w = 0.5$) is represented with the dot in the *MATCHED ID* column of Table 8.3.

Regarding the detection accuracy, as a direct comparison between the Naïve and the TMBoW method could not be made, the memory image was split differently. Here, a comparative analysis of the two solutions is conducted. First, when considering the unique document ID identified by the two methods, both reported exactly the same set of document IDs. Second, when we consider at the proportion of the *MATCHED ID* in column *A:B* in both tables, many similarities in the ratios of values reported for two document IDs, i.e. from time steps 3 to 10. Also, the similar trend is observed in the number of MATCH(es) discovered in images from different time steps. Third, one can notice that the natural appearance and disappearance of data loaded into the memory when using both *Naïve* and *TMBoW* methods. For instance, the data related to document IDs 1, 5, 6, 8, and 9 were discovered only at the time step 1, whereas document IDs 2, 3, 4, and 7 were found after the first use. Hence, the TMBoW method performs with 100% detection accuracy when compared to the baseline method.

8.5.4.2 Scalability

Figure 8.6 compares the increasing size of the $Dict_{BoW}$ data structure of *TMBoW* with the original string size when the number of sensitive documents ranges from 1 to 150,000 files. The scalability of *TMBoW* consists of two important data structures: $Dict_{BoW}$ and *SDR vector list* (i.e. *SDRList[]*). Since $Dict_{BoW}$ contains a set of unique original keywords and associated frequencies, the data structure size gradually increased from few hundreds bytes to around 16 MB when 150,000 documents were added to the sensitive database. The tendency of the increasing size is obviously $O(\log N)$. In contrast, the size of the original string from a sensitive document is linearly dependent on the number of documents in the database, i.e. $O(N)$. The total size steadily increases to approximately 75 MB when all documents are added to the database.

When considering the size of the SDR vector list, even though the size of the SDR vector is fixed and the total number of SDR is linearly dependent on the total number of sensitive files, the size of the SDR vector is trivial. For instance, if the size of each SDR is 100,000 bits, the total size of the SDR vectors will be only 1.8 MB for 150,000 sensitive files.

Figure 8.7 depicts the data size of the memory snapshots and the total number of SDR vectors extracted from the memory image per time step. The variation

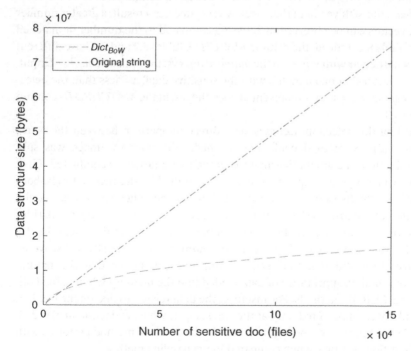

Figure 8.6 Data structure size comparison between original string and $Dict_{BoW}$.

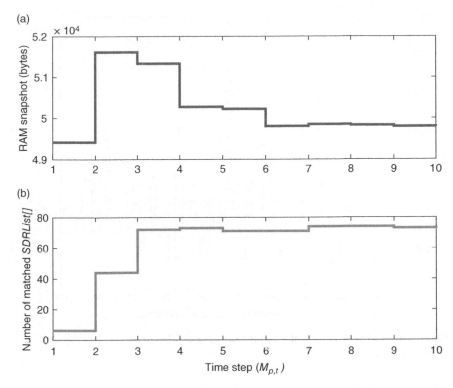

Figure 8.7 Size memory snapshot (a) and number of the extracted SDR from memory (b).

in the size of the memory snapshot between 4.9 and 5.2 KB, whereas the total number of SDR vectors extracted during each time step increased from less than 10 vectors at time step 1 to around 70 vectors at time step 3 and remained steady after that. Intuitively, some evidence of sensitive files which were used in the previous time step remained in the memory and mixed with the more recently used files. Hence, the number of SDRs increased at the beginning and steadied later. Therefore, the memory requirement for the real-time monitoring is considered constant regardless of the number of sensitive files in the database.

Due to the evidences that show a scalability of the memory requirement, particularly the size of data structures for (i) a sensitive database and (ii) incoming memory snapshots, the TMBoW method is scalable, especially in terms of memory footprint when more sensitive text files need to be monitored.

8.5.4.3 Robustness
In order to evaluate the robustness of the TMBoW method, the characteristics of the SDR vectors were examined, both the one that represents the sensitive file

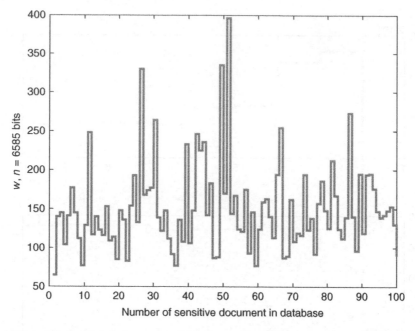

Figure 8.8 *w* of each document when the sensitive database contains 100 files and $|SDR| = 6585$ bits.

and the other from the memory snapshot. First, *w* or the total number of ON bits (i.e. $||SDR||_1$) of SDRs is measured, which represent sensitive documents. As shown in Figure 8.8, when the sensitive database contains up to 100 documents, the size of SDR vector is 6585 bits. The *w* of each individual sensitive file ranges from around 60 bits to approximately 400 bits ON.

After that, the characteristics of SDR vectors derived from the memory snapshots were monitored. Figure 8.9a shows details of SDRs generated from time steps 1 to 10. The top chart shows *w* of SDRs generated from the matched parts of memory snapshots. The total number of SDRs was around 85 vectors from 10 time steps. The number of SDRs from the memory snapshot depends on the number of splits per time step and the number of keywords in each split. The number of splits varies with each time step, as shown in Figure 8.9b. Overall, the *w* size fluctuated between around 40 and 140 bits. The *w* size of SDRs also reflected the tendency of matching and nonmatching when the sliding window moves over the memory image from the beginning to the end of the image. In other words, the number of *w* increased or decreased according to the number of keywords in the sensitive files.

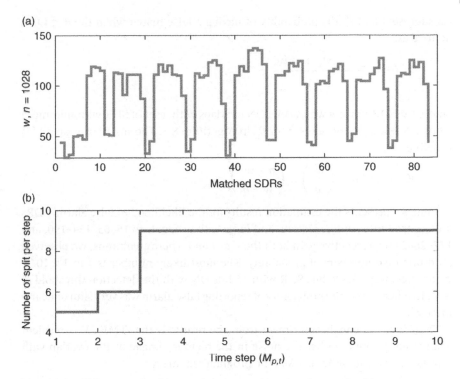

Figure 8.9 SDR vector size (a) over time step and memory image size (b).

Figures 8.8 and 8.9 show the characteristics of SDRs associated with the sensitive files and the memory snapshots. Therefore, the likelihood of TMBoW generating a false match is estimated to analyze the robustness of the TMBoW method. By doing so, the probability of randomly find information on RAM is analyzed, which exactly matches with any items in the sensitive file. The probability is simply computed as follows:

$$\binom{n}{w} = \frac{n!}{w!(n-w)!},$$

where n denotes size of the SDR (i.e. $|SDR|$), and w is the total number of ON bits (i.e. $||SDR||_1$).

In most cases, the detection was not an exact match. Therefore, the likelihood of obtaining inexact matches is also computed. The detection results shown previously in Table 8.3 were based on 50% detection threshold (i.e. $\theta = 0.5$).

As suggested by [5], the probability of having a false match when the $\theta < 1.0$ is defined as:

$$fp_w^n(\theta) = \frac{\sum_{b=\theta}^{w} |\Omega_x(n, w, b)|}{\binom{n}{w}},$$

where the SDR x size n with w bits ON overlaps with a set of SDR with minimum b bits ON. Here, b represents θ_w or β_w in Algorithm 8.3. The size of overlap set [5] is defined as:

$$|\Omega_x(n, w, b)| = \binom{w_x}{b} \times \binom{n - w_x}{w - b}.$$

Table 8.4 presents the estimation results for the likelihood of false alarm. SDRs are grouped into *small*, *medium*, and *large* with w equals to 15–65, 124–190, and 177–2802 bits, respectively. In both the *Exact* and *Approx.* columns, we observed all diminutive numbers of probability. The most likely number is 1 in 1×10^{-29} when matching 53,896 bits SDR with 15 bits ON with the detection threshold of 50%. In other words, the probability of reporting false alarm was very slim or nearly impossible.

Therefore, the conclusion drawn from the results is that TMBoW is resilient against noisy input – either the noise in the memory image or the overlap with unrelated text from other parts of the program's memory.

Table 8.4 Probability of false alarm: small, medium, and large based on sparsity of SDRs.

					Probability of false match	
w size	**# of file**	**n**	**w**	**# of patterns**	**Exact ($\theta = 1.0$)**	**Approx. ($\theta = 0.5$)[a]**
Small	10	1028	65	9.237×10^{103}	1.083×10^{-104}	1×10^{-44}
	100	6585	65	1.420×10^{157}	7.044×10^{-158}	1×10^{-71}
	1000	53,896	15	7.178×10^{58}	1.393×10^{-59}	1×10^{-29}
Medium	10	1028	124	8.916×10^{162}	1.122×10^{-163}	1×10^{-66}
	100	6585	151	8.191×10^{310}	1.221×10^{-311}	1×10^{-134}
	1000	53,896	190	7.328×10^{546}	1.365×10^{-547}	1×10^{-245}
Large	10	1028	177	3.849×10^{203}	2.599×10^{-204}	1×10^{-82}
	100	6585	396	3.011×10^{648}	3.332×10^{-649}	1×10^{-269}
	1000	53,896	2802	4.001×10^{4780}	2.499×10^{-4781}	1×10^{-1994}

[a]The term $\sum_{b=\theta}^{w} |\Omega_x(n, w, b)|$ was estimated by $|\Omega_x(n, w, \theta)|$ as its value far out weighted other terms in the summation equation. Hence, the accuracy in column *Approx.* is accurate at the order of ten.

8.6 Summary

This chapter described the TMBoW method to prevent temporal data exfiltration attacks. TMBoW creates a fingerprint of the sensitive data by using BoW and the SDR, which is not only scalable when the number of sensitive files is increasing, but is also capable of detecting the temporal data exfiltration. Furthermore, the work presented here on the TMBoW method is one of the first attempts made to detect data leakage threats by the direct monitoring of sensitive content in RAM. Experimental results showed that the TMBoW method is scalable and robust, particularly in detecting the sensitive text-based documents in the physical memory.

References

1 Denis Kolegov, Oleg Broslavsky, and Oleksov Nikita. Covert timing channels using HTTP cache headers. https://www.slideshare.net/yalegko/covert-timing-channels-using-http-cache-headers, 2015.

2 Google. Preventing Data Exfiltration. https://cloud.google.com/security/data-loss-prevention/preventing-data-exfiltration, 2021.

3 Michael Hart, Pratyusa Manadhata, and Rob Johnson. Text classification for data loss prevention. In *Proceedings of the Springer International Symposium on Privacy Enhancing Technologies Symposium*, pages 18–37, 2011.

4 Annarita Giani, Vincent H. Berk, and George V. Cybenko. Data exfiltration and covert channels. In *Sensors, and Command, Control, Communications, and Intelligence (C3I) Technologies for Homeland Security and Homeland Defense V*, volume 6201, page 620103. International Society for Optics and Photonics, 2006.

5 Subutai Ahmad and Jeff Hawkins. Properties of sparse distributed representations and their application to hierarchical temporal memory. *arXiv preprint arXiv:1503.07469*, 2015.

6 Yuri Shapira, Bracha Shapira, and Asaf Shabtai. Content-based data leakage detection using extended fingerprinting. *arXiv preprint arXiv:1302.2028*, 2013.

7 Hao Zhuang, Rameez Rahman, Pan Hui, and Karl Aberer. Optimizing information leakage in multicloud storage services. *IEEE Transactions on Cloud Computing*, 8(4):975–988, 2018.

8 Chunwang Zhang, Ee-Chien Chang, and Roland H. C. Yap. Tagged-MapReduce: A general framework for secure computing with mixed-sensitivity data on hybrid clouds. In *Proceedings of the 14th IEEE/ACM International Symposium on Cluster, Cloud and Grid Computing*, pages 31–40, 2014.

9 Hao Li, Zewu Peng, Xinyao Feng, and Hongxia Ma. Leakage prevention method for unstructured data based on classification. In *Proceedings of the Springer International Conference on Applications and Techniques in Information Security*, pages 337–343, 2015.

10 Sultan Alneyadi, Elankayer Sithirasenan, and Vallipuram Muthukkumarasamy. Detecting data semantic: a data leakage prevention approach. In *Proceedings of the IEEE Trustcom/BigDataSE/ISPA International Conference*, volume 1, pages 910–917, 2015.

11 Shuaiji Li, Tao Huang, Zhiwei Qin, Fanfang Zhang, and Yinhong Chang. Domain Generation Algorithms detection through deep neural network and ensemble. In *Proceedings of the World Wide Web Conference (WWW)*, pages 189–196, 2019.

12 Brian A. Powell. Malicious Overtones: hunting data theft in the frequency domain with one-class learning. *ACM Transactions on Privacy and Security (TOPS)*, 22(4):1–34, 2019.

13 Qi Li, Weishi Li, Junfeng Wang, and Mingyu Cheng. A SQL injection detection method based on adaptive deep forest. *IEEE Access*, 7:145385–145394, 2019.

14 Wei Song, Heng Yin, Chang Liu, and Dawn Song. DeepMem: Learning graph neural network models for fast and robust memory forensic analysis. In *Proceedings of the ACM SIGSAC Conference on Computer and Communications Security (CCS)*, pages 606–618, 2018.

15 Khudran Alzhrani, Ethan M. Rudd, C. Edward Chow, and Terrance E. Boult. Automated U.S diplomatic cables security classification: topic model pruning vs. classification based on clusters. In *Proceedings of the IEEE International Symposium on Technologies for Homeland Security (HST)*, pages 1–6, 2017.

16 David Sánchez and Montserrat Batet. Toward sensitive document release with privacy guarantees. *Elsevier Journal of Engineering Applications of Artificial Intelligence*, 59:23–34, 2017.

17 Oracle Corporation. Oracle VirtualBox. https://www.virtualbox.org/manual/ch08.html, 2017.

18 Aaron Walters. Volatility Wiki. https://github.com/volatilityfoundation/volatility/wiki, 2020.

19 Free Software Foundation Inc. strings - print the strings of printable characters in files. http://manpages.ubuntu.com/manpages/bionic/man1/arm-none-eabi-strings.1.html, 2020.

20 Jensen Baxter. (10)Dataset Text Document Classification. https://www.kaggle.com/jensenbaxter/10dataset-text-document-classification, 2020.

21 Deeplearing4j. Stopwords. https://deeplearning4j.konduit.ai/, 2020.

22 Oracle. Class String: Java API Docs. https://docs.oracle.com/en/java/javase/11/docs/api/java.base/java/lang/String.html, 2021.

23 Connor Zufelt. GitHub - cjzufelt/cppAES: C++ Cryptography Program Designed for Testing Anti-Ransomware Tools. https://github.com/cjzufelt/cppAES, 2019.

9

Conclusion

This chapter summarizes the work detailed in this book and its contribution for a better understanding of the data exfiltration detection technology and suggests future directions regarding three main methods of detection: behavior-based, memory-based, and temporal pattern-based.

9.1 Summary

This book began with background knowledge in Chapter 2 that is useful for the readers for the understanding of the cybersecurity methods described in the remaining chapters of the book. Several key concepts and methods were covered, such as hidden Markov model (HMM) and memory forensics. This is followed by a chapter that later provided details of cybersecurity threats so to enable readers to have a better understanding of the various concepts-related cybersecurity threats. Chapte 3 provided details of different concepts such as advanced persistent threat (APT) and cybersecurity attacks. Chapter 4 reported real-world data leakage and top cybersecurity attacks from 2020 to 2021 in all five continents. It covered the recent significant cyberattacks as well the malware development trends.

A detailed literature survey, with a focus on the recent research on the application of supervisory control and data acquisition intrusion detection systems (SCADA IDSs), was later provided in Chapter 5. Since SCADA is widely used for critical systems, numerous advanced supervised-based machine learning (supervised ML) methods have been proposed to detect cyberattack incidents. Many advanced supervised learning methods used in SCADA IDSs could also be applied in DLPs, as these are anomaly detection systems designed specifically for the detection of data leakage. This review of over a 100 of peer-reviewed papers yielded information on a broad variety of supervised ML methods that have been proposed for SCADA IDSs. The survey in Chapter 5 not only helps us identify the limitations of existing technologies in detecting data breaches from various

Data Exfiltration Threats and Prevention Techniques: Machine Learning and Memory-Based Data Security, First Edition. Zahir Tari, Nasrin Sohrabi, Yasaman Samadi, and Jakapan Suaboot.
© 2023 John Wiley & Sons, Inc. Published 2023 by John Wiley & Sons, Inc.

perspectives but also gives a wide and in-depth understanding of current state-of-the-art technologies. This knowledge is crucial for the later phases of our research. Furthermore, different methods have been proposed based on the various detection constraints (i.e. network traffic, program behavior, and cyber-physical signal). Therefore, from the survey, one can acquire some knowledge about the design of supervised-based data leakage detection solutions, in particular, of the specific characteristics of observable data of relevance to this thesis.

Then, an in-depth study was conducted for data exfiltration detection solutions. To begin with, we examined various data exfiltration issues caused by malware. Indeed, malicious software is one of the most crucial data-stealing tools used by adversaries as it allows them to search and exfiltrate sensitive information from millions of targets automatically. Chapter 6 focused on the detection of suspicious data leakages by examining dynamic behavior of the processes running in computer systems. Sequences of application programming interface (API) calls executed by the process were exclusively used to identify malicious behavior. In particular, the Sub-Curve HMM method was disrobed to extract fractions of the malicious program's behavior from the long API call sequences to detect a fraction of malicious behavior or the data-stealing activity that occurs over a brief period.

After that, the description moved from the behavior-based to the sensitive data-oriented approach. In particular, we challenged the general belief of the research in the field by proposing new ways of monitoring the presence of sensitive data in the physical memory instead of checking for malicious programs or scanning for sensitive data transmitted over the network. Since the random access memory (RAM) is the single point onto which all the data being processed by a computer system will be loaded, it is less likely that the adversary will be able to evade the memory-based detection. However, there are several challenges associated with examining the sensitive content in the RAM, especially under real-time constraints. Chapter 7 described in detail the Fast lookup Bag-of-Words (FBoW) method for detecting corpora of sensitive text documents in the RAM. It worked by compressing the text corpora to sequences of Bag-of-Words (BoW) and building the deterministic finite automaton (DFA) from the BoW sequence. Strings extracted from the memory space of each running process are then matched with the FBoW method to identify the processes that contain sensitive data on the memory space. FBoW was designed to be scalable and robust in monitoring a corpus of text documents/files based on the data extracted from the physical RAM. The output of the algorithm is a list of processes that contain sensitive data. This knowledge is crucial for the identification of suspicious behavior. Hence, a data-stealing activity can be detected regardless of the malicious or benign program being used to commit the data breach.

Finally, this book mitigated the strong data exfiltration attacks that have not been well studied thus far, known as temporal data exfiltration. Even though the leakage of sensitive data in the physical memory can be detected, advanced hackers can evade detection by reducing the size of the sensitive data being exfiltrated. However, although a tiny part of the sensitive data can still be captured by the detection model, since the size is too small, the matching likelihood could be smaller than the detection threshold, subsequently returning a false-negative result. The hacker can exfiltrate several tiny parts and, later on, combine them into one sensitive document. Chapter 8 described the Temporary Memory Bag-of-Words (TMBoW) method for dealing with this specific type of data exfiltration attack. TMBoW is basically the temporary memory of the BoW data structure: the temporary memory model allows fractions of sensitive text files being detected to accumulate over a period of time. This method is capable of detecting data-stealing behavior even if the process has been extended over a long time to evade the monitoring system.

9.2 What Is Innovative in the Described Methods?

The aim of this book was to explain and elaborate on the holistic data exfiltration detection approach. Throughout the work, several important new ideas and algorithms were described to the area of data leakage complex issues. Overall, the followings were elaborated: (i) conducted a comprehensive survey of the supervised ML methods for SCADA-specific IDSs and described several novel data exfiltration detection methods based on the holistic perspective, namely (ii) Sub-Curve HMM that is a software's behavior-based method; (iii) FBoW that is a memory-based sensitive data monitoring; and (iv) a temporal data exfiltration detection approach named TMBoW.

This book contributes *a comprehensive survey of the literature.* The extensive literature survey on supervised ML methods for the SCADA IDS demonstrated the development of such systems from industry perspectives, and it suggested a framework for categorizing various supervised ML methodologies. This survey not only helps researchers to quickly understand the operations of machine learning-based anomaly detection systems but also facilitates a much easier and faster understanding of the numerous technologies. The survey also provided qualitative and quantitative comparisons of several state-of-the-art literature to identify the directions of research that target different data auditing sources and attacking methods. Furthermore, we discussed additional issues and challenges for industrial IDSs using supervised learning methods and illustrated the development trends for such systems.

The main innovative ideas of *the behavior-based data exfiltration method* are as follows: the Sub-Curve HMM method is basically a novel feature extraction method that enables the extraction of subcontained malicious behavior from long

API call sequences. Existing methods cannot detect these malicious activities that occur over a brief period of time. We also tested the accuracy of current approaches in detecting such malicious programs. Compared to the results obtained by existing methods, Sub-Curve HMM outperformed baseline methods across six datasets of data-stealing malware with various average API sequence lengths. Results confirm the ability to detect interesting behavior from subsequences of the whole activities observed. Furthermore, the comparison of the detection rate of Sub-Curve HMM and 10 existing commercial antivirus scanners shows that the Sub-Curve HMM method is the best scanner for the malware family with the longer API sequence. Ultimately, in the context of real-time detection, the sequence of API calls is a continuous stream of input, which is unlikely to be able to gather all information from suspicious processes. Thanks to the dynamic API call analysis and the subcontained malicious extraction method, the Sub-Curve HMM method is capable of monitoring running processes in such a real-time situation. Therefore, by applying Sub-Curve HMM, the data-stealing behavior of the malicious program can be more efficiently detected and attackers are thwarted in a timely manner.

The memory-based data exfiltration detection method makes several contributions to this field of work. To the best of our knowledge, this work is the first attempt to mitigate data breaches by monitoring the sensitive content in the physical memory. Intuitively, if the RAM is efficiently monitored, it will be difficult for malicious activities to evade suspicion or detection. The Fast lookup Bag-of-Words (so-called FBoW) method is, basically, a novel approximate multi-pattern matching method. It addresses the scalability and robustness issues associated with the matching of sensitive text documents in the RAM. The scalability problem arises when there is a large number of sensitive documents that require monitoring. This not only reduces the runtime efficiency but also increases the memory footprint. The robustness issue is related to the inevitable noise resulting from the extraction of textual content from the binary image of the RAM snapshot. Moreover, FBoW allows the administrator to fine-tune the performance and security trade-off by using filtering thresholds, enabling an alternation or balancing of performance and accuracy levels. The experimental results showed that the FBoW method outperforms the state-of-the-art methods in regard to memory requirements and robustness against noise, with negligible reductions in runtime and accuracy. Furthermore, we tested the FBoW method with data extracted from an RAM snapshot, as well as keywords only and a plain text dataset to extensively investigate the performance and efficiency of FBoW in comparison with state-of-the-art methods. Hence, the novel FBoW method is a multiple pattern-matching method, which is scalable and can efficiently monitor a corpus of sensitive text documents in the physical memory.

The temporal-based data exfiltration detection method makes several innovations. The final part of this book tackles the long-existing and difficult issue of temporal data exfiltration attacks. Despite their occurrence for over a decade, only a few researchers have attempted to find solutions that will address this problem successfully; thus, it remains a challenging issue. The TMBoW method paves the way for researchers to continue developing sophisticated data exfiltration detection methods. TMBoW is based on the temporary memory data structure that is capable of memorizing fractions of small matching patterns over a certain period of time. This allows the time-delayed, data-stealing activity to be discovered. Apart from its main contribution to detect temporal data exfiltration, TMBoW is also a memory- and runtime-efficient method. TMBoW summarizes the sensitive documents in the database using BoW and condenses them to a sparse distribution representation (SDR) vector that allows each sensitive document to be represented as a binary vector. This is indeed memory-efficient. Furthermore, the bitwise similarity matching and data merging operations enable parallel computation. Hence, TMBoW can match multiple documents more efficiently on a multicore CPU system.

9.3 What Is Next?

Even though this book contributed substantial knowledge to the work on data exfiltration, ongoing work in this field is essential as new vulnerabilities are being discovered regularly and attackers continue to devise new attack methods, creating numerous avenues for future research.

9.3.1 Behavior-Based Method

Despite the promising outcomes of the Sub-Curve HMM method, one can notice that the feature extracting HMMs are sensitive to the training API sequences with indiscriminate features. As a result, the prediction accuracy is compromised by the false alarm rate. Further work could aim to develop a data preprocessing method that can efficiently reduce the overlapping features of benign software and data exfiltration malware families. Moreover, the method based on API call sequence could be evaded when malicious programs intentionally stop performing data-stealing activities or delay actions between commands. In other words, a temporal-based malicious behavior detection method will need to be developed to thwart an attacker attempting to launch a temporal attack on the program activities.

9.3.2 Memory-Based Method

This book is only the very beginning of the memory-based method. Since the idea is novel, an efficient framework for memory acquisition does not exist, especially for this memory-based data leakage detection approach. Moreover, the computer platforms of various industries and enterprises have numerous different constraints depending on whether they are cloud-based, edge-based, mobile-platform, single-server, distributed server, standalone, or special hardware. Furthermore, the same situation applies to software platforms, particularly as they are more diverse than the hardware systems. These issues raise challenging problems when developing a memory-based security system. Also, sensitive data can be stored in forms other than text documents; hence, more research is required concerning ways by which specific kinds of sensitive information can be protected. Possible future work could include larger-scale experimentation of the described methods over deployment environments and practical applications.

9.3.3 Temporal Pattern-Based Method

Undeniably, the advanced and sophisticated adversary poses the greatest threat to enterprises and government departments, particularly in regard to data exfiltration. However, hackers do not limit themselves to using one tool to compromise the target. Rather, they prefer to use various attack methods ranging from simple to advanced. One challenging direction for future work would be to investigate other variations of temporal attacks that use more than one channel to exfiltrate data. For instance, several programs may be used to gather data from different parts of the sensitive files. Finding solutions that will mitigate the possibility of such attacks remains a challenging task for researchers, since the advanced adversary is capable of developing one or more tools for the exfiltration of data or other types of cybersecurity attacks.

Index

Data Exfiltration Threats and Prevention Techniques: Machine Learning and Memory-Based Data Security,
First Edition. Zahir Tari, Nasrin Sohrabi, Yasaman Samadi, and Jakapan Suaboot.
© 2023 John Wiley & Sons, Inc. Published 2023 by John Wiley & Sons, Inc.

Printed and bound by CPI Group (UK) Ltd, Croydon, CR0 4YY

29/05/2023

03222460-0002